Joseph J. Mogan, Jr.

Chaucer and the Theme of Mutability

DE PROPRIETATIBUS LITTERARUM

edenda curat

C. H. VAN SCHOONEVELD

Indiana University

Series Practica, 3

CHAUCER

AND

THE THEME OF MUTABILITY

by

JOSEPH J. MOGAN, JR.

Texas Technological College

1969

MOUTON

THE HAGUE · PARIS

LIBRARY OF CONGRESS CATALOG CARD NUMBER: 68-29626

Printed in The Netherlands by Mouton & Co., Printers, The Hague.

To S. J. with gratitude

ACKNOWLEDGMENT

I gratefully acknowledge my indebtedness to Professor Thomas A. Kirby, "myn owene maister deere", who first enkindled my love for Chaucer and under whose guidance and direction this work was undertaken as a doctoral dissertation; to Professor Helen C. White, who read the manuscript and offered many detailed suggestions; and not least of all to my wife, whose contribution to the completion of this book "shul not here be told for me".

TABLE OF CONTENTS

INTRODUCTION

The theme of mutability is perhaps the most persistent theme in all literature. Especially is this true of English literature of the mediaeval, Renaissance, and Jacobean periods. When the idea of Progress finally settled, however, the ideas of mutability, mortality, decay of the world, and putrefaction were pushed into the corners of literature – only to be revived in the literature of disillusionment which followed in the wake of world wars and hitherto unimaginable scientific achievement; the god of Progress is no longer being universally worshipped.[1] Philosophers, writers, even the scientists themselves are demanding a reinterpretation of spiritual values; and while this reinterpretation is not intended to reproduce stoical indifference, the Gnostic or Manichean dichotomy of the principles of Good and Evil, or the mediaeval contempt of the world, it is similar to antiquity in this: it no longer accepts the Victorian dogma that "this is the best of all possible worlds"; and it is oriented to values which transcend both man himself and the material world.[2] Certainly then the god of Progress is being called to testify; and the scientific glorification of the material world is no longer without its dissenters. In a context such as this, therefore, the concept of mutability takes on much historical significance.

This is a study of the theme of mutability in the works of Geoffrey Chaucer. In view of the importance of mutability in Chaucer's poetry, it is in a way surprising that a study of this theme in his complete works has not yet been undertaken. In 1915, G. L. Kittredge wrote:

---

[1] I do not mean to imply here that the mutability theme completely disappeared from literature after the mid-seventeenth century. It is found, in fact, in the writings of Coleridge, Keats, Arnold, Thomas Wolfe, and others.

[2] See, for example, S. G. F. Brandon, *Time and Mankind: An Historical and Philosophical Study of Mankind's Attitude to the Phenomena of Change* (New York, 1951), pp. 186-88; J. B. Bury, *The Idea of Progress* (London, 1928), pp. 332-33; pp. 351-52; and Basil Willey, *The Seventeenth Century Background*, in Anchor Books (New York, 1953), pp. 17 ff.

Now this thought – that life and love and happiness are transitory – is not, with Chaucer, a commonplace reflection, with which he has only a concern that is conventional and impersonal and external. Nor is it, again, a dogma of experience, to which he has dispassionately adjusted his philosophic scheme. It is an element in his nature: it beats in his heart, and flows in his veins, and catches in his throat, and hammers in his head. All men are mortal, no doubt, but seldom do we find one in whom mortality is a part of his consciousness.[3]

But beyond pointing out the expression of mutability in one of Criseyde's speeches (*Troilus*, V, 1051-85; Kittredge, p. 129) he does not pursue the theme to any great extent.

In 1917, Bernard Jefferson, in *Chaucer and the Consolation of Philosophy of Boethius*,[4] studied many aspects of the mutability theme found in Chaucer's works, such as fortune, fame, true and false felicity. He also indicated all the passages in the works of Chaucer which find their sources in the *Consolation*, some of which deal with other aspects of the mutability theme; but these he merely catalogued. Jefferson was concerned, however, primarily with the *Consolation* as Chaucer's source. As a result, therefore, he rightfully takes no account of the large amount of mutability material in the works of Chaucer not found in the *Consolation*; nor does he analyze any of Chaucer's works very thoroughly (with the exception of four of the shorter poems, taken almost exclusively from the *Consolation*) in trying to show how mutability functions in the works themselves. For example, Jefferson says about the *Troilus*: "The entire poem abounds in allusions to the transitory nature of worldly joys, now brightening, now darkening, but ever fading entirely away in the end" (pp. 125-126). He makes little attempt to develop this idea; it is, in fact, almost incidental to his discussion of Troilus' fatalism, Criseyde's concern for true and false felicity, and the place of Fortune in the poem – all taken, of course, from the *Consolation*. In short, Jefferson's excellent study is concerned with the mutability theme in the works of Chaucer in so far as this theme appears in the *Consolation*.

Of course there have been a number of articles (or sections of larger works) which, directly or indirectly, treat of the mutability theme in individual poems, *The Parliament of Fowls* or *The Knight's Tale*, for example. These studies are by their very nature limited; often they are even erroneous because they fail to take into account not only the mediaeval attitude toward, and the mediaeval use of the theme of, mutability generally, but they also fail to consider the general pattern

[3] *Chaucer and His Poetry* (Cambridge, Mass., 1915), p. 72.
[4] Princeton, N. J., 1917.

of Chaucer's use of the theme throughout his entire works. These studies of the individual poems will be examined throughout the course of this work. There are, moreover, numerous *obiter dicta* on mutability in the works of Chaucer, such as in Willard Farnham's examination of the *Troilus* as a *De Casu* tragedy,[5] or in discussions of the character of Criseyde.[6] As yet, however, scholarship has not offered an adequate study of mutability as such, nor has Chaucer scholarship offered an adequate study of the theme as it is found and functions in Chaucer's poetry generally.

When one attempts to write about mutability, his first problem is to define the term. This statement is not so naive as it might appear. The *OED* defines mutability as "disposition to change, variableness, inconstancy". The adjective "mutable" is defined as "liable or subject to change or alteration"; "fickle; variable". Now this is obvious enough: this is the aspect of mutability which is most commonly associated with Fortuna. The problems, however, are two: the *OED*'s definition is not so broad as it might be and, secondly, some of the critics have used the term somewhat vaguely. As for the former, the idea of "transitoriness" should be included in the concept of "mutability"; no better evidence for this can be had than in Geoffrey Chaucer's translation of the *Consolation of Philosophy*: "But the schynynge of thi forme (*that is to seyn, the beute of thi body*), how swyftly passynge is it, and how transitorie! Certes it es more flyttynge than the mutabilite of floures of the somer sesoun." [7] It was Chaucer, incidentally, who first introduced the terms "mutability" and "mutable" into the English language, in his translation of Boethius' *Consolation*.[8] As for the critics' vague use of the terms, I shall cite but a few examples.

In Wells's *A Manual of the Writings in Middle English*, for example,

[5] *The Medieval Heritage of Elizabethan Tragedy* (New York, 1936), pp. 137 ff.
[6] See R. K. Root, ed., *The Book of Troilus and Criseyde* (Princeton, N. J., 1926), p. xlviii. See also Kittredge, p. 129; and Dorothy Bethurum, "Chaucer's Point of View as Narrator in the Love Poems", *PMLA*, LXXIV (1959), 511-20, for the best discussion to date of the mutability theme in some of Chaucer's works.
[7] F. N. Robinson, 2nd ed. (Boston, 1957), iii, pr. 8, 35-39. Throughout this study, all my references to Chaucer's works are from this edition. It might be conveniently mentioned here that at the first citation of a work I shall give full bibliographical information; thereafter I shall use abbreviated citation, and in the text when possible.
[8] Kittredge also uses the term to mean "transitory"; "Everything passes, mutability is the order of the world." *Chaucer and His Poetry*, p. 129. I am aware that "transitoriness" might be the effect or the nether aspect of "changeableness"; but this is not always the case and therefore the distinction should be made.

we read: "The 'ubi sunt' formula, on which is based the second section of this piece [*The Sayings of St. Bernard*], has well been said to be 'as universal as the themes of mutability and mischance.' " [9] Is "*ubi sunt*" something separate from "mutability" (to say nothing of the precise distinction between "mutability" and "mischance")? Benjamin Kurtz, in speaking of Bernard of Cluny's *De Contemptu Mundi*, says this: "But no extreme of horror is reached, and the theme dissolves into a long treatment of the mutability of all earthly glory, with much of the old *Ubi Sunt* formula." [10] Kurtz deals principally with the putrefaction theme and its presence in the Old English *Address of the Lost Soul to the Body*. In the process, he says that "Homer's reminder of the mutability of lovely manhood is not decayed flesh, but the generations of leaves scattered on the earth, while the forest puts forth again" (p. 250). This certainly implies that the theme of putrefaction is a part of, if not intimately related to, the theme of mutability. Moreover, what Kurtz implies, Huizinga explicitly states. In regard to the Middle Ages, he says:

All that the meditations on death of the monks of yore had produced, was now condensed into a very primitive image. This vivid image, continually impressed upon all minds, had hardly assimilated more than a single element of the great complex of ideas relating to death, namely, the sense of the perishable nature of all things. It would seem, at times, as if the soul of the declining Middle Ages only succeeded in seeing death under this aspect.

   The endless complaint of the frailty of all earthly glory was sung to various melodies. Three motifs may be distinguished. The first is expressed by the question: where are now all those who once filled the world with their splendour? The second motif dwells on the frightful spectacle of human beauty gone to decay. The third is the death-dance: death dragging along men of all conditions and ages.[11]

Huizinga's "motifs" are the clearest distinction of "themes" within the theme of mutability which have yet been made. But the fact remains that putrefaction and the death-dance are parts of the mutability theme; exactly where does one draw the distinction? And is not the death-dance itself part of the mortality theme and therefore separate from the mutability theme? Lest it be thought that I am deliberately confusing the issue, note George Williamson's observation on this point: "In seventeenth-century England the ideas of mutability and mortality unite

[9] J. E. Wells, *A Manual of the Writings in Middle English, 1050-1400* (New Haven, 1916), p. 389.
[10] "Gifer the Worm: An Essay Toward the History of an Idea", *University of California Publications in English*, II (1929), No. 2, 235-61.
[11] J. Huizinga, *The Waning of the Middle Ages*, in Anchor Books (New York, 1956), pp. 138-39.

in the quarrel about the decay of the world." [12] Mutability and mortality, then, are separate concepts. But is such actually the case? Immediately after Kittredge notes Chaucer's interest in mutability (transitoriness) he says: "All men are mortal, no doubt, but seldom do we find one in whom mortality is a part of his consciousness" (*supra*, p. 12).

In 1920, Edwin Greenlaw attempted to show that the predominant source of Spenser's *Two Cantos of Mutabilitie* is Lucretius' *De Rerum Natura*.[13] Having summarized the fifteenth book of Ovid's *Metamorphoses*, Greenlaw concludes: "Ovid deals with change; Spenser and Lucretius deal with Mutability" (p. 458). If this is not very clear, William P. Cumming, in his article "The Influence of Ovid on Spenser", shows precisely what Greenlaw means:

By this he means that Ovid represents things as endlessly changing into something new, while Lucretius and Spenser deal with struggles against supernaturalism as typified in Spenser by the arguments of Mutabilitie. Ovid is interested in mere Protean shifting from shape to shape; Lucretius and Spenser are concerned with the mortality of all things, physical and supernatural. Philosophically, the chief source of Mutability is Lucretius's *De Rerum Natura*.[14]

George Williamson, in discussing the viewpoints of Greenlaw and Cumming, speaks of "the confusion of philosophies in a mind like Spenser's"; points out evidence of this same confusion in Hakewill's *Apologie* (1927, pp. 113-114); and concludes "how easily Du Bartas, Hakewill, or Spenser could mingle or confuse the Lucretian theory of mortality with the Pythagorean philosophy of change".[15] The concept of "mutability", then, contrary to the *OED*, certainly involves more than simply the concept of change. Ovid's doctrine that "all things are ever changing; nothing perishes" can never be equated with the idea of mutability. The concept of mutability, properly speaking, involves the concept of mortality. More specifically, the concept of mutability always includes the concept of mortality; but the concept of mortality does not necessarily include that of mutability. In a word, one can consider the *fact* of death without seeing life as a transitory or a changing-toward-death process. The problem has to do with the concept of change; and each age has viewed change in the colors of its own milieu. Looked at from a historical perspective, Ovid's doctrine (that of Pythagoras, of course) is

[12] "Mutability, Decay, and Seventeenth-Century Melancholy", *ELH*, II (1935), 126.
[13] "Spenser and Lucretius", *SP*, XVII (1920), 439-64.
[14] *SP*, XXVIII (1931), 249.
[15] Williamson, pp. 135-36.

somewhat of an exception: not very many philosophers have ever taken the doctrine of the transmigration of souls very seriously; and certainly the doctrine has had little real influence in the history of Western literature. But there is a much more important consideration concerning this word "change", and the viewpoints of the different ages can best be seen in the light of the idea of Progress.

In general, one might say that until the idea of Progress began to take hold in the mid-seventeenth century, the whole Western world viewed any kind of change as a change for the worse, a process toward decay. What J. B. Bury says about the Greek philosophers holds, with some qualification perhaps, from ancient times until a short time beyond the end of the Renaissance:

The general view of Greek philosophers was that they were living in a period of inevitable degeneration and decay – inevitable because it was prescribed by the nature of the universe.

. . . .

Thus time was regarded as the enemy of humanity. . . . "time depreciates the value of the world", expresses the pessimistic axiom accepted in most systems of ancient thought.[16]

E. K. Rand testifies to the persistence of this same attitude throughout the Middle Ages: "If young and old in the Middle Ages saw visions and dreamed dreams, if they sometimes looked gloomily on the pleasures of the present, it was partly because they read the work of Cicero, glossed by Macrobius. They might have felt far less dismal had they not been so well read in the Classics of antiquity." [17] Finally, Richard Foster Jones discusses this attitude as it prevailed during the Renaissance and then concludes by pointing out some significant ramifications which evolved from this pessimistic attitude:

Perhaps, more than we discover in print, this lingering conception of universal decay was at the bottom of the worship of antiquity and the regard for Latin and Greek writers which characterized the criticism of the neo-classical period. Somewhere underlying the doctrine of imitation, which oppressed the age, must have been the feeling that modern minds were by necessity inferior to ancient. . . . Though the critics of the day seldom express the theory directly, it is not improbable that in their subconscious minds resided the conviction of inevitable inferiority through the decline of nature. How else could a critical theory like that of close imitation secure such a strong hold upon intelligent people, or how could there have been such extravagant and servile worship of men who had lived many ages before?

---

[16]   Bury, *Idea of Progress*, pp. 9-12.
[17]   "Mediaeval Gloom and Mediaeval Uniformity", *Speculum*, I (1926), 257.

... Edward Young's *Conjectures on Original Composition*, which in places
sounds startlingly like the mid-seventeenth century, proves that in order to
overthrow the doctrine of imitation Young felt compelled to combat the idea
of universal decay.[18]

It is precisely this concept of change which prevailed, and in fact almost
exclusively predominated, from classical antiquity to the rise of the idea
of Progress in the mid-seventeenth century. And Williamson, more than
Greenlaw or Cumming, reveals delicate sensitivity to the mediaeval and
Renaissance consciousness when he points out "how easily Du Bartas,
Hakewill, or Spenser could mingle or confuse the Lucretian theory of
mortality with the Pythagorean philosophy of change" (*supra*, p. 15).
The fact that these writers found it unnecessary to distinguish (perhaps,
were not even aware of a distinction) between change and mortality
shows, I think, their concept of mutability: the Renaissance, and especially the Middle Ages, were never troubled by the assimilation of disparate concepts into their own peculiar sensibility. It is all right, therefore, for a critic to distinguish the themes of "mutability" and "mortality",
and usually their contexts justify the distinction, but it is important to
realize that when one is dealing with pre-Progress literature, the concepts are usually not mutually exclusive.

There is a reason, however, why these terms and themes – decay of
the world, *ubi sunt*, mutability, mortality, contempt of the world, putrefaction, and the others – are often not clearly defined and sometimes
are used interchangeably in the writings of most of the critics and in
the literary works themselves. First, the critic's ultimate thesis determines his point of view toward these various concepts. It is understand-
able and correct, for example, for Willard Farnham, in contrasting the
mediaeval contempt for and the Renaissance acceptance of the world,
to say that the mediaeval tragical narrative, such as Boccaccio's *De
Casibus Virorum*; the putrefaction theme which predominated all other
aspects of death at the end of the fourteenth and the beginning of the
fifteenth centuries; and the *ubi sunt* poems and the *Ars Moriendi*
treatises – to say that all these are forms of the contempt of the world
theme.[19] He is speaking broadly and we know what he means. It is all
right too, for example, for Huizinga to relate, and for Kurtz to separate,
the mutability and the putrefaction themes: such clarification of con-

[18] *Ancients and Moderns: A Study of the Background of the "Battle of the
Books", Washington University Studies in Language and Literature*, N. S., No. 6
(St. Louis, 1936), p. 42.
[19] Farnham, *Medieval Heritage*, pp. 41-42.

cepts is completely justifiable in the contexts of their over-all theses. If, therefore, it is confusing to the uninitiated who are seeking a clarification of these terms, it is, nevertheless, unavoidable. The second reason that these terms are not always clearly defined is the very nature of the ideas themselves. Any one of these themes, or terms, can in a given context be used as a common denominator for the others: it is largely a question of emphasis. One can view putrefaction, for example, as a *memento mori* or as a *memento vitae brevae*. One can view the *De Casibus* form as the mutability of the goddess Fortuna; as revealing the transitory nature of worldly goods; or as a form of contempt of the world, because the world's goods are illusory and can ensnare man to his damnation. The points of view are endless.

The concept of mutability, however, is more common to all these themes, and it is therefore more valid as a common denominator than any other of these concepts. If I may follow Huizinga's suggestion, and broaden it, I should say that all of these other themes are motifs of the theme of mutability. I say this because the classical, mediaeval, and Renaissance attitudes toward change are basic in, and are subsumed under, all these other concepts. The concept of mutability is much more basic than the attitude toward death; for the classical and Christian attitudes toward death were quite different. It is this concept which has the most firm philosophical basis, and which has occupied thinkers from the time of Heraclitus to the time of Lipsius; even to the time of Alfred North Whitehead, who prophesied that "that religion will conquer which can render clear to popular understanding some eternal greatness incarnate in the passage of temporal fact".[20] It is this concept more than any of the others which is contained in the genres such as the *ubi sunt*, contempt of the world, the *De Casibus*, and the Golden Age, but which is itself too broad and too abstract to be fully contained in any one genre.

The mediaeval concept of mutability (and attitude toward change) was not essentially different from that of classical times. It was, certainly, more conscious and therefore more intense, chiefly because Christianity emphasized those elements in Greek and Roman philosophies which lay at the basis of the concept of mutability. It was, too, more complex because their heritage was an amalgamation of Greek, Roman, Jewish, and Christian (both Biblical and Patristic) thought. In brief, the mediaeval concept of mutability cannot be completely understood apart from its origins and influences. For this reason, I have

[20]   *Adventures of Ideas* (New York, 1935), p. 41.

devoted the chapter which follows to the study of the history of the concept. At the end of this investigation, I have appended illustrations of the various motifs of the theme of mutability, such as the *ubi sunt* and the decay of the world variations of the theme; this, partly because of the critics' confusion of the "motifs" with the "theme", but chiefly because these motifs can be identified in the works of Chaucer. In view of the fact that there is no study of the history of the concept of mutability as such, this chapter might possibly have an incidental usefulness of its own.

The second chapter makes a study of mutability in the *Consolation of Philosophy*, in Innocent III's *De Contemptu Mundi*, and in *Le Roman de la Rose*; the first two Chaucer translated completely, and the last, at least in part. These are not only representative works of the Middle Ages, but they strongly influenced Chaucer's thought; and since he translated these works, the suspicion is well founded that they are extremely valuable in illuminating his sensibility.

Chapters Three, Four, Five, and Six study the theme of mutability in the works of Chaucer: in relation to his sources and in its artistic function in each of the poems in which it appears. The various motifs of the theme are identified in his poetry. The aim of these chapters is threefold: first, to show that the theme of mutability is much more important in Chaucer's poetry than has been hitherto realized; second, to formulate some generalizations, at least tenuously, which will not only illumine his works generally, but which might suggest a background, if not indications, for interpreting his poems in particular; and third, to arrive at some insight into Chaucer's poetic sensibility, that complex mechanism which unifies his entire poetic vision and which inspires the delicate balance or tension in his poetry between the truly earthly and the truly spiritual, the truly worldly and the truly supernatural.

I have said that in a way it is surprising that a study of mutability in the works of Chaucer has never been adequately undertaken. In another way, however, this is not surprising. The final impression of Chaucer's poetry is life-in-fullness and life-in-abundance; the epitome in fact of action, of movement, of humor, of *joie de vivre*, of love: in short, we rarely think of Chaucer as a tragic poet. The theme of mutability is not so important on the surface of Chaucer's poetry as it is at the core of his poetic vision. It determines his *Weltanschauung*, it reveals his sensibility, it restrains his complete commitment to life; it even restrains his final commitment as a poet. The mediaeval concept of mutability is quite different from the modern concept of disillusionment and its vast Wasteland.[21] The mediaeval man knew that this was a wasteland all along, but he also saw life as a pilgrimage. Beyond the horizon he saw another world. It was the eternal city, out of the reach of time, of change, of decay. And if these eternal shadows forever outlined the transitoriness of the world and forever informed the immediacy of time, this did not mean that the pilgrims could not have fun along the way; in fact, this eternal shrine, always lingering in the background, "gave to the incidents of life a zeal and color which they might otherwise have lacked" and "added intensity to thought and energy to passion".[22] Chaucer was such a mediaeval man; but beneath all the *joie*, and *gladnesse*, and *jolitee*, he never for a moment forgot that it was *half-way pryme*.

---

[21] It is interesting to note Willard Farnham's expression that T. S. Eliot "performs a Dance of Death through the Waste Land of our existence". His remark immediately following this establishes the difference between the mediaeval and modern wastelands: "He sees our fruitfulness gone and an utter lack in us to produce anything but an incongruous juxtaposition of useless activities." In *Essays in Criticism by Members of the Department of English, University of California* (Berkeley, 1929), p. 29.

[22] Theodore Spencer, *Death and Elizabethan Tragedy: A Study of Convention and Opinion in the Elizabethan Drama* (Cambridge, Mass., 1936), p. 37. For a similar idea, see Dorothy Sayers' "Introduction" to her translation of Dante's *Il Purgatorio*, in The Penguin Classics (Edinburgh, 1955), p. 23.

I

THE CONCEPT OF MUTABILITY FROM ANTIQUITY
THROUGH THE MIDDLE AGES

The mediaeval attitude toward mutability is a complex of many influences. It was inherited essentially from Greek and Roman philosophy and literature, influenced by Jewish thought handed down in the Old Testament and in the writings of the Fathers of the Church, and finally, influenced most importantly by Revelation and the whole structure of Christianity. In fact, as the idea of an immutable God and the promise of eternal happiness became more real to the people of the Middle Ages, in that proportion did life and happiness become more transitory and the world more insignificant. The theology of Christianity, however, was formulated largely in terms of the pre-Christian philosophies, and the classical influence in general was never absent in the Middle Ages. Since mutability is primarily a philosophical concept or, more accurately, since the meaning of "mutability" depends upon a particular philosophical attitude toward change, the mediaeval sensibility of change-toward-decay cannot be adequately studied apart from its influences.

For this reason, therefore, this chapter presents an outline of the history of the concept of mutability. The theme of mutability, as I have pointed out in the Introduction, permeates and manifests itself in the motifs of the Golden Age (the nether aspect of the decay of the world), *ubi sunt*, putrefaction, and contempt of the world. After this outline will follow a brief explanation and a few examples of each of these motifs of the mutability theme. Thus their relationship to the general theme of mutability and to each other will perhaps be made clearer.

MUTABILITY

The phenomenon of change has been remarked from the very beginning of mankind, but the first person to attempt a philosophical explanation of it was Heraclitus of Ephesus (536-470 B. C.). For Heraclitus, all things were in a continual state of flux: "It is not possible to step twice into the same river";[1] and "Those who step into the same river have different waters flowing ever upon them" (12). Man himself participates in the flux: he too is changing, as is the river, so that, "In the same river, we both step and do not step, we are and we are not" (49a). "When they are born, they are willing to live and accept their fate (*death*); and they leave behind children to become victims of fate" (20). "Time is a child playing a game of draughts; the kingship is in the hands of a child" (52); ". . . everything comes about by way of strife and necessity" (80). This tension is thus expressed: "The bow is called Life, but its work is death" (48).

The flux, then, is a major part of the philosophy of Heraclitus. But Heraclitus never attempts to give an ultimate reason for the flux, nor in his philosophy does this change imply a loss; life and death are one in the circular continuum of change: "The way up and down is one and the same" (60; see also, for example, 30, 76, 88, and 90). Such a philosophy can only be optimistic about the hurrying toward death since death does not imply a loss.[2] The concept of mutability, as opposed simply to change, becomes significant only when this world is seen as transitory (implying a loss) in contrast to another world of permanence and fixity: this contrast is found in Plato.

In Plato we find for the first time the emphasis on individual immortality and the unqualified assertion of the supersensuous and invisible Hereafter: "A more supersensuous and abstract Hereafter than Plato's cannot be conceived." [3] Plato, by his construction of the World of Ideas, made an absolute distinction between the world of sense, becoming and visible, and the place of the mind or being, invisible and unchangeable. Timaeus says: "First then, in my judgment, we must make a distinction and ask, What is that which always is and has no becoming, and what is that which is always becoming and never is? That which is apprehended by intelligence and reason is always in the same state, but that which is conceived by opinion with the help of

[1] Heraclitus, 91 (Diels), translated in Kathleen Freeman, *Ancilla to the Pre-Socratic Philosophers* (Oxford, 1948). I am indebted to this work for all my references to Heraclitus (hereafter cited in the text). For an excellent analysis of Heraclitus, see Eric Voegelin, *The World of the Polis*, in *Order and History* (Baton Rouge, 1957), II, 220-40.
[2] See Voegelin, *ibid.*, pp. 236-37.
[3] Karl Vossler, *Mediaeval Culture: An Introduction to Dante and His Times* (New York, 1929), I, 36.

sensation and without reason is always in a process of becoming and perishing and never really is." [4] The changing world of phenomena, in fact, merely confuses the intellect.[5] The pure soul, liberated from the body and from this world of change, "departs to that place which is, like itself, invisible, divine, immortal, and wise, where, on its arrival, happiness awaits it, and release from uncertainty and folly, from fears and uncontrolled desires, and all other human evils, and where . . . it really spends the rest of time with God" (ibid., 81). The greatest achievement and at the same time the very nucleus of Plato's theology is the idea of immortality. The human soul comes from the divine realm of Ideas and, like the Ideas, is without beginning or end. Its contact with the body and other material phenomena defiles it, and only through abstinence and contemplation of the Good can it again become pure. Thus, "the denial of what is ephemeral is in itself and for itself virtue, immortality, and blessedness" (Vossler, I, 27).

In brief, the only reality for Plato is the World of Forms; the material world is devoid of essence and is therefore non-existent.[6] Henceforth, this absolute transcendence of the divine, spiritual realissimum will give to mankind its true place and perspective. The consciousness of the flux and the transitoriness of the material world, as opposed to the permanence and the eternity of the other world, will have a fixed place in the history of ideas. Christian thought will assume this Platonic distinction and emphasize it; the awareness of the mutability of this world and of the things of this world will reach its climax in the late Middle Ages and in the Renaissance.

The Aristotelian influence was no less important during the Middle Ages. The notions that the region beneath the moon is changeable and full of corruption and that the region beyond the moon is unchangeable is perhaps Pythagorean in origin.[7] The Aristotelian De Mundo, however,

---

[4] Timaeus, 28 (Jowett's translation, 4th ed., in The Collected Dialogues of Plato, ed. Edith Hamilton and Huntington Cairns [New York, 1961], Bollingen Series, 71).

[5] Phaedo, 79 C; 80 B (Tredennick's translation in Hamilton and Cairns).

[6] For further evidence of this dichotomy in the works of Plato, see especially the Republic, 514-517 E and the Symposium, 207 D-212. See also A. O. Lovejoy, The Great Chain of Being, in Harper Torchbooks (New York, 1960), pp. 31-66, et passim. It should be noted, however, that while this dichotomy of Plato in fact deprecates the world of matter and of appearance and is the philosophical source for the later contempt of the world, for Plato himself the world is good, beautiful, the best possible in a world of matter, and not therefore to be completely despised. See Timaeus, passim.

[7] William Harris Stahl, trans., Macrobius: Commentary on the Dream of Scipio (New York, 1952), p. 131, n. 7.

became the heritage of the Middle Ages. Having described the celestial region with the fixed stars and the six planets which are below them, fixed and unchangeable, the author speaks next of "the element that is through the whole of its extent liable to change and alteration, and is, in short, destructible and perishable".[8] Henceforth the mutable sublunary earth, "this turbulent, troubled place", will forever be conscious of its own mortality in the presence of the celestial region, which itself is "removed from all darkness and disorderly motion" and is "never changed or altered" (400a). The breakdown of this theory is ultimately responsible for the Renaissance preoccupation with the decay of the world and, consequently, for Renaissance melancholy.

Of all the classical writers, however, Lucretius (ca. 99-55 B. C.) is the most immediately and graphically occupied with the fact of mutability. An Epicurean, he denied the spiritual in any form. Life itself was the result of atoms and death was simply the displacement of these same atoms. Change, decay, death were all parts of an endless process of movement or displacement of atoms. The universe itself would eventually decay; the atoms, themselves indestructible, would eventually separate and fall into an infinite void – this would be the dissolution of the universe. But like the continual generation and decay of this epoch, a new universe would someday be generated; and thus the endless circle would have begun again (this, incidentally, was also held by the Stoics). The theory is rather uncomplicated, even if it does not answer satisfactorily many difficulties, since Lucretius always remains on the mechanical level.

One of the major preoccupations of Lucretius in his *De Rerum Natura* is mortality: It is useless to fear death; it will come inevitably. If one understands the universal law whereby Nature remains immortal while her visible aspects are destroyed, that "fear of Acheron" will be "sent packing which troubles the life of man from its deepest depths, suffuses all with the blackness of death, and leaves no delight clean and pure".[9] In the process of unveiling these horrors of death and of calling attention to the mortality of all the visible manifestations of Nature, Lucretius has much to say about mutability. The dominant theme in the following passage is that of mortality, but the concept of mutability creeps in and

---

[8] *De Mundo*, 392 b (ed. and trans. D. J. Furley, in *The Loeb Classical Library* [Cambridge, 1955]).
[9] *De Rerum Natura*, trans. W. H. D. Rouse, in *The Loeb Classical Library* (New York, 1928), p. 173. There is evidence that Lucretius was read during the Middle Ages; see Albert S. Cook, "Chaucerian Papers I: Prologue 1-11", *Transactions of the Connecticut Academy of Arts and Sciences*, 23 (1919), 19.

the two concepts are, ultimately, intricately related: "There is an end fixed for the life of mortals, and death cannot be avoided, but die we must. . . . one unchanging thirst of life fills us and our mouths are for ever agape: and it is uncertain what fortune the next years may bring, what chance has in store, what end awaits us" (p. 245). The farmer, for example, seeing the decayed and shrivelled vine, accuses "the progress of time and wearies heaven; not comprehending that all things gradually decay, and go to the tomb outworn by the ancient lapse of years" (p. 169). It is indeed foolish to rail against the nature of things.

The bulk of Lucretius' work treats of mortality: he argues that since the parts which compose the whole (the *kosmos* and everything in it) are mortal, the whole is therefore mortal. His arguments for the decay of the parts, however, are based primarily on the concept of birth-growth-decay: "For certainly we must own ourselves convinced that many elements flow away and pass out from things; but still more must be passed in, until they have touched the pinnacle of growth. *After that by minute degrees age breaks the strength and mature vigour, and melts into decay*" (p. 165; *underscoring* my own). Thus the concepts of age, change, and time are usually involved in Lucretius' discussions of mortality; this is in fact symptomatic of the general difficulty of attempting to distinguish the two concepts of mutability and mortality in the pre-Progress writers. Unlike Plato, Lucretius obviously does not contrast the mutable world with a transcendent immutable reality; rather he contrasts the indestructible atoms with their mutable quantitative manifestations, and the calm equanimity which one should possess in the face of Nature's laws of mutability and mortality.

If Lucretius emphasizes mortality, the writings of Seneca and Marcus Aurelius emphasize mutability. In his *De brevitate vitae*, Seneca points out that mortals have but a brief span of life and that "even this space that has been granted to us rushes by so speedily and so swiftly that all save a few find life at an end just when they are getting ready to live".[10] His main thesis is that life can be long if one knows how to use it (p. 229); that they alone really live who take time for philosophy, for in this way they assume the wisdom of every age to their own (p. 333): this "is the only way of prolonging mortality – nay, of turning it into immortality" (p. 339).

Seneca's philosophy was primarily ethical: the study of philosophy should orient the soul toward virtue. Life can be lengthened by "the love

[10]   *Seneca: Moral Essays*, trans. John W. Basore, in *The Loeb Classical Library* (New York, 1932), II, 287. The quotations in my text are from this edition.

and practice of the virtues, forgetfulness of the passions, knowledge of
living and dying, and a life of deep repose" (p. 351). This dichotomy
between the spirit (ideally in repose, calm and at rest in the practice of
virtue) and the external world gives to Seneca's consciousness of the
transitoriness of all things (and the rush of time itself) an intensity
equalled only in Boethius' *Consolation of Philosophy*. This intensity
is evident in the following excerpt: "Present time is very brief, so brief,
indeed, that to some there seems to be none; for it is always in motion,
it flows and hurries on; it ceases to be before it has come, and can no
more brook delay than the firmament or the stars, whose ever unresting
movement never lets them abide in the same track. The engrossed,
therefore, are concerned with present time alone, and it is so brief that
it cannot be grasped, and even this is filched away from them, distracted
as they are among many things" (p. 319). If one follows a life of vice,
on the other hand, then "a thousand years . . . will shrink into the
merest span; your vices will swallow up any amount of time" (p. 303).[11]

Marcus Aurelius of course, in his *Meditations*, evidences the same
viewpoint towards external reality as does Seneca, and is treated here
chiefly for the direct and interesting manner in which he expresses the
world's mutability. In no other book perhaps has there been gathered
together so many and various expressions of the mutability and mortality
concepts as appear in these *Meditations*. "Everything is only for a day,
both that which remembers and that which is remembered." The greatest
love of the Universe is to change and to renew the things that are.
"Everything that exists is in a manner the seed of that which will be."
"Thou art a little soul bearing about a corpse. . . ." The familiar image
of time as a river is here, but "a violent stream", the author adds.
Human beings are "ephemeral" and "worthless" and "what was yesterday a little mucus, to-morrow will be a mummy or ashes".[12] The following passage, for example, gathers together three of the often-used
images associated with mutability:

Some things are hurrying into existence, and others are hurrying out of it;
and of which is coming into existence part is already extinguished. . . . In
this flowing stream then, on which there is no abiding, what is there of the
things which hurry by on which man would set a high price? It would be
just as if a man should fall in love with one of the sparrows which fly by,

[11]   See also the *Moral Epistles*, nos. 4, 12, 24, 26, 49, 61, 101, 117, and 118 for
further instances of the mutability theme; and Victor Goldschmidt, *Le système
stoïcien et l'idée de temps* (Paris, 1953), especially pp. 168 ff.
[12]   *The Meditations of Marcus Aurelius*, trans. George Long, in *Harvard Classics* (New York, 1909), II, 220-22.

but it has already passed out of sight. Something of this kind is the very life of every man, like the exhalation of the blood and the respiration of the air. ... just the same it is with the whole respiratory power. (Pp. 236-37)

Here we find the images of time as a stream, the transitory and precarious flight of the sparrow, and the transitory (almost illusory) nature of the breath of air. To this mutability and vicissitude, Aurelius opposes and urges a conformity to and the acceptance of nature, "to end thy journey in content, just as an olive falls off when it is ripe, blessing nature who produced it, and thanking the tree on which it grew" (p. 222).

To mutability then the Stoics oppose a permanent, unchanging self-identity which finds its full realization in the practice of virtue (i. e., living "according to nature", which means accepting whatever happens as good or indifferent); the truly virtuous man therefore becomes perfectly identified with, or submerged into, the divinity or Providence. Thus does Georges Poulet describe this contraposition in Stoicism:

To the spontaneous flight of the self Stoicism advises the opposing of a voluntary maintenance of the self; and that by an anticipated acceptance of the future, and especially of the future extremity, of death. Thus the permanence of being would be realized. The acceptance of death would at the same stroke imply the acceptance of the whole course of one's life. Such a position would put thought on a level with the ensemble of existence, and further, with the eternal cosmic order whose execution is entrusted to time. This would be a total adherence to destiny.[13]

In a sense Plato's "shadows" are still here, but his *realissimum* has been brought into the human will itself.

The work of yet another Stoic had an incalculable influence on the Middle Ages: "Scipio's Dream", the closing portion of the sixth book of Cicero's *De re publica*. Modeled upon Plato's *Republic* in its broader outlines (Cicero traces the development of the Roman Republic and discusses the ideal state with Rome always in mind), "Scipio's Dream" is obviously an imitation of the Vision of Er. This work of Cicero was known to the Middle Ages only through the *Commentary* of Macrobius.

In the dream the younger Africanus finds himself with his grandfather (the elder Scipio Africanus) in the region of the Milky Way. Africanus the Elder points out to him the happy abode wherein the souls of the good rulers of the commonwealth will be happy forever; and he urges him to cultivate virtue and to ignore the praise and esti-

---

[13] *Studies in Human Time*, trans. Elliott Coleman, in Harper Torchbooks (New York, 1959), p. 41.

mations of mortals, for only virtue leads to true and lasting glory. They look down from above the seven spheres and the elder man tells the younger: "Below the Moon there is nothing except what is mortal and doomed to decay, save only the souls given to the human race by the bounty of the gods, while above the Moon all things are eternal." [14] Thus is expressed once again the idea of sublunar mortality. We have already seen how closely the concepts of "mutability" and "mortality" are related in this cosmological scheme. To make the heavens immortal, Aristotle had to think up a "quint" essence, which was not subject to change and alteration. Africanus informs Scipio that the body is really a prison (a notion at least as old as Plato) and that "that life of yours, which men so call, is really death" (section xiv, p. 267); then he lectures him on the insignificance of worldly fame (sections xxi-xxiii, pp. 277-79).

Just as man's life and reputation are limited in time, so is he limited in space. Scipio relates about his dream that "the starry spheres were much larger than the earth; indeed the earth itself seemed to me so small that I was scornful of our empire, which covers only a single point, as it were, upon its surface" (section xvi, p. 269). Finally, Africanus advises him to "scorn the earthly" and to keep his gaze fixed upon heavenly things (section xix, p. 273). As with Seneca and Marcus Aurelius, Cicero again opposes the permanence of virtue to the mutability and mortality of the earthly. Of all the works which have been examined, it is this of Cicero which will have the most influence upon the Middle Ages and will constantly be called forth to reinforce their gazings at eternity.

The philosophers which have been surveyed thus far make up the more significant influences upon the thought of the succeeding ages. They also present a brief survey of the classical writers' views toward change. Philosophically, Heraclitus was the first to broach seriously the problem of change; for him all things were always in a constant state of flux. Behind this flux was a cosmic urge which manifested itself in the strife of opposites. There was furthermore no loss; the change amounted to a chemical change, wherein a loss is not actually involved, but one thing really, totally, and completely becomes something else. This doctrine of Heraclitus was, in fact, an optimistic one and was strongly contrary to the popular pessimism in regard to change which prevailed in Ephesus and in all of Greece.

[14] Trans. C. W. Keyes, in *The Loeb Classical Library* (London, 1928), section xvii ff. of *The Republic*, p. 271.

Influenced by Heraclitus' theory of flux and in opposition to Parmenides' unchanging Being, Plato posited his World of Forms as opposed to the world of phenomena. Plato's attitude toward matter and toward the phenomenal world became irrevocably fixed in the history of ideas, and reinforced by Neoplatonism, this attitude passed on to Christianity and to the Middle Ages. What the popular belief had been in regard to change until this time was now philosophically formulated, but formulated in such a way that change gave reason for even more pessimism. Now, matter, opposed to the Good and to the World of Forms, is unreal; it lacks being; it is in fact a hindrance to the complete liberation of the soul.

Aristotle abandoned Plato's transcendental realm of ideas; he considered these separate forms an unnecessary duplication. His forms are immanent in reality itself. For Aristotle "there is no essential being except the essences which we discern as such in the stream of reality . . . but essence begets essence in the infinite, uncreated stream of reality itself" (Voegelin, III, 274). But while Aristotle abolished Plato's transcendent universals, he did distinguish between prime matter and substantial form.

More important in the history of thought was Aristotle's distinction between the celestial and the terrestrial realms. For Aristotle the world was eternal. The heavenly spheres were composed of a "fifth matter", a quintessence, which did not change or decay. The earth, made up of earth, air, fire, and water, was always changing and subject always to generation and decay. This process on the earth itself was endless since the heavens, which were themselves divine and eternal because of the matter from which they were made, could exercise an unending influence on this our mortal earth (for Aristotle himself only the sun influenced the earth; this statement, however, is correct for the later Aristotelians). This distinction became absorbed into mediaeval cosmology mainly, as was pointed out, through the *Commentary* of Macrobius and remained fixed until it was discarded by the scientific notions of the seventeenth century.

Shortly after Aristotle philosophy fell into a decline. At this time appeared the Epicureans and the Stoics, of whom Lucretius on the one hand and Seneca and Marcus Aurelius on the other are the representatives. Both Epicurus and Lucretius were concerned primarily to rid men of their superstitions, particularly their fears of the gods and of death. In this way would man have inner calm and security, which is the best of pleasures. Thus Lucretius' emphasis upon mortality: death is simply the dispersion of a certain combination of atoms which make up the human soul; it is part of a universal law of all things and hence should not be feared. The Stoics likewise occupied themselves with change but, as in the case of the Epicureans, it did not occupy the focal point of their philosophy. The philosophy of the Stoics was ethically orientated: virtue was their primary study and all else was subordinate to this. Essentially, the Stoics repudiated the world. And the fact that the world was always changing and that life and the things of the world were transitory – these ideas which are seen so clearly in Marcus Aurelius' *Meditations* – proved to the Stoic that the world had little value and deserved only contempt. In this way virtue could be more seriously cultivated; it was the only thing, in fact, which was worth cultivating because only virtue is permanent, as opposed to the external world of fleeting shadows. At the basis of this whole problem of mutability therefore lies the distinction, perhaps incipient in Heraclitus but irrevocably made explicit in Plato, of change and permanence, matter and form, mortal and eternal.[15]

These ideas of the transitoriness of life and the inevitability of death are not particularly prominent in the Old Testament, but they are present and the fact remains that the Old Testament influenced the

[15]   The mutability and mortality themes also appear in Greek literature, but usually in a dramatic situation; certainly there is never the morbid preoccupation with these themes (as in the literature of the Christian era). Homer compares the generations of men to the generation of leaves but is quick to add that others come forth in the spring. See *The Iliad*, trans. A. T. Murray (New York, 1928), VI, ll. 146-52, p. 273. For other examples see the following: *The Greek Anthology*, trans. W. R. Paton, in *The Loeb Classical Library* (New York, 1925), Vol. II, Book VIII, no. 327, p. 175. *Agamemnon*, ed. Dudley Fitts, *Greek Plays in Modern Translation* (New York, 1947), p. 46. Sophocles' *Oedipus at Colonus*, ibid., p. 410; and *Ajax*, in *Sophocles*, trans. F. Storr, in *The Loeb Classical Library* (New York, 1924), II, 19. In the Roman poet Horace the theme appears of course on nearly every third page. See Steele Commager's discussion of this theme in the works of Horace in *The Odes of Horace: A Critical Study* (New Haven, 1962), pp. 235-306.

Perhaps at least some mention should be made here of the metempsychosis doctrines of the Pythagoreans and Empedocles, the influence of the former made significant mainly by the fifteenth book of Ovid's *Metamorphoses* (widely known in the Middle Ages), which probably influenced Spenser's *Two Cantos of Mutabilitie*. The doctrine of the Pythagoreans had no importance during the Middle Ages and constitutes mere change as opposed to mutability. See *The Metamorphoses of Ovid*, trans. A. E. Watts (Berkeley, 1954), pp. 350, 352-53; and *supra*, Introduction, pp. 15-16. To the extent that Ovid influenced Renaissance thought in regard to change, however, to that extent did Renaissance thought tend toward the idea of Progress and away from the concept of change as a corruptive phenomenon. Cf. the *carpe diem* theme in Ovid's *Art of Love*, trans. J. H. Mozley, in *The Loeb Classical Library* (Cambridge, 1947), III, 59 ff.

Middle Ages, especially through the New Testament and through the writings of the Fathers. It should not be surprising that the concept of mutability is not so prominent in the Old Testament. The reasons for this are many, only the more important of which I shall mention here. The concept of mutability usually prevails in the literature of a people with a vivid sense of the spiritual and a strong sense of their own individualities. Certainly this was not the case with the Israelites. Yahweh was essentially inscrutable. The attempt to explore the metaphysical possibilities of "He who is" was not made until Christian times. Voegelin points out that: "The God of Israël revealed himself in his wrath and his grace ... in natural phenomena as well as in his messengers in human shape; he spoke audibly, distinctly, and at great length to the men of his choice ... but he was not the unseen Measure of the soul in the Platonic sense" (I, 240-41). Furthermore, this same primitivism in regard to the speculation about the soul also prevailed in Israel: it is not clear that the Israelites ever conceived of the soul as something spiritual, a permanence within the flux.[16] Nor did they believe that the soul survived after death.[17] When, in the third century and only under Persian influence, the concept of immortality did enter Jewish thought, its expression was crude indeed. The Greeks would have been horrified at the idea of the resurrection of the old body (Vossler, I, 39). In brief, the Israelites could not clearly conceive of, certainly could not formulate an idea of, a spiritual substance. This deficiency is seen in their emphatic, ever-present Messianic hopes, wherein they dreamed of the realization of an earthly kingdom.

The transience of life, furthermore, is usually found in the awareness

[16] "For the most part, we are accustomed to think of man in the dualistic terms derived from Greek philosophy, in which the spiritual and material natures are sharply distinguished. In the Bible no such dualism exists. Man is a vital unity composed of various interdependent elements. ... The word *néphesh*, translated 'soul', is most commonly used to designate a person's vitality, the total self as a self-conscious unit which is activated by the mysterious principle of life; thus it does not have reference to the 'soul' at all in the Greek sense of the term." G. Ernest Wright, "The Faith of Israel", *The Interpreter's Bible* (Nashville, 1952), I, 367-68. H. Wheeler Robinson says: "The Hebrew conceived man as an animated body and not as an incarnate soul." *Inspiration and Revelation in the Old Testament* (Oxford, 1946), p. 70. An excellent and succinct study of this problem appears in Aubrey R. Johnson's *The Vitality of the Individual in the Thought of Ancient Israel* (Cardiff, U. of Wales Press, 1949), especially pp. 88 ff.

[17] See G. Ernest Wright, *Interpreter's Bible*, I, 370; and R. H. Charles, *Eschatology* (New York, 1963), in Schocken Books, pp. 48 ff. This is not to discount man's existence in Sheol, however, where he existed in a very weak, inactive, non-vital state.

of a people who have a strong sense of their own individualities. The Jews' adherence to clans and tribes, their consciousness of being a chosen people, their belief that the spirit of Yahweh "is present with the community and with individuals in their capacity as representatives of the community, but . . . not present as the ordering force in the soul of every man" (Voegelin, I, 240): these obviously absorbed any personalized, brooding sensibilities into the nationalistic, epic existence of Israel.[18] It was, incidentally, this tendency of the Jews to identify themselves with the tribe and their disbelief of the soul's survival after death which made them experience triumph and defeat "with a poignancy hitherto unknown to man" (R. H. Charles, p. 241). The concept of mutability is not strong in ancient epic (there is only one expression of it in Homer); nor is it frequent in the epic of the Jewish race. There are, nevertheless, some expressions of this concept in the Old Testament, such as in Psalm 38: "And indeed all things are vanity: every man living. Surely man passeth as an image: yea, and he is disquieted in vain. He storeth up: and he knoweth not for whom he shall gather these things." [19] In Psalm 89 the Psalmist compares time and eternity, wherein he uses the familiar image of the withering grass: "For a thousand years in thy sight are as yesterday, which is past. And as a watch in the night, things that are counted nothing, shall their years be. In the morning man shall grow up like grass; in the morning he shall flourish and pass away: in the evening he shall fall, grow dry, and wither. . . . Our years shall be considered as a spider: the days of our years in them are threescore and ten years. But if in the strong they be fourscore years: and what is more of them is labour and sorrow" (4-10). In Psalm 101, the poet sings that his days "are vanished like smoke", "have declined like a shadow", and that he is "withered like grass" (4, 12). Psalm 102 again uses the same image of the withering grass (note, incidentally, the inseparability of the notions of "mutability" and "mortality" here): "He [the Lord] remembreth that we are dust: man's days are as grass, as the flower of the field so shall he flourish. For the spirit shall pass in him, and he shall not be: and he shall know his place no more" (14-16).

---

[18]   R. H. Charles says: "The self-centredness, if not selfishness, that marked the Greek doctrine of immortality is conspicuous by its absence in the religious forecasts of the faithful in Judaism. In true religion unlimited individualism is an impossibility. The individual can only attain to his highest in the life of the community alike here and hereafter." *Eschatology*, pp. 80-81. See especially his long note on p. 81.

[19]   The Douay-Rheims version, vv. 6-7. The Douay-Rheims version is used throughout this study since it is based on the Vulgate.

In Isaias, "All flesh is grass, and all the glory thereof as the flower of the field" (xl, 6-8). In Ecclesiasticus, Jesus the son of Sirach again expresses the idea by means of the same image: "Remember that death is not slow. ... All flesh shall fade as grass, and as the leaf that springeth out on a green tree. Some grow, and some fall off: so is the generation of flesh and blood, one cometh to an end, and another is born. Every work that is corruptible shall fail in the end: and the worker thereof shall go with it" (xiv, 12, 18-20). And who is not familiar with the ever-recurrent theme of Ecclesiastes: "Vanity of vanities, and all is vanity" (i. 2)? "One generation passeth away, and another cometh", says the Preacher (i, 4). One of the major themes of Ecclesiastes is expressed thus: "All things have their season, and in their times all things pass under heaven" (iii. 1).

A few other passages in the Old Testament express the transitoriness of life and the vanity of all earthly things, but these are the more typical ones. It is interesting to note that these instances of mutability are relatively late, after other cultures have shown their influences on Hebrew thought. It might be noted too that the mutability of the grass, the leaves, and the flowers is among the more popular images used to express the mutability of human life: this is true from Homer to Boethius and beyond, into the Middle Ages. One might be reminded at this point that Chaucer introduced the term "mutabilite" into the English language (in his translation of the *Consolation of Philosophy*) when he pointed to the "mutabilite of floures of the somer sesoun" (iii, pr. 8, 11. 38-39) to show the transitoriness of bodily beauty.

Classical and Jewish thought each played its part in the development of Christianity. If classical thought bequeathed a clear-cut concept of the spiritual, Israel bequeathed the concept of monotheism: Plato's *Bonum* was Israel's Yahweh, a personal God vitally interested in the affairs of men. And perhaps what is just as important in a study of mutability, the Israelites bequeathed to Christianity the story of Creation. Aristotle believed that the world is eternal, that it was never created. Plato also probably believed that the world is eternal but that it was generated. His teachings, however, regarding the initial generation of the world are not very clear. There is, on the other hand, never any question about the creation of the world in the minds of the Israelites; Genesis makes it clear that God created Adam and Eve in time. These concepts – plus the Platonic inherent defect of matter – were absorbed into the teachings of Christianity and, within the framework of Christian revelation, took on a meaning capable of electrifying the Christian sensibility with an awareness of the transitoriness of life and of the world heretofore unrealized.

It would be tedious to itemize the expressions of mutability that appear in the New Testament. The transitoriness and the vanity of this world as contrasted with the permanence and the eternal happiness of the next is the major burden of the Gospels and the Epistles. The problem is to discover what particular factor or factors in Christianity made for this deeper intensity and stronger impetus. Perhaps part of the answer lies in the Christian viewpoints toward creation and death.

The concept or doctrine of creation once and for all instilled into the popular consciousness the idea that man was contingent and dependent. Man was created in the image of God and destined to return to God. The revelation of Christ and the Apostles gave this assurance. This realization, in fact, was intensified by the mediaeval teaching in regard to the preservation of existence. Georges Poulet states very clearly the mediaeval teaching along these lines:

> If from being nothing they [the Christians of the Middle Ages] came to be something, if from the possible they passed to the actual, if their existence remained contingent and dependent, that was because such existences were created existences. In one sense they were being created every moment; not that God was obliged each moment to create them anew, but rather that in all the range of their existence, by the same act of will, the Creator caused them to be and to endure. . . .
>
> Thus sustained by the permanent continuity of substantial form, the moving continuity of time unrolled itself, so mobile and so fluid that it was impossible to distinguish consecutive moments. No doubt, such fluidity implied a part of nonbeing. But what distinguished this time from Heraclitan time or even Platonic time – time of pure mobility – was that it was a movement toward an end. The finality of the movement gave it in return something that transcended its materiality. Even in his body the Christian of the Middle Ages felt a continuous orientation toward a spiritual perfection. Time had a direction. Time finally carried the Christian toward God. (pp. 3-6)

Creation was therefore more than just a historical fact. In the mediaeval consciousness, the existence of each man found its beginning and its continuance in this single action of God. Specifically, the end of this divine action was, from man's point of view, the enjoyment of the beatific vision, supreme and eternal happiness. But all that

> was naturally spontaneous and instantaneous in spiritual life – the act of comprehending, the act of feeling, the act of willing or of enjoying – all of this was being achieved in man only through time, only with the help of time, only as if borne by time toward its completion. But in proportion as

this act was brought close to its point of perfection, in proportion as it approached its own completion in time, it tended to release itself from time. At the very moment it attained its fullness, all its temporality disappeared. It was brought to perfection in an instant which transcended time and which, as long as it lasted, lasted within a duration that was permanent. (*Ibid.*, p. 6)

Poulet concludes that: "For the man of the Middle Ages, then, there was not one duration only. There were *durations*, ranked one above another, and not only in the universality of the exterior world but within himself, in his own nature, in his own human existence" (p. 7). It is therefore not surprising that human time took on an immediacy in the mediaeval consciousness which it had not had in the consciousness of the ancients. Time was no longer man's own, to do with as he pleased; it was no longer mere mobility, hurrying past man's vision. It was now a means of salvation, a fleeting opportunity which appeared more fleeting amid the urgency of the spiritual "now". Life had a beginning and an end: it was in fact a pilgrimage toward an eternal duration. It was this eternal duration ceaselessly haunting the mediaeval consciousness that made the temporal duration always seem vain and transitory. The two durations were always counterpoised in the mediaeval mind.

The second factor which was responsible for this new impetus in regard to the sensibility of the transitoriness of life and of the world was the Christian attitude toward death. There was for the most part among the Greeks "the impersonal and graceful sadness of minds accustomed to acquiesce in the natural cycle of life and death" (Kurtz, p. 250). Plato looked upon death as a welcome release from contaminating matter. The Epicureans taught that "we may be sure that there is nothing to be feared after death, that he who is not cannot be miserable" (Lucretius, iii, ll. 866-67). The Stoics accepted the fact of death with the same equanimity that they accepted the fact of life. These are only random instances of the attitudes of the ancients toward death. Perhaps the *Greek Anthology* most adequately approximates the Greek attitude toward death, and here death is never pictured as hideous or something to be especially feared. This attitude persisted from Homer down to and beyond Seneca.

The Christian concept of death, however, was vastly different from that of the Greeks and Romans. Christianity taught that death is a penalty for the Fall: through the sin of Adam death entered into the world, says St. Paul. In Book XIII (Ch. 15) of *The City of God*, Augustine argues that death is penal and had its origin in Adam's sin. He says: "And therefore it is agreed among all Christians who truthfully hold the catholic faith, that we are subject to the death of the body, not by the law of nature, by which God ordained no death for man, but by His righteous infliction on account of sin; for God, taking vengeance on sin, said to the man, in whom we all then were, 'Dust thou art, and unto dust shalt thou return.' " [20] Theodore Spencer observes that:

Christianity added one remarkable doctrine which pagan disillusionment and transcendental philosophy had never mentioned. It taught that death was a punishment for man's sin. This was a notion entirely foreign to Greece and Rome; as Lessing remarked, "to deem death a punishment, could not of itself have occurred to the brain of a man who only used his reason, without revelation". . . . when death was considered a punishment, it became at once the most critical moment of life. To think of death was to think of sin, and to think of sin was the only way to purify the soul. Death was no longer merely a step across a threshold or the closing of a door, it was the crucial event in human experience. (P. 5-6)

Spencer's statement can hardly be denied; it is natural and even inevitable that this view of death should be a major factor in contributing to Christian pessimism. Add to this the Christian teachings of personal immortality, its teachings of Heaven and Hell (the visionary descriptions of which are found early in Christian history), and its constant reminders that man must die to the world in order to gain heaven (Baptism, for example, is itself a symbol of man's death to the world), it was inevitable that there appear in Christian literature a more intense and refined sensibility of the mutability of all earthly things. This new intensity can be seen in almost all the writings of the early Fathers of the Church, of which only a few instances need be evidenced here.

In his letter to Heliodorus, for example, St. Jerome writes that "every day we are changing, every day we are dying, and yet we fancy ourselves eternal. The very moments that I spend in dictation, in writing . . . are so much gone from my allotted time".[21] In like manner St. Ambrose in the *Hexaemeron* remarks that:

Today you may see a strong, maturing young man, flourishing in the greenness of life, with a pleasing appearance and an attractive complexion; tomorrow, changed in appearance and face he meets you; and he who on the preceding day seemed to you most splendid because of his comely form, on

---

[20] *A Select Library of the Nicene and Post-Nicene Fathers of the Christian Church*, ed. Philip Schaff (Buffalo, 1886-87), II, 252.
[21] *A Select Library* . . ., eds. Philip Schaff and Henry Wace, Second Series (Grand Rapids, 1954), VI, 131.

another day appears wretched and wasted by the weakness of some illness. Hardship breaks very many, or want weakens them, or miserable condition vexes them, or wines destroy them, or old age weakens them, or pleasures make them unmanly, or study deprives them of their blooming complexions. Is it not true that the grass has become dry and the flower has fallen? . . . Behold, it is true that just as the grass withers before it is pulled up, so it is with the life of man.[22]

St. Augustine, in the well-known passage from *The City of God* (Ch. 10), speaks of mutability in terms which betray a Senecan influence:

For no sooner do we begin to live in this dying body, than we begin to move ceaselessly towards death. For in the whole course of this life (if life we must call it) its mutability tends toward death. Certainly there is no one who is not nearer it this year than last year, and to-morrow than to-day, and to-day than yesterday, and a short while hence than now, and now than a short while ago. For whatever time we live is deducted from our whole term of life, and that which remains is daily becoming less and less; so that our whole life is nothing but a race towards death, in which no one is allowed to stand still for a little space, or to go somewhat more slowly, but all are driven forwards with an impartial movement, and with equal rapidity.[23]

Thus did the early Fathers set the pattern and the pace for the treatment of the theme of mutability in the literature of the later Middle Ages. Henceforth literature will abound with references to the mutability of life, of fame, and of fortune until the end of the Renaissance. The theme of mutability appears in religious and secular literature alike. In the next chapter, the theme will be discussed as it appears in Boethius' *Consolation of Philosophy*, the *Romance of the Rose*, and Innocent III's *De Contemptu Mundi*; these are important for this study not only because they were Chaucer's sources and because he chose to translate these works, but also because they are fairly representative of the Middle Ages generally.

At this point, however, the theme is cited in a few other works of the Middle Ages simply to show how widespread and commonplace the

---

[22] *Patrologiae Cursus Completus*, ed. J. P. Migne, *Series latina* (Paris, 1879-87), XIV, col. 123; translation my own. Unless otherwise indicated, translations throughout this study are my own.

[23] *A Select Library*, Orig. Series (1886-87), II, 249. See also Book XI of the *Confessions*; and the excellent treatment of Saint Augustine's concept of time in H.-I. Marrou, *L'Ambivalence du Temps de l'histoire chez Saint Augustin* (Paris, 1950); Jean Guitton, *Le Temps et L'éternité chez Plotin et Saint Augustin* (Paris, 1959), especially pp. 271 ff. For the importance of the dichotomy between Immutable Being and mutable creation in Augustine's philosophy and his influence, see Etienne Gilson, *History of Christian Philosophy in the Middle Ages* (New York, 1955), pp. 70 ff.

concept really was.[24] Here the attitude is always personal, practical, and preoccupied with death (in contrast with the preoccupation of the ancients, which was usually speculative. Of all the ancients, in fact, only Seneca was preoccupied with the thought of death). So commonplace was the mutability theme that it even appears in public documents:

I Stephen, Count of Boulogne and Mortain . . . in this year of our Lord's incarnation 1126 – seeing that the bounds of this our age are breaking and falling daily into decay – seeing, again, how all the transitory pomp of this world, with the flowers and rosy chaplets and palms of flourishing kings, emperors, dukes and all rich men do wither from day to day; how, again, death casts them all into one mingled mass and hurries them swiftly to the grave – seeing all this, I give, grant, and make over to God and to St. Mary of Furness, and to the abbot of that monastery. . . .[25]

The mutability theme also appears in one of the more important religious works of the Middle Ages, the *Ayenbite of Inwyt*. Note how the Senecan idea, that we begin to die as soon as we begin to live, takes on a more immediate meaning in a context which visualizes the torments of hell. It is again clear from this passage that it was this vivid visualization of an eternal afterlife which informed the mediaeval consciousness with the realization of the transitoriness of all earthly things:

This life is but a wending, for sooth, for sooth: a wending well short. For all the life of a man, though he lived a thousand years, were but a point compared to the other life that shall last ever without end, either in sorrow or in bliss without ending.
  The king, the earl, the prince, the emperor who formerly had bliss in the world, and are now in hell, weeping, crying, yelling, sorrowing – these bear us witness of this. "Alas", they say, "what is our power, nobility, riches,

[24] The mutability theme is frequent in Old English literature and the "Anglo-Saxon melancholy" is well-known. It appears in *Beowulf* (ll. 1758-68); the "Elegy of the Lone Survivor", ll. 2247-66; and the "Lament of the Father" (ll. 2444-62a), the *Ruin*, the *Wanderer*, the *Seafarer, Deor's Complaint*, to cite but a few instances of the theme; and of course there is the famous passage wherein man's life is compared with the "swift flight of a lone sparrow through the banqueting-hall" in *Bede: A History of the English Church and People*, trans. Leo Sherley-Price, in Penguin Books (Baltimore, 1955), pp. 124-25. For brief discussions of this theme as a heathen motif, see Stopford Brooke, *English Literature From the Beginning to the Norman Conquest* (London, 1930), p. 100; and E. K. Chambers and F. Sidgwick, eds., *Early English Lyrics* (London, 1911), pp. 284-85. For fuller discussions of the mutability theme as a Christian element, cf. Bernard F. Huppé, "*The Wanderer*: Theme and Structure", *JEGP*, 42 (1943), 516-38; and J. E. Cross, " 'Ubi sunt' Passages in Old English – Sources and Relationships", *Vetenskaps-Societetens i Lund Arsbok* (1956), 25-41. Huppé very perceptively distinguishes the Christian and the heathen elements, pp. 526 ff.
[25] G. G. Coulton, *Life in the Middle Ages* (New York, 1933), IV, 108; Coulton's translation is from the *Monasticon*, V, 247.

boasting worth to us now? All is gone, more quickly than the shadow, or the flying bird, or the arrow of the crossbow. And thus goes all our life. We were born and very quickly borne to our graves. Our whole life is but a little prick. Now we are in sorrow without end. Our bliss is turned into weeping and our carols into sorrow. Our garlands, robes, partying, dishes, and our other goods have failed us." Such are the songs of hell. As the writings tell us (and show us), this life is but a wending, and living is but a wending. To live therefore is but to die; and this is as true as the Pater Noster. For when you begin to live, you begin to die. And all your age and time that has passed, death has won from you, and holds them. You say that you have sixty years, but death has them and will never yield them. ... For you die day and night as I have said.[26]

Perhaps no devotional work of the Middle Ages is so filled with the mutability theme as *The Imitation of Christ*, thought to be by Thomas à Kempis (1380-1471). It is significant in determining the extent to which mutability was a part of the mediaeval outlook that some twenty editions of Richard Whitford's translation of this work appeared in England from 1530 to 1585.[27] It was during this period of the Renaissance that the mediaeval sensibility regarding change generally still prevailed.

The main theme of *The Imitation of Christ* is that all things are passing but Christ. In the first chapter of the book Thomas says: "How great a vanity is it . . . to love things that shortly shall pass away, and not to haste thither where joy is everlasting." Almost every chapter of the work is a variation of this one basic theme, the contrast of the temporal and the eternal states. Temporal joy is as nothing compared to that joy which is eternal (ii, 6). In the first chapter of the second book, we find: "Thou hast here no place of long abiding, for wheresoever thou be come thou art but a stranger and a pilgrim and never shalt thou find perfect rest till thou be fully joined to God. Why dost thou look to have rest here since this is not thy resting place? Thy full rest must be in heavenly

[26] *Ayenbite of Inwyt*, ed. Richard Morris, in EETS, Original Series, 23 (London, 1866), p. 71; see also p. 81 for the idea of the transitoriness of beauty. It might conveniently be mentioned here that there are expressions of mutability in the *Divine Comedy*, even though the *loci dramatis* are obviously outside of mortal time. See the Modern Library College edition, trans. Carlyle-Okey-Wicksteed, *Inf.*, vii; *Purg.*, xi, xx, xxxi; *Para.*, v, xv, xvi, xvii, xxvi, xxvii, xxix; especially *Para.*, xii. for a modified concept of the Aristotelian doctrine of the unchanging heavens and the mutable earth. For an excellent statement of the theme as it is expressed in mediaeval religious lyrics, see E. K. Chambers and F. Sidgwick, *Early English Lyrics*, pp. 282-85; and for other statements of its expression in mediaeval literature generally, Huizinga, *Waning*, pp. 138 ff.; H. S. Bennett, *Chaucer and the Fifteenth Century* (New York, 1947), p. 100.
[27] See Richard Whitford's translation of *The Imitation of Christ*, ed. Edward J. Klein (New York, 1941), Introduction, p. xxxi; all future citations of the *Imitation* are from this edition.

things, and all earthly things thou must behold as things transitory and shortly passing away." Thomas almost leads the reader to believe that "sin" and "delight in transitory things" are identical: "Think all the world as naught, and prefer my service [the author is impersonating Christ here] before all other things; for thou mayst not have mind on me and therewithal delight thee in transitory pleasures" (iii, 53). In the same chapter he writes: "O how sure a trust shall it be to a man at his departing out of this world, to feel inwardly in his soul that no earthly love nor yet the affection of any passing or transitory thing hath any rule in him!" And in another place, "Forsake the love of transitory things and seek things that be everlasting. What be all temporal things but deceivable?" (iii, 1). All things should be suffered for eternal life, for "an hour shall come when all thy labours and troubles shall cease. And truly that hour is at hand, for all is short that passeth with time" (iii, 47). The spirit of truth teaches those who have it "to love heavenly things, to forsake the world that is transitory, and to desire both day and night to come thither where joy is everlasting" (iii, 4). In short, there is hardly a book which betrays this mediaeval sensibility of the transitoriness of life and of the world more than this work of Thomas à Kempis. He writes that "the end of all men is death, and the life of man as a shadow suddenly slideth and passeth away" (i, 23). Why should one fear the vain judgments of mortal man? "This day he is, and tomorrow he appeareth not" (iii, 36). In truth, "man is but as grass, and all his glory is as a flower in the field which suddenly vanisheth away" (ii, 7). These are but a few of the references to the theme of mutability in *The Imitation of Christ*; there are many others.[28] The Platonic contrast between the permanent World of Ideas and the mutable World of Shadows has come a long way; and *The Imitation of Christ* is the exact measure of the limits which this contrast reached within the framework of mediaeval Christianity.[29]

[28] See I: 3, 11, 20, 22, 23, 25; II: 6, 7; III: 14, 16, 33. There are also numerous references to man as a pilgrim and an exile, to the woe which always follows joy, and to related themes.
[29] The mutability theme so abounds throughout the Middle Ages that one hardly needs to cite further instances of its appearance. I might simply mention here, however, its prevalence in the Middle English lyrics. See the general indices (under "mutability", "transitoriness", and the various cross-references), for example, of Carleton Brown and R. H. Robbins, *The Index of Middle English Verse* (New York, 1943); and Brown's *A Register of Middle English Religious and Didactic Verse* (Oxford, 1916-20). The frequency of the theme may also be seen in John E. Wells, *A Manual of the Writings in Middle English 1050-1400* (New Haven, 1916), pp. 385-96.

GOLDEN AGE AND DECAY OF THE WORLD

In this chapter particularly and throughout this study, I refer to "Golden Age" and "decay of the world" interchangeably. The Golden Age is but the poetical expression of the idea of the decay of the world and, until the Renaissance, was its foremost expression. It has been pointed out that Plato and Aristotle believed that the world is eternal. The idea of the world's mortality, however, was expressed most fully and with the greatest power by Lucretius, who argued that decay in the elements, the parts, necessarily meant decay in the whole.[30] The idea of the world's growing old is also expressed in the Psalms.[31] The notion of the world's mortality is, certainly, consonant with the general attitude of the Greek and Roman philosophers toward change, as a deteriorative process. Given this fact and the early Christian idea that the end of the world was near at hand, it is easy to see why St. Cyprian's influence, along with Lucretius, was very important in disseminating the concept of the world growing old. In the following, Cyprian speaks vividly about the world's mortality in his over-all context that the end of the world is imminent:

And this [to come willingly when the Lord calls in death] ... much more ought to be done now – now that the world is collapsing and is oppressed with the tempests of mischievous ills; in order that we who see that terrible things have begun, and know that still more terrible things are imminent, may regard it as the greatest advantage to depart from it as quickly as possible. If in your dwelling the walls were shaking with age, the roofs above you were trembling, and the house, now worn out and wearied, were threatening an immediate destruction to its structure crumbling with age, would you not with all speed depart? ... Lo, the world is changing and passing away, and witness to its ruin not now by its age, but by the end of things.[32]

Except for an occasional reference here and there throughout the Middle Ages,[33] however, the views of Lucretius and Cyprian did not reach the

[30] See especially the final passage of Book II of Rouse's translation. Only generally related to this point but extremely useful for illuminating the whole concept of change in ancient and early Christian times is Theodor E. Mommsen's chapter "Augustine on Progress", in *Medieval and Renaissance Studies* (Ithaca, 1959), pp. 265-98.
[31] Psalm 101, v. 27.
[32] "On the Mortality", in *The Ante-Nicene Fathers*, eds. A. Roberts and J. Donaldson (Buffalo, 1886), V, 475.
[33] See, for example, Coulton's excerpt which he translated from Walther v. der Vogelweide, Lachmann, 124, 1, in *Life in the Middle Ages*, III, 16. The belief that the end of the world was imminent was certainly not general after the fourth or fifth centuries. See A. Vasiliev, "Medieval Ideas of the End of the World: West and East", *Byzantion*, 16 (1942-43), 462-502.

popular imagination until the Renaissance, when the discovery of change in the heavens greatly accelerated the belief in the world's decay. Until this time the poetical expression of the Golden Age was the most prominent manifestation of this theme.

In his *Apologie* (1627), George Hakewill not only holds Lucretius and St. Cyprian responsible for the idea of the decay of the world, but, he says, what has led to this false opinion "is that *idle tale* and *vaine fancie* forged by *Poets*, & taken up by some *Historians*, & beleeved by the *vulgar* of the *foure ages of the world*".[34] He then quotes this "idle tale" from Ovid's *Metamorphoses* and points out Boethius' and Juvenal's borrowing of it in the *Consolation* and Thirteenth Satire, respectively.

The story of the Golden Age entered literature in Hesiod's *Works and Days*, in the eighth century B. C. The work is essentially an exhortation to industry. After the Fable of Pandora, Hesiod writes of the four races of men, the first of which is the golden race:

First of all the deathless gods who dwell on Olympus made a golden race of mortal men who lived in the time of Cronos when he was reigning in heaven. And they lived like gods without sorrow of heart, remote and free from toil and grief: miserable age rested not on them; but with legs and arms never failing they made merry with feasting beyond the reach of all evils. When they died, it was as though they were overcome with sleep, and they had all good things; for the fruitful earth unforced bare them fruit abundantly and without stint. They dwelt in ease and peace upon their lands with many good things, rich in flocks and loved by the blessed gods.[35]

He then describes the silver, bronze, and iron races, the last two interrupted by his description of the Homeric race of heroes, which is obviously out of place. Through the four ages of men the condition of the world deteriorates, so that the poet says, "Would that I were not among the men of the fifth generation" (p. 15). Thus begins the literary genre that expresses the desire for the stable, changeless order which existed in the world before it began to decline and decay.

Since the Golden Age will be treated in the following chapter in connection with its appearance in the *Consolation of Philosophy* and *Le Roman de la Rose*, it is sufficient here merely to indicate its wide-

[34] *Apologie or Declaration of the Power and Providence of God in the Government of the World, Consisting in an Examination and Censure of the Common Error Touching Nature's Perpetual and Universal Decay*, p. 323. Quoted from Willamson, "Mutability, Decay", p. 132.
[35] *Hesiod: The Homeric Hymns and Homerica*, trans. Hugh G. Evelyn-White, in *The Loeb Classical Library* (New York, 1926), p. 11.

spread appearance in literature after Hesiod and to show its relationship to the concept of mutability generally.

It has already been stated that the theme appears in Ovid's *Metamorphoses*, Juvenal's Thirteenth Satire, the *Consolation,* and *Le Roman de la Rose*. It is also found in Virgil's *Aeneid*, Dante's *Inferno*, in the works of Deschamps, and, as will be seen, in Chaucer's *Former Age*. The Garden of Paradise in Genesis is, in fact, related to this genre.[36] In all these influential works, the depiction of the Golden Age is essentially the same: no diseases, no labor, no misery of old age, no wars, happiness in full, brotherhood inspired by love, no greed, no competition or commercialism – in short, the Golden Age is the literary expression of mankind's universal yearning to be free from all the ills which plague mortality.[37]

It also reveals an attitude toward change. If indeed change involves deterioration and decay, it stands to reason that any age, seeing its own miserable condition of mortality, should look upon the beginning of the human race as a state of ideal earthly perfection. (This is especially true in the absence of the doctrine of original sin, which accounts for man's impoverished condition in terms other than time and change.) Here again appears the intimate connection between mutability and mortality. It is the element of change in this ideal order of the Golden Age, the fact that this order was subject to mutability, which has effected the present condition of man's mortality.

UBI SUNT

The *ubi sunt* formula is perhaps as old as mankind. Of all the motifs or variations of the theme of mutability, this is the easiest to distinguish because it is stereotyped; "C'est probablement la question plaintive: *Ubi sunt* . . . etc., qui forme le point de départ de notre motif poétique",

[36] It is interesting to note that St. Bernard (?) describes even the celestial paradise in terms of the Golden Age: "Nulla erit ibi tristitia, nulla angustia, nullus dolor, nullus timor, nullus ibi labor, nulla mors, sed perpetua sanitas semper ibi perseverat." *Meditationes Piissimae de Cognitione Humanae Conditionis* (attributed to St. Bernard and printed with his works). Migne, *Pat. Lat.*, clxxxiv, col. 505.
[37] For the fullest treatment of this subject, which I have merely outlined here, see *A Documentary History of Primitivism and Related Ideas*, eds. Lovejoy, Chinard, Boas, and Crane (Baltimore, 1935), I.

says Gilson.[38] This theme is found rather sparsely in classical literature, more frequently in the Old Testament, still more frequently in the Patristic writings, and abounds throughout the literature of the Middle Ages. In *The Greek Anthology*, for example, we find: "Where is now Praxiteles? Where are the hands of Polycleitus, that gave life to the works of ancient art? Who shall mould Melite's scented ringlets, or her fiery eyes and the splendour of her neck? Where are the modellers, the carvers in stone?" [39] Another illustration of the theme is found in Ovid's *Metamorphoses*, when Ajax exclaims, "Where now is the eloquent Ulysses?" [40]

The most influential source of the theme, however, is the Old Testament. "Where is the learned? where is he that pondereth the words of the law?" where is the teacher of little ones?" asks Isaias (xxxiii, 18). In IV Kings, the author asks, "Where is the king of Emath, and the king of Arphad, and the king of the city of Sepharvaim, of Ana and of Ava?" (xix, 13). In Baruch, the author tells his hearers to "learn where is wisdom" that they may "know also where is length of days and life" (iii, 14). Then he says that few have found the treasure of wisdom and asks: "Where are the princes of the nations, and that rule over the beasts that are upon earth? That take their diversion with the birds of the air? That hoard up silver and gold, wherein men trust . . . They are cut off, and are gone down to hell . . ." (16-19). In First Corinthians, St. Paul echoes Isaias: "Where is the wise? Where is the scribe? Where is the disputer of this world? Hath not God made foolish the wisdom of this world?" (i, 20). From the Bible the Church Fathers took up the formula.

The formula entered Christian literature with the Syrian Saint Ephrem (306-373), whose influence is seen in the writings of Saint Cyril of

---

[38]   Étienne Gilson, *Les Idées et les Lettres* (Paris, 1955), p. 20n. Gilson's first chapter, "De la Bible à François Villon", deals exclusively with the history of the *ubi sunt* theme. In my treatment of the theme here, I rely upon Gilson's work very heavily. I have, however, also consulted the following: C. H. Becker, *"Ubi sunt qui ante nos in mundo fuere"*, *Islamstudien*, I (1924), 501 ff.; James W. Bright, "The '*ubi sunt*' Formula", *MLN*, VIII (1893), 94; Frederick Tupper, Jr., "The *ubi sunt* Formula", *ibid.*, pp. 253-54; Clark S. Northup, "*Ubi Sunt* Heroes?", *MLN*, XXVIII (1913), 106-107; Kr. Nyrop, "Note sur une Ballade de Villon", *Bulletin de l'Académie royale des Sciences et des Lettres de Danemark*, II (1907), 73-82. Nyrop's article furnishes many examples of the theme; see also Professor Creizenach's "Das 'Gaudeamus' und was daran hängt", *Verhandlungen der 28 Versammlung der Philologen und Schulmänner* (Leipzig, 1872), pp. 203-208.

[39]   *The Greek Anthology*, II, 175.

[40]   Trans. Frank Justus Miller, in *The Loeb Classical Library* (New York, 1926), II, xiii, 9, p. 235.

Alexandria (370-444); both writers appropriated the formula from First Corinthians (quoted above), in its exact form. Isidore of Seville (d. 636), however, used the theme creatively and abundantly and is perhaps responsible for its wide diffusion; the *Etymologiae* and the *Synonyma* were popular source-books for mediaeval preachers and poets. In the *Synonyma*, for example, he writes: "The happiness of this world is short and its glory scanty, worldly power is fragile and transitory. Tell me, where are the kings? where are the princes? where are the emperors? Where are the wealthy? where are the powerful and the opulent of the world? They have passed as shadows, and vanished as a dream." [41] From this time on, the theme is found abundantly in the Patristic writings, especially in those of Saints Prosper of Aquitaine, Augustine, Anselm, Bonaventure, and Bernard. The following excerpt from the writings of St. Bonaventure provides an excellent illustration of the full development of the theme and an indication of the course that it will take in mediaeval poetry generally:

All things have passed away as shadows and as a ship that has traversed the waves, and not a trace is to be found. They have indeed been brought to nothingness; and, alas, how few have left behind even so much as a sign of accomplishment! Where are the rulers of nations and those who have commanded the beasts of the earth, who have gathered and collected silver and gold, who have vanquished cities and encampments and have separated kings from their kingdoms? Where is the wise, where is the scribe, where is the disputer of this world? [Note the influence of I Cor. i, 20; *supra*, p. 44.] Where is Solomon the most wise? Where is Alexander the most powerful? Where is Samson the most strong? Where is Absalon the most beautiful? Where is Assuerus the most glorious? Where are the most powerful Caesars? Where are the kings and the renowned rulers? What profits them their empty fame, their fleeting pleasures, their worldly power, famous family, carnal pleasures, the deception of riches, and the sweetness of concupiscence? Where is the laughter, where is the joy, where the bragging, where the presumption, where the nobility of birth, the beautiful body, the fine appearance, where is the youthful comeliness, the large estates, the splendid palaces, where is the wisdom of the world? All these things are of the world and the world loves its own; and yet these things will not remain with the world for very long. For the world and its desires will pass away.[42]

This excerpt from Bonaventure makes abundantly clear how the primitive biblical theme grew to rather large and detailed proportions. Bonaventure instances here the popular tendency to recall the names of famous men and women; for at about this same time there appeared

[41] *Synonyma, Pat. Lat.*, lxxxiii, col. 865.
[42] Quoted from Gilson, *Les Idées*, pp. 17-18.

"l'insistance plus marquée sur la fragilité de la beauté féminine" (Gilson, p. 19). It is unnecessary to multiply instances of the theme as it appears in the literature of the Middle Ages.[43] "Hwer is Paris and Heleyne,/ That weren so bryht and feyre on bleo?" and "Were beth they biforen us weren,/ Houndes ladden and hauekes beren ... ?"[44] are only random instances of the formula's ubiquitous occurrence. At least five of Deschamps' *balades* deal with this theme.[45] It is found in Lydgate's *Like a Midsomer Rose* and was in fact, even as early as the twelfth and thirteenth centuries, a theological and poetical banality. Whatever form or combination of forms the *ubi sunt* might have taken, however, the phrase itself echoed throughout the Middle Ages until it reached its climax in the works of Villon. His "Ballade of the Ladies of Bygone Times" remains the lasting monument of this empty formula:

> Tell me where, or in what land
> is Flora the lovely Roman,
> or Archipiada, or Thaïs
> who so resembled her,
> or Echo speaking when one called
> across still pools or rivers,
> and whose beauty was more than human.
> But where are the snows of bygone years?
>
> Where is Héloïse, so wise, for whom
> Pierre Abelard was gelded
> and made a monk at Saint-Denis?
> For her love he bore these trials.
> And where now is that queen
> by whose command Buridan
> was thrown in a sack in the Seine?
> But where are the snows of bygone years? [46]

The final stanza of the ballad names seven more illustrious women of the past. With the exception of the later Middle Ages when the theme became almost exclusively trite and banal, typified in Villon, it is not too far-fetched to remark that the frequency of the occurrence of this formula is the approximate measure of the prevailing sensibility of the transitoriness of all things.

---

[43] Gilson, pp. 31-38, lists the principal works in which this theme occurs.
[44] Chambers and Sidgwick, *Early English Lyrics*, pp. 285 and 163-64, respectively.
[45] Gilson, p. 36; Huizinga, *Waning*, p. 140.
[46] *The Complete Works of François Villon*, trans. Anthony Bonner (New York, 1960), p. 39.

PUTREFACTION

The putrefaction motif is in a sense the vividly depicted answer to the question, *Ubi sunt qui ante nos in mundo fuere*? This motif is not found in Greek and Roman literature; [47] its first significant appearance is in the Book of Job. "I have said to corruption", says Job, "Thou are my father; to the worm, my mother and my sister" (xvii, 14); "They shall lie down alike in the dust and the worms shall cover them" (xxi, 26). Kurtz considers Job the main source of this theme: "Straight from *Job*, then, and a few passages scattered in *Ecclesiasticus*, *The Wisdom of Solomon*, and other books of the Old and New Testaments – with no tradition bridging the centuries between, and with no important source in any other ancient literature of the West – comes a theme that, misunderstood, ignobly transformed, and applied to a new purpose, develops into the Gifer-theme of the Middle Ages" ("Gifer the Worm", p. 256).

This theme first appeared in English literature in the *Address of the Soul to the Body*; here the poet is attempting to teach with power the lesson that life in the world, vain as it may be, determines the soul's destiny in the afterlife. The name of the worm in the poem is Gifer, whence the term "Gifer theme".

> The worm is a glutton,   one whose jaws
> are sharper than a needle,   He is the first
> to creep down   into the earth cave.
> He slits the tongue,   bores through the teeth,
> eats the eyes   up in the head,
> and to that wealth of feasting   opens a wide way
> to other worms,   when the wretched body
> has grown cold,   that for a long time
> was clothed in robes. It is now worm's meat,
> his food in the earth;   and everyone
> who is a wise man   will remember this.[48]

[47] Empedocles, lamenting the necessity of being born in various aspects of dying, approaches the theme only slightly: "And I wept and shrieked on beholding the unwonted land [of this life] where are Murder and Wrath, and other species of Fates, and wasting diseases, and putrefaction and fluxes." "On Purifications", trans. Arthur Fairbanks, in *The First Philosophers of Greece* (London, 1898), ll. 385-88. The reason that the putrefaction theme does not appear in the literature of the Greeks and Romans stems ultimately perhaps from their attitudes toward death. This difference in the classical and mediaeval attitudes toward death I have explained in the study of mutability. Job's complaint is not a *memento mori*, to be sure. The theme is incidental to his expression of complete denigration of self and his abhorrence to God, as he sees it.

[48] Margaret Williams, *Word-Hoard* (London, 1946), p. 175.

The *Address of the Soul to the Body* offers the only example of the putrefaction theme in Old English literature.

The Gifer theme is only a part of the more general theme of putrefaction. Any depiction of physical decomposition after death constitutes the putrefaction theme. In the *Sayings of Saint Bernard* (1250-1300), for example, both the worm imagery and other imagery expressive of decay are found:

> Saint Bernard seith in his bok:
> That mon is worm and wormes cok,
> And wormes he schal feden.
> Whon his lyf is him bireved,
> In his rug and in his heved
> Wol foule wormes breden.
>
> The flesch schal melten from the bon,
> The senewes sundren everichon,
> The bodi schal defyen.
> And ye that wolen the sothe sen,
> Under the graves, ther they ben,
> And loketh hou thei lyghen.[49]

Of the Patristic writings dealing with this theme, the most influential were Innocent III's *De Contemptu Mundi* and St. Bernard's *Meditationes Piisimae de Cognitione Humanae Conditionis*. The theme as it appears in Innocent's work will be pointed out in the following chapter. As for Bernard's Latin work, the *Sayings* itself testifies to its vast influence. This work is not nearly so morbidly detailed as is the work of Innocent. This excerpt might well suggest the method and theme of the *Meditationes*: "The flesh, of such great intimacy and importance to you, is not other than foam made into flesh, clothed in fragile beauty; but when it becomes a corpse, it will be ugly and putrid and worms' meat" (Migne, 184, col. 489). Up to this point, it is clear that the purpose of the putrefaction imagery is to incite a *memento mori*.

Actually, the putrefaction theme is not very dominant in Middle English literature to 1400. Outside of a few relatively insignificant poems, such as *Signs of Death*,[50] its most complete and vivid expression is found in the *Sayings of St. Bernard*. It is not until the late Middle Ages following upon the Black Death that the theme becomes wide-

---

[49] Hermann Varnhagen, "Noch einmal zu den sprüchen des heiligen Bernhard" (from the Vernon and the Auchinleck MSS), *Anglia*, III (1880), 285-86.
[50] *An Old English Miscellany*, ed. Richard Morris, EETS, O. S. 49 (London, 1872), p. 101.

spread, not only in literature but also in painting and sculpture.[51] At this time, in fact, the preoccupation with the physical horrors of death ceases to be a *memento mori* and is enjoyed in and for itself. Huizinga testifies to this and offers, I think, an adequate explanation for the fact: "The imagination of those times relished these horrors, without ever looking one stage further, to see how corruption perishes in its turn, and flowers grow where it lay. A thought which so strongly attaches to the earthly side of death can hardly be called truly pious. It would rather seem a kind of spasmodic reaction against an excessive sensuality" (*Waning*, pp. 140-41). Perhaps no poetry better illustrates this enjoyment of the horrible details of decay and the lack of the pious purpose of this imagery than that of Villon. The following is from *The Testament* (1461-62):

> Death makes him tremble and turn white,
> curls his nostrils, stretches taut his veins,
> puffs out his neck, makes flesh turn flabby,
> joints and nerves dilate and swell.
> O woman's body, so tender,
> smooth, soft and precious,
> do these ills await you too?
> Yes, unless you go alive to heaven.
>
> (*Works*, tr. Bonner, p. 39)

When the putrefaction theme was used for a *memento mori*, it was closely related to mutability. It functioned as a reminder of the fleeting moments of time and of the inevitability of death. Not used for this purpose, the putrefaction material has no relation to the theme of mutability.

CONTEMPT OF THE WORLD

Of all the mutability motifs under consideration in this study, the critics' use of the contempt of the world idea is most likely to lead to confusion. This is so primarily because some critics use the expression generically to embrace not only the general concept of mutability but also the different variations of this theme, the *ubi sunt*, for example.[52]

---

[51] See E. Mâle, *L'art religieux à la fin du moyen âge en France* (Paris, 1908), pp. 347-437.
[52] See, for example, Huizinga, *Waning*, p. 141; Farnham, *Medieval Heritage*, pp. 80 ff.; and Donald Howard's unpublished University of Florida doctoral dissertation, "The Contempt of the World: A Study in the Ideology of Latin Christendom with Emphasis upon Fourteenth Century Literature" (1954), *passim*.

Second, because of the popularity of the theme during the Middle Ages, particularly from the twelfth to the fifteenth centuries, some critics tend to give the impression that the idea is uniquely Christian. It is all right to use the expression generically, provided its relation to the concept of mutability and its various motifs is understood; but as for the second source of confusion, the contempt of the world has its origin in Plato's dichotomy of the changeable world and the fixed, stable World of Ideas. Karl Vossler says: "A more supersensuous and abstract Hereafter than Plato's cannot be conceived. Man cannot more firmly detest the contamination of things material" (*Med. Culture*, II, 36). It was the "contemptible", contaminating world of change, in fact, which led Plato to postulate the World of Forms and to deny existence to the world of phenomena. The Stoics were more emphatic about their repudiation of the world. From these philosophies, ultimately, and from Neo-Platonism, Gnosticism, and Manicheism, immediately, "early Christianity acquired ready-made descriptions of the world as irrational and civil disorder" (Farnham, *Medieval Heritage*, p. 14). Add to these the Aristotelian despair for the sphere "beneath the moon", the doctrine of original sin, and intense certitude about the afterlife and a vividly conceived hope of attaining it, and it becomes clear why Christianity effected a new and vigorous emphasis on the classical contempt of the world. The popularity of the theme was indeed inevitable.

With Christianity the dichotomy between a personal, all-good God and the sinful, transitory world became very practical and very specific, as is seen for example in Isidore of Seville: "If you despise the things that are present, you will certainly find the eternal; if you scorn worldly and mundane things, you will easily and lightly receive heavenly grace, and you will reign with him who rules the living and the dead. Wealth is never served without sin. No one, in fact, deals in earthly matters without sin. . . . Whoever is assiduous in the love of things is in no way delighted in God" (Migne, 83, col. 866). While the specific motive for contempt of the world, however, might be that the world is a source of sin and therefore an obstacle to one's union with God, the philosophical basis for this motive is the instability and the inherent transitoriness of the world itself. This idea continually appears in the contempt of the world treatises throughout the Patristic and the mediaeval periods, both in the formally entitled *De Contemptu Mundi* treatises and in those which are *de contemptu mundi* in substance. Another aspect of the contempt of the world motif which appears in some of these works is the vilification of the body. This too stems ultimately from Plato's dichotomy and his insistence upon the contamination of matter. In short, the Christian contempt of the world is not essentially different from that of the classical thinkers; but it is much more extravagant and exaggerated because of Christianity's rigid asceticism.

The expression of the world's transitoriness in these treatises usually takes the form of viewing man's life here upon earth as a pilgrimage or any other image which might express the difference between man's temporary and permanent abodes. In "On the Mortality", for example, St. Cyprian writes: "We should consider, dearly beloved brethren – we should ever and anon reflect that we have renounced the world, and are in the meantime living here as guests and strangers. . . . Who that has been placed in foreign lands would not hasten to return to his own country? . . . What a pleasure is there in the heavenly kingdom, without fear or death; and how lofty and perpetual a happiness with eternity of living!" (*Ante-Nicene Fathers*, V, 475). The same idea appears in Bernard's *Meditationes*, a genuine *de contemptu mundi* treatise even though it is not labeled as such. "No one is a stranger there, but whoever merits to come there will remain secure in his own country, forever joyful, and forever filled with the vision of God" (Migne, 184, cols. 505-6). Innocent's *De Contemptu Mundi*, certainly the most important representative of this genre, will be studied in the following chapter. It is sufficient here simply to glance at a few of the chapter headings to see how much of his contempt of the world stems from the world's transitoriness. The following are but a few of these headings: *De incommodis senectutis et brevitate vitae hominis* (x), *De brevi laetitia hominis* (xxii), *De vicinitate mortis* (xxiv), and *De incertitudine divitiarum* (xvi). Clearly the transitory theme is an integral part of the idea of the contempt of the world.

Innocent's work was the most popular and influential of a genre which is found as late as the English Renaissance. A few of the more important works are Bernard of Moras' *De Contemptu Mundi*, that of St. Anselm, of Jacopone da Todi, and the *Augustinus De Contemptu Mundi*, written in England in the fifteenth century. Stephen Langton wrote a Latin poem on contempt of the world, and Petrarch's *Secretum* is more popularly known as his *De Contemptu Mundi*. Of these I shall point out only two: that of Bernard of Moras, because it is next in importance to Innocent's work; and that of the unknown author in fifteenth-century England, because it is the first genuine example of the genre written in English. F. J. E. Raby sums up Bernard's work thus: "Of Bernard of Moras it can be said that no one before him, even the unknown author of the *Urbs beata Hierusalem,* or Hildebert in his *Me receptet Syon illa,* had risen to such heights in describing the longing of the pilgrim for his home. *Non habemus hic manentem civitatem!* – the true monk should have his eyes fixed on the world to come. . . ." [53] In the *Augustinus De Contemptu Mundi* the author, as the title indicates, lends authority to his sayings by attributing them to Augustine. The motives furnished for the "contempt" are almost exclusively the transitoriness of the world and of its joys. The author makes liberal use of the *ubi sunt* formula, speaks of the world's "schorte gladnes", says that "hys welthis been vncerteyne", that its power slides away "as doth a brokele potte that fresshe ys and gay". In fact, says he, "Truste ye rather to letters wrytten in yis: than to the wrecched worlde that fulle of synne ys"; and, "The ioye of this wrecched worlde ys a schorte feeste, yt ys lykened to a schadewe that may not longe laste." Near the end of the poem, he advises, "Sette thin herte in heuene aboue and thenke what ioye ys there, and thus to dyspyse the worlde y reede that thou leere." [54] It is natural and significant that this work, the last important *De Contemptu Mundi* in the history of English and Latin literature, should cite Augustine, the great Platonist, as the authority for the contempt of the world.

The second aspect of the contempt of the world motif is, as was pointed out, the vilification of the flesh. The most significant treatises in this regard are Innocent's *De Contemptu* and Bernard's *Meditationes.* No author equalled Innocent's vitality and vividness in the defilement of the body. For him, man is "conceived in lust, in the heat of passion, in the stench of luxury and, what is worse, in the infamy of sin"; he is born "to labor, fear, and sorrow", and what is even more miserable, "to death" (*infra,* p. 63). Innocent delights in piling up dung-images but this is not quite true of Bernard. Allowing for the obvious rhetoric, these words of Bernard are perhaps the strongest in his entire treatise: "As for the exterior man, I come from those parents who condemned me before I was even born. Sinners bore a sinner in their sin and they nourished him with sin. The miserable bore a miserable one into this misery of light. I have nothing from them except sin and misery, and this corruptible body which I carry about. . . . What am I? . . . weeping and wailing I am given over to the exile of this world; and behold I die full of sins and iniquities" (Migne, col. 487). Such description, however, is sustained in only one chapter of the entire work. The vilification of the body, as in

[53]   *A History of Christian-Latin Poetry from the Beginnings to the Close of the Middle Ages* (Oxford, 1953), p. 317.
[54]   In *Yorkshire Writers,* ed. C. Horstmann (London, 1896), II, 374-75.

these works of Innocent and Bernard, finds its ultimate philosophical basis in Plato's attitude toward matter. This brings us back to the philosophical basis of the entire concept of mutability in all its colorations: the spiritual, eternal transcendence as opposed to the material, finite world. In the following chapter, it will be seen how this dichotomy, implied in the concept of mutability and all its motifs, is operative in three of the most representative works of the Middle Ages, works, furthermore, which Chaucer translated.

II

THE THEME OF MUTABILITY IN CHAUCER'S TRANSLATIONS

Chaucer translated Boethius' *De Consolatione Philosophiae*, Innocent III's *De Contemptu Mundi*, and at least part of *Le Roman de la Rose* of Guillaume de Lorris and Jean de Meun. Not only are these among the most representative works of the Middle Ages, but the first two are perhaps the most important of all mediaeval documents one may consult to determine the mediaeval attitude toward mutability and to delineate the various themes of mutability which make up this complex attitude. *Le Roman de la Rose*, perhaps more widely read even than the philosophical and the theological treatises, contains a surprising amount of mutability material for a love poem and is important in showing that this aspect of the mediaeval mentality was not limited to philosophical or devotional works.

We can only conjecture why Chaucer translated these particular works. In the case of the treatises of Boethius and Innocent, he must have been attracted by their content, which, as will be seen, is almost exclusively concerned with various aspects of mutability. As for the *Rose*, this indeed was the major courtly love document of the Middle Ages and, to be sure, it was this aspect of the book which led Chaucer to begin, at least, its translation. But Chaucer also knew the mutability theme in the *Roman de la Rose* and he knew it well.[1] While Chaucer's initial attraction for the content of these works led him to translate them, it is natural that they should have influenced his thought; and in fact they did, especially the *Consolation* and the *Rose*. A close analysis of these works, therefore, will help to clarify the mediaeval attitude toward mutability generally, and will illumine not only Chaucer's sensibility in particular but also the function of this theme in his poetry.

[1] See D. S. Fansler, *Chaucer and the Roman de la Rose* (New York, 1914), pp. 179-80; 205-14; 223.

Richard Morris, in the Introduction to his edition of Chaucer's translation of the *De Consolatione Philosophiae*, says: "No philosopher was so bone of the bone and flesh of the flesh of Middle Age writers as Boethius. Take up what writer you will, and you will find not only the sentiments, but the very words of the distinguished old Roman." [2] And I might add that no other writer was "so bone of the bone and flesh of the flesh" of Chaucer, as Jefferson's book makes abundantly clear. The concept of mutability, furthermore, is of the very essence of the *De Consolatione Philosophiae*. Perhaps there is no better description of the work itself than that which George Colville in the sixteenth century wrote on the title page of his translation: "And this boke is in manner of a dialoge or communication betwene two persones, the one is Boecius, and the other is Philosophy, whose disputations and arguments do playnly declare the diversitie of the lyfe active, that consisteth in worldly, temporell, and transitory thynges, and the lyfe contemplatyue, that alwayes dyspyseth the worlde, and all thinges therein, and beholdeth almyghtye God, and all heavenlye thynges." [3] Many of the variations of the mutability theme which appeared in classical antiquity recur in Boethius; the *Consolation of Philosophy* might even be viewed in some ways as a synthesis of classical and Christian pessimism. The most dominant aspect of the theme, however, is the mutability of Fortune. After a prosperous and successful career in the government service of Rome, Boethius is now in prison awaiting his death. Book I of the *Consolation* opens with Boethius' complaint against unfaithful, deceitful, the now-beclouded Fortune, "for he that hath fallen stood noght in stedefast degre". [4] Amid his complaint Lady Philosophy, whom he had formerly reverenced and followed but has temporarily forgotten in his suffering, appears, admonishes him for his self-pity, diagnoses his malady, and sets about applying light and easy remedies in the beginning. The truth is that Boethius has forgotten what he is and has not recalled the purpose of things; "for thow", continues Lady Philosophy, "hast foryeten by whiche governementz the werld is governed, forthy weenestow that thise mutacions of fortunes fleten withouten governour. Thise ben grete causes, noght oonly to maladye, but certes gret causes to deth" (I, pr. 6, 77-82). Thus does Book I of the *Consolation* set the stage and state the subject for the entire work: the object and nature of

---

[2] "Chaucer's Translation of Boethius's 'De Consolatione Philosophiae' ", in EETS, Extra Series, No. 5 (London, 1868), p. ii.
[3] Ed. by Ernest Belfort Bax (London, 1897), *Tudor Library*, V.
[4] I, m. 1, 20-32. Citations of Chaucer's translation of the *Consolation* in my text are from *The Complete Works*, ed. F. N. Robinson, 2nd ed. (Boston, 1957).

man's happiness. In Book II Lady Philosophy goes into great detail to show that the goods of Fortune are worthless, chiefly because they are transitory; only that man is secure, in fact, who has been forsaken by Fortune. Book III concerns itself with the Immutable Good, the Supreme Good, or God. This is the end to which all men aspire, the good which contains within itself all the other lesser goods, the good which men are really seeking when they choose false worldly goods. But, and this is the concern of Book IV, if God is the Supreme Good and omnipotent, why is there evil in the world? Especially, why is it that the good and virtuous people often suffer evil and the wicked often prosper and apparently go unpunished? To this question (for they are really one), Philosophy answers that in a sense the wicked or vicious do not really exist and that their very wickedness is their own punishment. If (in Book V) God's providence rules all things so that chance is only illusory, what becomes of man's free will? Philosophy answers that God sees all things in an eternal present, and that God's foreknowledge does not influence or destroy man's freedom. True happiness, therefore, lies in following the path of virtue, which itself brings happiness, and which leads to man's possession of the Supreme Good, the perfect and lasting happiness. The main theme of the *Consolation* then is the dichotomy between the true and the apparent or deceptive happiness or the immutable and the mutable or transitory goods; perhaps no treatise in the Middle Ages treats more thoroughly the mutable nature of worldly goods. For this reason, and even more importantly because the *Consolation* figures so significantly in Chaucer's poetry, an examination of this work will not be unrewarding.

That one should not trust to worldly pleasures because they are transitory (and therefore deceptive) and that he should put his trust in virtue and in God (the ultimate reward of virtue) because only these are permanent are written large on every page of the *Consolation*. Especially is this true when Philosophy discusses the nature and habits of the goddess Fortune (in Book II): Boethius' malady results from the loss of his former good fortune but Philosophy well understands the "felefolde colours and desceytes of thilke merveylous monstre Fortune". Boethius is wrong in thinking that Fortune has changed toward him; she is merely acting according to her nature, says Philosophy: "Sche hath rather kept, as to the-ward, hir propre stablenesse in the chaungynge of hirself. Ryght swich was sche whan sche flateryd the and desseyved the with unleful lykynges of fals welefulnesse" (pr. 1, 52-6). Change therefore is of the nature of Fortune. Boethius should either accept this two-faced, blind goddess as she is and quit complaining; or he should reject her entirely and thereby be indifferent to either good or bad fortune. Fortune is a fickle mistress, the wind which violently blows the sails here and yon; her swiftly turning wheel cannot be stopped. "O thow fool of alle mortel foolis!" Philosophy tells her patient. "Yif Fortune bygan to duelle stable, she cessede thanne to ben Fortune" (pr. 1, 113-115). She is, furthermore, "cruel Fortune", so hard that she laughs at and scorns the tears of those whom she has made weep; "thus sche pleyeth, and thus sche proeveth hir strengthes" (m. 1, 14-15). When Philosophy speaks to Boethius *in persona Fortunae*, she remarks, "Yif thou maist schewen me that ever any mortel man hath resceyved ony of tho thynges to ben his propre, thanne wil I graunte freely that thilke thynges weren thync whiche that thow axest" (pr. 2, 9-14). Thus man by his very nature is subject to mutability; this is rather obvious, of course, but Boethius must realize this before Philosophy can offer him stronger medicine. Fortune continues her sermon to Boethius – and here Chaucer introduces the term "mutabilite" into the English language: "What eek yif my mutabilite yeveth the ryghtful cause of hope to han yit bettere thynges?" (pr. 2, 81-3). How, asks Philosophy, can Boethius believe that "any stedfastnesse be in mannes thynges, whan ofte a swyft hour dissolveth the same man (*that is to seyn, whan the soule departeth fro the body*)" (pr. 3, 82-5)? Man becomes completely "unfortunate" at his death: "therfore what wenestow thar rekke, yif thow forleete hir in deyinge, or elles that sche, Fortune, forleete the in fleynge awey?" (Pr. 3, 89-92). The seasons change, the sun and stars wax beautiful and then disappear, the calm sea is often changed into "boylynge tempestes"; if therefore the form of this world is "so seeld stable, and yif it torneth by so manye entrechaungynges", how can one trust in "the tumblynge fortunes of men" and in "flyttynge goodes"? Thus, concludes Philoso-phy: "It is certeyn and establissched by lawe perdurable, that nothyng that is engendred nys stedfast ne stable" (m. 3, 15-23). Even the little happiness that man has "is spraynd with many bitternesses" (pr. 4, 119). In short, favorable Fortune (Fortune debonayre) always lies, but ad-verse Fortune "is alwey sothfast, whan sche scheweth hirself unstable thurw hir chaungynge. The amyable Fortune desceyveth folk; the con-trarie Fortune techeth" (pr. 8, 11-19). In Book III Philosophy concludes the negative side of her argument, that happiness does not or cannot lie in the possession of transitory goods, with one of the most striking passages in the entire book:

Now is it thanne wel yseyn how litil and how brotel possessioun thei coveyten that putten the goodes of the body aboven hir owene resoun. ... Byhoold the spaces and the stablenesse and the swyft cours of the hevene, and stynt somtyme to wondren on foule thynges. The whiche hevene certes nys nat rather for thise thynges to ben wondryd upon, than for the resoun by which it is governed. But the schynynge of thi forme (*that is to seyn, the beute of thi body*), how swyftly passynge is it, and how transitorie!

Certes it es more flyttynge than the mutabilite of floures of the somer sesoun. ... preise the goodes of the body as mochil as evere the lyst, so that thow knowe algatis that, whatso it be (*that is to seyn, of the godes of the body*) which that thou wondrist uppon, mai ben destroied or dissolvid by the heete of a fevere of thre dayes. Of all whiche forseide thynges Y mai reducen this schortly in a somme: that thise worldly goodes, whiche that ne mowen nat yeven that they byheeten, ne ben nat parfite by the congregacioun of alle goodis; that they ne ben nat weyes ne pathes that bryngen men to blisfulnesse, ne maken men to ben blisful. (Pr. 8, 23-61)

Against the mutability of Fortune and the transitoriness of earthly goods Philosophy opposes virtue and the awareness of God's providence. The negative side of virtue which she emphasizes is not unlike the Stoical tranquility of mind which comes from the indifference to, even the contempt of, external fortunes and one's own emotions. Boethius' sufferings have come about, says Philosophy, because "many tribulacions of affeccions han assailed the, and sorwe and ire and wepynge todrawen the diversely" (I, pr. 5, 68-70). Whoever is virtuous and "hath put under fote the proude weerdes, and loketh, upright, upon either fortune, he may holden his chere undesconfited" (I, m. 4, 1-5). Not even the "unstable" Vesuvius, which can destroy high towers, can move this man. "Hope aftir no thyng, ne drede nat; and so schaltow desarmen the ire of thilke unmyghty tiraunt", says Philosophy, but if anyone fears or desires anything that "nys noght stable of his ryght", he throws away his shield and himself fastens the chain with which he will be drawn (I, m. 4, 15-22). In fact, concludes Philosophy, "Yif thou wolt loken and demen soth with cleer lyght, and hoolden the weye with a ryght path, weyve thow joie, dryf fro the drede, fleme thow hope, ne lat no sorwe aproche (*that is to seyn, lat non of thise foure passiouns overcomen the or blenden the*)" (I, m. 7, 14-19). "For withinne is ihidd the strengthe and the vygour of men, in the secre tour of hir hertes, (*that is to seyn, the strengthe of resoun*)" (IV, m. 3, 39-42).

This strength (tranquility) of reason is possible because there is a divine providence operating throughout the universe, wherein there is no room for chance. Philosophy thanks God that her patient has the best medicine in "the sothe sentence of governance of the world, that thou bylevest that the governynge of it is nat subgit ne underput to the folye of thise happes aventurous, but to the resoun of God" (I, pr. 6, 85-8). Thus Boethius need not fear: this is the little spark from which his heat will shine. Philosophy's arguments for divine providence in the *Consolation* are well-known and I shall refer to only a few of those passages which indicate how the mutability of this world is actually only a part of the stableness of the divine plan.

Such, for example, is the famous poem in Book III (m. 9) where Philosophy addresses the creator of heaven and earth, "that governest this world by perdurable resoun ... thow that duellest thiselve ay stedefast and stable and ... formedest this world to the lyknesse semblable of that faire world in thy thought" (1-14). Perfect harmony reigns throughout the universe, the end of all things are subject to their beginning; and Philosophy prays that this harmony may prevail over man too:

O Fadir, yyve thou to the thought to steyen up into thi streyte seete; and graunte hym to enviroune the welle of good; and, the lyght ifounde, graunte hym to fycchen the clere syghtes of his corage in the; and skatere thou and tobreke the weyghtes and the cloudes of erthly hevynesse; and schyn thou by thi bryghtnesse, for thou art cleernesse, thow art pesible reste to debonayre folk; thow thiself art bygynnynge, berere, ledere, path and terme; to looke on the, that is our ende. (38-49)

When man seeks earthly goods, he is actually seeking the supreme good (III, pr. 10, 236-39), that is, the supreme happiness. Insofar as man is virtuous he is truly happy and to that extent participates in divinity itself: "Thanne is every blisful man God" (III, pr. 10, 146-47). "Her schal ben the reste of your labours, her is the havene stable in pesible quiete; this allone is the open refut to wreches" (III, m. 10, 4-7). In short, says Philosophy, "the engendrynge of alle thinges ... and alle the progressiouns of muable nature, and al that moeveth in any manere, taketh his causes, his ordre, and his formes, of the stablenesse of the devyne thought" (IV, pr. 6, 42-7). Looked at in the mind of God the temporal order is called providence; looked at as unfolding in the order of time, this order is called destiny. And "yif the thing clyveth to the stedfastnesse of the thought of God and be withoute moevynge, certes it surmounteth the necessite of destyne" (IV, pr. 6, 136-39). A man grounded in virtue, therefore, escapes the mutability of fortune and of time because he actually participates in the immutability of God.

Besides the Fortuna and the transitoriness themes in the *Consolation*, there are three other motifs of the mutability theme which appear in this work. First, that of the Golden Age which, as I have already shown, plays a prominent part in the development of the theme of the decay of the world: "Blisful was the firste age of men. They heelden hem apayed with the metes that the trewe feeldes broughten forth. They ne destroyeden ne desseyvede nat hemself with outrage. They weren wont lyghtly to slaken hir hungir at even with accornes of ookes. . . . I wolde that our tymes shold torne ayen to the oolde maneris!" (II, m. 5, 1-30). Another motif, the *ubi sunt*, appears in the same book when Philosophy is discoursing on the vanity of fame: "Where wonen now the bones of trewe Fabricius? What is now Brutus or stierne Caton? The thynne fame yit lastynge of here idel names is marked with a fewe lettres. . . . And yif ye wene to lyve the longer for wynd of yowr mortel name whan o cruel day schal ravyssche yow, than is the seconde deth duellynge unto yow (. . . *the styntynge of the renoun of fame*)" (m. 7, 17-33).

The contempt of the world motif so prevails throughout the *Consolation* that one must suspect the inadequacy of his definition when he attempts to distinguish this particular motif in the work. What could be more contemptuous of the world than the disdain of earthly fortune which, as has been pointed out, inspires the very spirit of the *Consolation*? It is in this work certainly that the mutability and the contempt of the world themes confuse and become well-nigh indistinguishable. There are, nevertheless, specific overt instances and formulations of the contempt theme in the *Consolation* which, when viewed closely, enable one to better grasp its tradition and spirit.

There are, first of all, all of those passages where Lady Philosophy tells Boethius to cast away joy, fear, hope, and sorrow and to forget his concern for anything "that nys noght stable of his ryght": these have been sufficiently examined. The gifts of Fortune are not only "brutel" and "transitorie", but they are furthermore in themselves "fowl" (II, pr. 5, 4-8; glory is "foul", III, pr. 6, 1). The body, for example, is weak and frail: "Yif thou looke wel upon the body of a wyght, what thyng shaltow fynde more freele than is mankynde; the whiche men ful ofte ben slayn by bytynge of smal flyes, or elles with the entrynge of crepynge wormes into the pryvetees of mannes body?" (II, pr. 6, 36-42). Again, human souls are most free when they are without the body contemplating the divine mind directly; less free when they "slyden" into the bodies, and still less free when they are bound by earthly bonds (V, pr. 2, 26-32). Of all the animals only man stands erect, with his head toward heaven, looking down and despising the earth under him (V, m. 5, 16-19). In Book IV (m. 1) Philosophy tells Boethius that her wings are swift and are able to mount beyond the heavens. When this swift thought has thus taken flight, "it despiseth the hateful erthes" (3-4). After the thought (that is, man's philosophical contemplation) eventually passes beyond the last sphere, there "he schal be makid parfit of the worschipful lyght of God . . . stable in hymself" (26-31). If Boethius' own mind pursues this same road, which he has now forgotten, then, continues Philosophy, "wiltow seye that that is the contre that thou requerist, of which thou ne haddest no mynde – 'but now it remembreth me wel, here was I born, her wol I fastne my degree (*here wol I duelle*)'. But yif the liketh thanne to looken on the derknesse of the erthe that thou hast forleten, thanne shaltow seen that these felounous tirantz, that the wrecchide peple dredeth now, schullen ben exiled fro thilke faire contre" (34-44). And finally there appears perhaps one of the clearest contempt of the world expressions found in literature. Lady Philosophy says:

Yif the soule, which that hath in itself science of gode werkes, unbownden fro the prysone of the erthe, weendeth frely to the hevene, despiseth it nat thanne al erthly ocupacioun; and, beynge in hevene rejoyseth that it is exempt fro alle erthly thynges? (*As who seith, thanne rekketh the soule of noon othir thyng, ne of renoun of this world.*) (II, pr. 7, 151-59)

Closely allied with the mutability theme in the *Consolation* and significantly prevalent throughout is the theme of mortality, that is, man as a victim of his human condition. The problem of the suffering of the innocent and the prosperity of the wicked is of course a major theme of the *Consolation* (especially in Bks. I and IV). Man's helplessness is often depicted by means of sea-imagery. Boethius prays to God: "O thou . . . loke on thise wrecchide erthes. We men . . . ben turmented in this see of fortune" (I, m. 5, 49-54). Boethius should not wonder though Philosophy "in the byttere see of this lif, be fordryven with tempestes blowynge aboute" (I, pr. 3, 63-5); whoever looks upon either (good or bad) fortune indifferently cannot be moved even by "the rage ne the manaces of the see" (I, m. 4, 5-6). Fortune is as unpredictable as "the boylynge Eurippe" (II, m. 1, 2-3); and Boethius is helpless, says Philosophy, "yif thou committest and betakest thi seyles to the wynd" (II, pr. 1, 101-2).[5] Philosophy addresses men as "erthliche bestes" (II, pr. 6, 29-30; III, pr. 3, 1-2). Men's eyes are "so wont to the derknesse of erthly thinges" that they cannot see "the light of cler sothfastnesse" (IV, pr. 4, 183-85); the members of the body cloud the soul in darkness and confusion (V, m. 3, 12-17; 42-45). Philosophy speaks of "the trubly

[5] For further sea-imagery see: I, pr. 5, 74-77; II, m. 3, 13-16; II, pr. 4, 53-54; II, m. 4, 4-5; II, pr. 5, 60.

errour of our ignoraunce" (IV, m. 5, 32-33) and the "so schorte bowndes of this lif" (IV, pr. 4, 41-2). Philosophy says, happy is he who "mai unbynden hym fro the boondes of the hevy erthe!" (III, m. 12, 2-3). Further, "Ful anguysschous thing is the condicioun of mannes goodes" since happiness is never complete or long-lasting when it does come (II, pr. 4, 75 ff.). In fact, "every delit hath this, that it angwisscheth hem with prykkes that usen it" (III, m. 7, 1-2). The term "mortal" or "mortal folk" as applied to man is used so often throughout the *Consolation* that this very reminder constantly reinforces the mortality theme.[6] Man therefore is subject not only to Fortune, innocent-suffering, fears, anxieties, ignorance, unhappiness, and death; he is, finally, limited in space and in time. In explaining to Boethius "how litel and how voyde of alle prys" is fame, Philosophy says that "al the envyrounynge of the erthe aboute ne halt but the resoun of a prykke at regard of the gretnesse of hevene; that is to seyn that, yif ther were maked comparysoun of the erthe to the gretnesse of hevene, men wolde juggen in al that the erthe ne heelde no space" (II, pr. 7, 20-30). Furthermore, only one-fourth of this earth, dwarfed by the heavens, is inhabited; subtract from this the seas, marshes, and the deserts and man is "envyrouned and closed withynne the leeste prykke of thilke prykke" (II, pr. 7, 42-3). How then can glory which is so narrowly limited be very valuable?

As the true perspective of the earth is from the heavens, so is the true perspective of time to be viewed from eternity. Whatever lives in time, says Philosophy, "is present, and procedith fro preteritz into futures (*that is to seyn, fro tyme passed into tyme comynge*), ne ther nis nothing establisshed in tyme that mai enbrasen togidre all the space of his lif". Whatever lives has not yet reached tomorrow and has already lost the time of yesterday; even "in the lif of this dai ye ne lyve namore but right as in this moevable and transitorie moment" (V, pr. 6, 17-26). Nor should Plato's view that the world is endless be mistaken for eternity. God experiences everything in an immovable present: this is eternity. Even if the world were endless it would be "perpetuel" and not "eterne" since "it ne mai nat han togidre al the plente of the lif . . . and byndeth itself to som maner presence of this litle and swifte moment" (V, pr. 6, 76-83). In short, man experiences only transitoriness: this is time. God sees everything in an immovable present: this is eternity. It is the divine simplicity which defines the many-fractured, transitory nature of man and his affairs.

This, the *Consolation of Philosophy*, is the document which Chaucer

[6]   See for example, I, pr. 6, 61; II, pr. 2, 10; II, pr. 4, 128; and II, pr. 7, 2.

translated and used extensively in his works. It is not my purpose to determine the influence of Boethius on Chaucer – B. L. Jefferson has done this most admirably.[7] But I am attempting to deal with Chaucer's sensibility; and I think that a study of the concepts of mutability and mortality in the *Consolation* might help to explain and to define Chaucer's own attitude toward life and the world much more clearly.[8]

Another document which is important in determining the mediaeval attitude in regard to mutability is Innocent III's *De Miseria Humane Conditionis*, which Chaucer translated perhaps between 1386 and 1394. Chaucer's use of this treatise in his poetry is only another indication of its wide influence on mediaeval literature generally.

Innocent's work is divided into three books: the miserable origin and condition of man (*ingressus*); the culpable and turbulent progress that is man's during his earthly pilgrimage (*progressus*); and, finally, man's death and the misery that awaits him after his departure from life (*egressus*).[9] The work is generally a hodgepodge of scriptural quotations grouped together under various subjects (*capita* or headings), all of which ultimately relate more or less to his general theme. This theme might be indicated by his quotation from Jeremias in the opening line of the treatise: "Why have I come out of the womb of my mother to see labor and sorrow and to spend my days in confusion?" How much more does this apply to man who, far from being sanctified in the womb like Jeremias, is begotten in sin? Better that one should die in the womb of his mother; or if he is born at all that he be carried straightaway from the womb to the grave (p. 7). Thus is indicated the general theme of the treatise which Kurtz calls "as thoroughgoing a blackening of man as one can anywhere find" ("Gifer the Worm", p. 239). Nowhere is man's mortality more horribly set forth than in this work. Man, for example, "is formed from dust, clay and ashes; and what is even more vile, from the filthiest of seeds. He is conceived in lust, in the heat of passion, in the stench of luxury and, what is worse, in the infamy of sin. He is born to labor, fear, and sorrow and, what is more wretched, to death" (p. 2).

The close relationship of the mutability and the mortality themes has already been pointed out: Innocent's chapter "The Brevity of this Life"

---

[7] *Chaucer and the Consolation of Philosophy of Boethius* (Princeton, 1917).
[8] See Jefferson, pp. 165-66, for an excellent expression of Chaucer's temperamental kinship to Boethius.
[9] All references to the *De Miseria* in this study are to the edition of Michele Maccarrone (Lugano, 1955), in *aedibus Thesauri Mundi*. For convenience I cite only the page numbers in this edition, where the texts and biblical references may easily be found.

offers a good example of this relationship. He begins by saying that in
the early stages of the race it is said that men lived nine hundred years
and more. He then points out that God said to Noah: "My spirit will not
remain in man forever because he is flesh, and his life span will be
reckoned at a hundred and twenty years." This, says Innocent, can be
understood as referring to a period for doing penance as well as to the
life span. The human life span receded more and more until the Psalmist
could say: "The days of our life number seventy years; if, however, life
should extend to eighty years, there would only be that much more labor
and pain." He then complains: "But now the scarcity of my days will be
ended in a short time. 'Our days pass more swiftly than the cloth which
is cut by the weaver'. 'Man is born from woman, living a short life
which is filled with many miseries. He comes forth and is crushed as the
flower, and flees as a shadow and never remains in the same state'. Now,
few live for sixty years and fewer still for seventy" (pp. 15-16). Thus in
this short chapter of eighteen lines, Innocent has touched upon the theme
of the Golden Age; has focused primarily on the mutability theme; and
has developed the mortality theme, in speaking of man's labor, suffering
and pain, almost indistinctly from the theme of transitoriness.

The chapter "Concerning the Labor of Mortals" offers another
example of the merging of these two themes (although the mortality
theme strongly predominates) and is especially interesting for Innocent's
observation on time:

The bird is born to fly but man is born to labor. All his days are filled with
labor and troubles, and even at night his mind does not rest. And is this not
vanity? There is nothing under the sun without labor, there is nothing under
the moon without infirmity, there is nothing in time which is without vanity.
For time is the delay of the change [*motus*] of changeable things. "Vanity
of vanities and all is vanity", says Ecclesiastes. (P. 17)

The coupling together of the concepts, "*non est sine defectu sub luna,
non est sine vanitate sub tempore. Tempus enim est mora motus rerum
mutabilium*" is significant. It has been pointed out in Chapter I of this
study that the region beneath the moon was considered the realm of
mortality and, therefore, whatever is sublunar is "*non sine defectu*".
Now whatever is sublunar is "*sub tempore*", and therefore "*non sine
vanitate*". Thus Aristotle's statement that whatever is beneath the moon
is mutable. Innocent follows this with "*Tempus enim est mora motus
rerum mutabilium*": time is the delay of the movement (or change) of
all mutable things. It is interesting to note that, in contrast to Boethius,
Innocent looks upon time here as static. It is somewhat of an inversion

of the concept of mutability as we have seen it expressed by other authors. But the intensity of the transitoriness of earthly things is still implied; it is as if he were to say that "time is the temporary stay of all mutable things", or, "whatever lives in time is temporary and vain".

Like Boethius, Innocent treats of the brevity of life and of joy, of the uncertainty of riches, and of the short and unhappy life of great men. "Time passes and death approaches. . . . mortal life is nothing save a living death. . . . Life passes quickly and is unable to be held back." He states the paradox that "as much as a man increases, so much the more he decreases" (pp. 30-31). No man has ever spent even one full day without some kind of disturbance, he says; and he refers to Ecclesiastes: " 'Time will be changed from morning to evening' "; and to Job: " 'They hold a tymbral and harp, and rejoice at the sound of music. They spend their days in good things and in a moment they go down to the nether world' " (p. 29). Furthermore, "sudden sorrow always follows worldly joy. What begins in joy ends in sadness. Worldly happiness is spattered with much bitterness" (p. 29). At this point Innocent relies heavily upon Job and Ecclesiastes to paint the woeful situation of man. In his condemnation of wealth he points out that it is against nature to be avaricious: man was born naked and will go down into his grave naked. " 'Do not fear therefore when a man becomes rich, and when the glory of his house is multiplied, because when he dies he will not take along all these things, nor will his glory descend along with him' " (p. 48). He condemns ambition and enumerates the worries and distresses of great men and again quotes Ecclesiastes: " 'Every power is short lived' " (p. 62). He warns that " 'a man does not know his own end; but as fish they are caught by the hook and as birds they are snared by the trap, in like manner are men seized at a bad time, when it shall come upon them immediately' " (p. 33). Finally, in speaking of man's adornments, he is careful to recall again that man is complete vanity and that: " 'All flesh is grass, and all its glory is as the flower of the field' because 'as grass they quickly wither and as the green herbs they quickly fall' " (p. 71). One can readily see from these extracts that the mutability concept underlies and furnishes much of the *raison d'être* of the contempt of the world. It is perhaps more accurate to suggest, however, that in Innocent's hands the mutability concept is used to furnish an added "proof" of the world's worthlessness and another reason for its condemnation. For Innocent's focus is not transitoriness so much as the despicable plight of man (his mortality): he is subject to sickness, warfare, various kinds of torments, terrible dreams, every sin imaginable, the devil, old age, death, physical decay, and even hell. In fact, it is Innocent's ferret-like virtuosity for unearthing every species of human misery which makes his work a permanent curiosity.

Another mutability motif which figures prominently in Innocent's treatise is that of putrefaction. I mention this not because this element in the work of Innocent influenced Chaucer – Chaucer never uses the theme of putrefaction – but because Innocent's *De Contemptu Mundi* is one of the landmarks in "vermifluous" literature. Benjamin P. Kurtz says correctly and humorously about the deacon's vermifluous learning: "One need hunt no further in the Old and New Testaments for passages on worms. All the Old Testament worms are here" ("Gifer the Worm", p. 239). Innocent, simply to cite one example, has an entire chapter entitled "On the Rottenness of Dead Bodies" (pp. 79-80). Here he points out that it is natural that whatever is material be resolved into matter; that man is earth and will be returned therein. He continues thus:

When, however, man dies, he will inherit the animals, the snakes and the worms. "For all will sleep in the dust, and the worms will cover them." ... How foul is the father, how vile the mother, how abominable the sister! For man is conceived from blood made putrid through the burning of lust, at whose corpse the worms, as belonging to the funeral, will be present. Living, he generated lice and belly worms; dead he will generate earthworms and flies. ... He will produce rottenness and stench ... he will fatten many worms. What therefore is more rotten than the human corpse?

Certainly this is a black picture of man. But one must be careful about accepting unqualifiedly Kurtz's remarks that the Latin texts on the contempt of the world are themselves enough to earn for the twelfth century the title of "the savage twelfth"; and that "no Manichean, no bitterest pessimist or most perverted decadent has ever defiled the life of man so horribly and indecently" ("Gifer the Worm", pp. 239-40). One must remember that the *Contemptus Mundi* was a devotional exercise; it attempted to inspire men to right-living and to the ultimate salvation of their souls. The last part of the chapter "On the Rottenness of Dead Bodies" clearly indicates its rhetorical intent: "Therefore", concludes Innocent, "of what advantage are riches, banquets, pleasures, honors?" Secondly, Innocent upheld the dignity of man, a Christian dignity, based upon man's ideal relationship with God and his neighbor.[10]

[10]   See Robert Bultot, "Mépris du monde, misère et dignité de l'homme dans la pensée d'Innocent III", *Cahiers de civilisation médiévales (X-XII siècles)*, IV (1961), 441-56. It is to be noted that in his Prologue Innocent says that he has undertaken his treatise to stamp out pride, "the head of all the vices"; and that he will undertake a treatise on the dignity of man if his patron suggests it

Basically it is the question of the *"hoc mundus"* and the *"alter mundus"* seen in the *Consolation of Philosophy*: the one passes away and the other is eternal. It is therefore anachronistic for John L. Lowes to call Innocent's work "fiercely misanthropic".[11] Willard Farnham's statement about contempt of the world generally is more to the point: he recognizes that it is true devotion in its religious aspects, bad if "indulged in fanatically". The average layman of the Middle Ages, he says, "knew full well that he had to spend much of his life pursuing the things of the world, but he believed more firmly than we do now that thereby he jeopardized his soul, and he balanced his sense of values by a form of meditation which reviled his ordinary pursuits. He did not spend all his time praying; neither did he spend all his time in such meditation. If this is so, it is gratuitous on our part to 'defend' Innocent III and Chaucer in this connection by seeking to find in them an ideal consistency" (*Medieval Heritage*, pp. 45-46).

It is natural and appropriate to find mutability expressions in Boethius' *Consolation of Philosophy* and in Innocent's *De Contemptu Mundi*, for these are a philosophical and a religious treatise, respectively. But the mutability theme is also prominent in the greatest courtly-love poem of the Middle Ages, *Le Roman de la Rose*. That Chaucer translated at least part of this long poem (it is over 22,000 lines) we know from the *Prologue to the Legend of Good Women*. He translated it, most probably, in the very earliest part of his literary career.[12] *The Romance of the Rose* is "one of the great germinal books of the Middle Ages"[13] and "remains Chaucer's primary literary source. . . ."[14] C. S. Lewis remarks that "as a germinal book during these centuries it ranks second to none except the Bible and the *Consolation of Philosophy*".[15] Certainly one might

---

(Maccarrone, p. 3). Bultot's work considers this aspect in Innocent's "unwritten book" and in his other works at considerable length. Bultot has projected a series of works on the contempt of the world theme from Ambrose to Innocent III and a study on the dignity of man in the Middle Ages and in the Renaissance. See the Bibliography at the end of this study for the volume (pts. 1 and 2) which has appeared.

[11] *Geoffrey Chaucer* (Oxford, 1934), p. 89.

[12] Most probably Chaucer translated only 1705 lines of this poem, but A. Brusendorff in *The Chaucer Tradition* (London, 1925), pp. 308 ff., argues that Chaucer translated the entire work. For problems as to Chaucer's translation of the poem and the probable date, see F. N. Robinson, ed., *The Complete Works*, 2nd ed. (Boston, 1957), pp. 872-73; W. W. Skeat, ed., *The Complete Works of Geoffrey Chaucer*, 2nd ed. (Oxford, 1899), I, 1-14.

[13] Lowes, *Geoffrey Chaucer*, p. 67.

[14] John Speirs, *Chaucer the Maker* (London, 1954), p. 35.

[15] C. S. Lewis, *The Allegory of Love* (New York, 1958), p. 157.

determine much about mediaeval consciousness and sensibility from a thorough study of this work. And in regard to Chaucer, J. L. Lowes' statement that "the *Roman de la Rose* was one of the half-dozen books most closely woven into the very texture of his mind and art" (*Geoffrey Chaucer*, p. 60) is unquestionable.

In the beginning of *The Romance of the Rose*, the Dreamer describes the different figures which he sees painted along the garden wall. Among these is Old Age, who is described in a kind of declarative aspect of the interrogative *ubi sunt* convention:

> Faded her once bright lustrous eye;
> Wrinkled the cheeks once soft and smooth;
> And those once pink-shell ears, forsooth,
> Now pendent hung; her pearl-like teeth
> Alas! had long since left their sheath.[16]

This somewhat naturally occasions a digression on Time:

> Time speedeth over night and day,
> No rest he taketh nor delay
> Of briefest movement makes, but steals
> So warily along, man feels
> His going nought, but fondly deems
> Time standeth still; but while he dreams,
> Half-waked, Time's foot hath passed, I trow,
> For none can say that time is – NOW!
> Ask thou some learned clerk, while he
> Maketh response, the time shall be
> Gone and departed three times o'er,
> For Time aye passeth, but no more
> Returneth: e'en as water flows
> For ever onward, but ne'er goes
> Back to its source. No thing can 'dure
> Against the force of time, though sure
> As adamant or iron. Time
> Each thing devoureth when its prime
> Is reached. 'Tis Time that maketh grow
> All new-born things, and Time doth show
> How all things change, and wear and waste;
> 'Tis he that hath our fathers chased
> From off the earth. Of mighty kings
> and emperors the dirge he sings,

---

[16] *The Romance of the Rose*, trans. F. S. Ellis (London, 1940), ll. 360-64. Since it is generally agreed that Chaucer translated only part of the incomplete Middle English version of the *Roman*, all quotations are given from Ellis' translation. At the end of this chapter (note 22) are listed the corresponding lines of the *Le Roman* text.

And all, through Time must pass away,
For he 'tis marks our dooming day.

(ll. 367-92)

This passage makes it clear that time and change (mutability) and decay are inextricably woven together, if in fact these concepts are not actually identical, in the mediaeval consciousness. Guillaume de Lorris has much to say about the transitory and capricious nature of love, but there are no other instances in his section of the *Romance of the Rose* which significantly contribute to the understanding of the mediaeval sensibility in regard to mutability. This is, of course, as it should be. Guillaume's poem is exclusively a love poem; the poem is executed in a highly artistic manner and there are therefore remarkably few digressions. This is certainly not the case with the 18,000 lines of Jean de Meun. His section of the poem "is practically nil" (Lowes, p. 65) so far as the action is concerned; C. S. Lewis, in fact, numbers ten digressions (most of them varying from one to four thousand lines) in this section (*Allegory*, pp. 138 ff.). In these digressions De Meun discusses at length almost all the subjects which might be of interest to the mediaeval man; Lowes says that all the elements of the Middle Ages are there "in something of their own warring chaos" (p. 67). And for C. S. Lewis, this "explains why the *Romance* is the typical poem of the Middle Ages in a sense in which the *Comedy* is not – typical in its richness and variety, and typical also in its radical vices" (p. 155). It is therefore not surprising to find that much of De Meun's matter is pertinent to the theme of mutability.

Near the first part of De Meun's section of the *Romance*, Reason gives the Lover a lecture on his folly. In the process Reason describes Eld, who has wasted her youth in sin:

Who all her years of vigour spent
In folly; now doth she repent
Her wasted preterite, and would fain
By painful penance seek to gain
Future forgiveness of the sin
Committed long ago, and win
Sweet heaven thereby, and thus redeem
Those days, that now so worthless seem
When youth and all its joyance drew
Her feet from virtue's paths, and slew
Remembrance of how quickly pass
The glorious hours of youth; alas!
Too late she sees how brief a time
Endure those days of golden prime.

(ll. 4811-24)

Thus time is very precious. It is a period of trial wherein man, through a virtuous life, merits heaven; and through a life of vice, on the other hand, merits hell. Time is brief and fleeting because it is always viewed in the shadow of eternity; indeed it is irrevocable. The consciousness of the immediacy of time is perceivable throughout this whole discourse of Reason, who says:

> sad thy fate
> Would prove, if all thy youth should be
> Consumed in Love's wild revelry,
> And thou shouldst all too late behold
> Thy life laid waste. If thou so bold
> And strong art found that thou canst cast
> And break Love's bonds, thou then time past
> Mayst mourn, but canst recover never.
>
> (ll. 4900-07)

That love which the lover is seeking is carnal; he should not "let that love inmesh/ His soul, whose trammels wake the flesh" (ll. 4883-84). One's life is wasted if it is not spent in the pursuit of virtue and the *Summum Bonum*. Even "if gaunt famine face him, he/ Welcomes his end right manfully" (ll. 5323-24); for death "grants heaven in change for earth's dull sod" (l. 5328).

> Pythagoras hath said the same
> Within that noble book men name
> "The Golden Verses", fair and bright
> They shine throughout the ages' night.
> "When of thy body thou art quit,
> Forthwith to heaven thy soul shall flit,
> And freed from human grossness be
> Absorbed within the Deity."
> Wretched the fool who dreams that this
> Poor earth our only city is.
> Let one demand of some wise clerk,
> Well versed in that most noble work
> "Of Consolation", 'foretime writ
> By great Boethius, for in it
> Are stored and hidden most profound
> And learned lessons: 'twould redound
> Greatly to that man's praise who should
> Translate that book with masterhood.
>
> (ll. 5329-46)

Non habemus hic manentem civitatem: this is the spirit which informs this long, rambling digression of Reason, as it is the spirit which also informs the *Consolation of Philosophy*. So strong is this vision of the

Summum Bonum in fact for De Meun, that Reason concludes with Lady Philosophy: "The plain corollary is then,/ That less than nought are evil men" (ll. 6699-6700). If this passage prompted Chaucer to translate the work of Boethius, as Skeat thought, is it not likely that it was a sensibility akin to that of Boethius which led him to a further and so thorough an inquiry?

De Meun's concept of Fortune and of external goods is the same as that of Boethius: "External goods have no more worth/ Than some poor horse's outworn girth" (ll. 5645-46); and no man "can own throughout a long life's span/ The value of a garden leek" (l. 5648). Beauty is "a thing/ Unstable, frail, and perishing/ As flowerets that bedeck the lawn,/ Faded at eve, though blown at dawn" (ll. 8737-40). Examples of and statements about the mutability of Fortune are scattered plentifully throughout the entire poem. Even the Rose which the Lover seeks is a gift of Fortune: "Forsake/ Thy cruel God of Love, and make/ No count of Fortune and her wheel/ (Not worth a prune is she)" (ll. 6171-74); this love "doth wane/ Or wax with Fortune . . . as doth the moon/ Whose brightness dims and fades . . ." (ll. 5083-86). Reason's well-known discussion of Fortune, however, occurs in this first digression and occupies approximately 1,100 lines (ll. 6171-7280). Suffice it to say that all the conventional aspects of Fortune are here: her mutability, blindness, snares, her wheel, and numerous examples of great men who have been in turn raised up and betrayed by her. Finally, the attitudes of Boethius and De Meun toward earthly happiness are similar: "No man such great happiness/ Can boast him, but that some distress/ Shall come to dash his cup of joy" (ll. 7215-17), says Reason. In short, I venture to say that there is no secular author in the Middle Ages (with the exception possibly of Chaucer, as will be seen later) who typifies the influence of the *Consolation of Philosophy* better than Jean de Meun. I have mentioned here only a few of De Meun's borrowings from Boethius.[17]

De Meun also implies the decay-of-the-world theme when he discusses the Golden Age: "How pleasant were earth's simpler ways/ In our progenitors' first days!" (ll. 8767-68), the Friend tells the Lover. In the Golden Age men lived simply, and "the fruitful earth no need to ear/ Had they, it foisoned 'neath God's care" (ll. 8799-8800). There were no seasons then, but "one unvarying tide of spring" (l. 8821); there was no seigniorage, no jealousy, and typically De Meun, the evil

[17] For the influence of Boethius on De Meun, see Ernest Langlois, *Origines et Sources du Roman de la Rose* (Paris, 1891), pp. 93-96; 136-39; and 185 ff.

institution of marriage had not yet been divised. But, alas! Dan Jupiter
"changed all things from good to bad,/ And bad to worse" (ll. 21041-
42).

> Into four parts the eternal spring
> He clove, and made the rolling year
> To vary as the times came near
> Of spring's delight and summer's heat,
> And autumn's bounteousness replete
> With fruits, and winter's bitter cold,
> When men seek house and flee the wold.
> But the unending spring no more
> Men revelled in as heretofore. . . .
> And soon the silver age, alas!
> Declined to that of baser brass.
> And ever as time went, I trow,
> Mankind fell lower and more low,
> Till in the iron age at last
> His lot, fulfilled of woe, is cast. . . .
>
>   (ll. 21044-62)

This section is perhaps not merely conventional since it appears in a
context which contrasts this fallen age with a new Golden Age (Paradise), which Genius promises to those who follow Nature's commands.
This concept of the Five Ages of Man is, as has been pointed out in
previous sections of this chapter, another aspect of the concept of
mutability; for it views change as aging deterioration, degeneration and,
for the Christian (as opposed to some of the ancients who held to a
theory of world-cycles), gradual extinction.

The theme of mutability, moreover, becomes prominent when Nature
enters, at line 16655. The barons had made an oath to support Venus
and Cupid in their assault on the castle wherein Fair-Welcome is imprisoned. The author then tells how this made Nature happy, who "into
her workshop entered straight,/ Where swinketh she both rathe and
late,/ To forge such pieces as may be/ Used for the continuity/ Of life"
(ll. 16649-53). Here follows a long account of the life-and-death race
and of Nature's ceaseless attempt to preserve the species:

> For she doth mould things so
> That ne'er shall any species know
> The power of death, but as one dies
> Forthwith another may arise
> To fill his place. In vain doth death
> With hurrying footsteps spend his breath;
> So closely Nature followeth him. . . .
>
>   (ll. 16653-59) [18]

This can be viewed as the theme of mutability, properly speaking, rather than the theme of mortality because the emphasis here is upon generation rather than upon death; on the continuity rather than on the cessation of the different species of life; at the least on the recurrent polarity, the systole and the diastole of existence. On the surface this might seem similar to Ovid's (Pythagoras') doctrine of change as set forth in the *Metamorphoses*: "Nothing, I say, the form it has can hold:/ Inventive nature fashions new from old." But De Meun's doctrine of change is something entirely different.[19] For Pythagoras, "nought is lost the cosmos through:/ Things merely change and take an aspect new".[20] Nature, however, works night and day to preserve the *species*; she "abhors and hates Death's envious mood" (l. 16770) and laments the loss of the lives of individuals of the species; for unlike Pythagoras' doctrine De Meun's holds that the individual undergoes a final death and death is not merely a change of aspect. Nature thinks of the ensuing battle and death in general; De Meun then writes:

> Then busy Nature, whose desire
> Is ever to keep bright the fire
> Of life in all her works, raised high
> Her voice and wept so plaintively. . . .
> (ll. 16917-20)

When Nature confesses to Genius (the god of reproduction), her priest, she speaks with benign approval of the harmony of the heavens, the planets, and the elements; then she says:

> But those who closely look will see
> That howsoever good may be
> The harmony, from day to day
> The sap of life must waste away,
> Till Death's sure step will lastly come
> By nature's course to bear men home. . . .
> (ll. 17783-88)

---

[18] C. S. Lewis says about this Genius-Nature passage (nearly five thousand lines with numerous digressions): "In its earlier phases this unwieldy passage is nothing less than a triumphal hymn in honour of generation and of Nature's beauty and energy at large. It has really nothing to do with courtly love" (*Allegory*, p. 149).

[19] Cf. *Le Roman de la Rose*, ed. Ernest Langlois (Paris, 1922), IV, ll. 15891 ff., and Notes, pp. 296 ff. The sources for most of this section are *De Planctu Naturae*, *Breve breviarium de Dono Dei*, and the *Summa perfectionis magisterii*. Apparently Ovid does not in any way influence this Nature-Genius passage; see Langlois' *Origines et Sources du Roman de la Rose*, pp. 119-27.

[20] *The Metamorphoses of Ovid*, trans. A. E. Watts (Berkeley, 1954), p. 352. See *supra*, note 15 in Chapter I of this study.

She indeed realizes, and calls upon Plato as witness to the fact, that however great her power of generation, she deals but with mutable stuff:

> Nature before the Almighty power
> Of God hath but a passing hour,
> He as in lightning flash doth see
> Time past, time present, time to be.
>
> (ll. 19901-05)

She is God's minister but she has no power over man's immortal and incorruptible part:

> For nought there is by Nature made,
> But what must in due season fade
> And perish, whatso care thereto
> She gives, but whatsoe'er is due
> To God's right hand is pure, and clear
> Of all defect, and hath no peer,
> Nor ever can corruption see,
> Since made 'tis incorruptibly.
>
> (ll. 19917-24)

Thus, even though De Meun is concerned here primarily with the generative power and the fecundity of Nature, this is nevertheless as good a statement of the mediaeval concept of mutability – the transitoriness of life and the inevitability of death – as can be found anywhere in mediaeval literature. The main difference between this particular digression and most of the other treatments of the theme in mediaeval literature is that this passage treats the theme impersonally and therefore makes no attempt to reflect human sentiment in regard to mutability.

What is more important to the poem, however, and more important in discovering the depth of mediaeval consciousness regarding mutability, is the speech of Genius to Venus, Cupid, and his barons, whose cause Nature is supporting. Nature had deputized Genius to tell them to increase the race and to pay homage to love (ll. 20223-26), and this he does at great length (ll. 20353-21545): "Bend all your powers to multiply/ The human race, and so defy/ The work of Atropos, though she/ Strive hard to win the mastery" (ll. 20659-62), is the gist of what he has to say. But he also tells them to strive to lead a virtuous life and to bow before God, Nature's master; "and he I trow/ Your Heart's door against fear will shut/ When Atropos your thread shall cut" (ll. 20741-50). Genius then sets out to describe at length (ll. 20787-21545, with brief interruptions) the Heavenly Paradise and its splendor which is beyond comparison, what "no thought of man could hold in view,/ Nor tongue give utterance to" (ll. 21239-40). In fact, "from the lips of Genius we learn for the first time that the Garden of Love and Delight is, after all, only the imitation of a different garden; and not only a copy, but that misleading kind of copy which the philosophers call *Schein* rather than *Erscheinung*" (Lewis, p. 151).

> For whoso of that garden fair,
> Closed with the little wicket, (where
> The Lover saw by happy chance
> Sir Mirth and Pleasure lead the dance,)
> Should make comparison with this
> Bright spot I tell of, would, ywis,
> Err greatly, for no mortal sight
> Hath e'er beheld such radiant light
> As shines therein; it were, forsooth,
> Fable to pledge 'gainst spotless truth.
>   (ll. 21137-46)

And just as the Garden of Love (an Earthly Paradise, ll. 650 ff.) has such hideous figures as *Eld, Vilanye*, and *Papelardie* carved upon its outer wall, "on the wall of the 'good park', as we should expect, are the sins and the devils ... the earth and the stars, and in fact the whole material universe. But Jean de Meun is right.

He is talking of the *realissimum*, of the Centre, of that which lies beyond the "sensuous curtain": and to that, not only in hell and sin and courtly love, but the world and all that is in it, and the visible heaven, are but painted things – appearances on the outside of the wall whose inside no one has seen. What the wall shows from without are, in fine, phenomena. ... This is the outer face of the wall, the side we know.[21]

Whoever passes through the gates of this Heavenly Paradise, then, will be beyond the reach of time, of the world, of phenomena, of mutability; and it is always in terms of mutability and permanence that De Meun views the two gardens:

> Nor record how Time speeds I wot,
> Is kept in that all-blissful spot.
> For day endures, yet nothing it
> Of future knows or preterite,
> For, in good truth, the tenses three
> Are ordered so that they may be

---

[21] C. S. Lewis, *Allegory*, pp. 152-53. See Ellis, ll. 21164-198 (or Langlois, *Le Roman de la Rose*, 20305-34) for the imagery which Lewis discusses.

> All present, which can never die
> Into the past, nor open lie
> As future – 'tis one sphere-like day,
> Which can nor fade nor pass away,
> Preterite, present, future, all
> Into one blissful moment fall,
> Which wasteth not nor passeth by,
> But beams through far eternity.
>
> (ll. 20865-78)

But no matter how beautiful this Garden of Love is, it is not abiding because it is of the world:

> Fair sirs, but vain imaginings
> Were these fair sights and sounds, I trow,
> A vain and fleeting worldly show
> Which soon must perish, for on all
> That joyous crew dim death must fall
> Ere long, and, dance and dancers spent,
> An end be of their merriment;
> Since things corruptible amain
> Must into dust return again.
>
> (ll. 21214-22) [22]

And it is this garden of the Heavenly Paradise which man has been seeking all along; the Garden of Love, which Cupid would have him seek, will fade away. It is this vision of eternity which makes the world and love and the gifts of Fortune at times seem insignificant to the mediaeval consciousness. Whether this was Jean de Meun's final view of love or not really makes little difference: I suspect that his "formless-ness" is a much surer guide in discovering the mediaeval sensibility than we might think. The fact remains of De Meun's clearly-seen and, I suspect, deeply-felt distinction between the infinite and the finite. This

---

[22]   The lines from *Le Roman de la Rose* corresponding to the translated passages of Ellis which I have used in this discussion appear in parentheses and are from the edition of Ernest Langlois, SATF (Paris, 1914-24): 360-64 (352-57); 367-92 (361-86); 650 ff. (635 ff.); 4811-24 (4533-44); 4883-84 (4600-03); 4900-07 (4617-24); 5083-86 (4783-88); 5323-46 (5019-40); 5645-48 (5337-40); 6171-74 (5844-46); 6171-7280 (5844-6898); 6699-6700 (6341-42); 7215-17 (6835-40); 8737-40 (8316-22); 8767-68 (8353-59); 8799-8800 (8381-84); 8821 (8403-06); 16649-59 (15895-905); 16770 (16005-09); 16917-20 (16149-53); 17783-88 (16975-81); 19901-05 (19070-76);19917-24 (19089-97); 20223-21545 (19385-20667); 20659-62 (19801-04); 20741-50 (19885-98); 20787-21545 (19931-20667); 20865-78 (20010-26); 21041-62 (20185-204; 21137-46 (20279-88); 21214-22 (20349-58); 21239-40 (20375-78).

is the poem that was bequeathed to Geoffrey Chaucer, and which he, at least in part, translated. It is this dichotomy between the infinite and the finite, the permanent and the temporal, so clearly expressed in these works which Chaucer translated, which will now be studied in his poetry.

III

THE SHORTER POEMS

The extent to which the mutability theme occupies the shorter poems of Chaucer is perhaps not very surprising. The problem, however, is in determining the extent of Chaucer's originality in these generally conventional pieces. Relatively little scholarly attention has been given to them, but I think it can be determined that Chaucer, even from the beginning of his writings, was vitally concerned with the mutability theme.

The *Complaint of Mars*, perhaps the finest in this group of poems, affords a clear-cut illustration of this fact. Here Chaucer skillfully combines mythological and astrological elements in a poem clearly in the Valentine-, the aubade-, and the complaint-traditions. Most of the critics have been so concerned with the personal allegorical interpretation of the poem that they have entirely neglected its artistic brilliance. Others have dismissed it as merely "conventional", and have said little more about it. Two critics have significantly discussed the poem as a work of art.[1] Gardiner Stillwell examines the *Mars* by comparing it with its analogue, the *Ovide moralisé,* and other Valentine poems, especially Graunson's *Songe saint Valentin.* "Not only in the Proem", he says, "but in the Story and Complaint as well, the general movement is one of deliberate descent from an aristocratic dream-world to sober truth" (p. 81). Stillwell points out that Chaucer's "use of the literary type – the complaint – and of the conventions of courtly love is . . . highly original" (p. 74). Unlike the *Complaint unto Pity* and the *Complaint to his Lady,* the *Mars* is not simply the conventional portrayal and telling of lovers' woes. "The hero is indeed, up to a point, the typical lover experiencing woe because of his sovereign lady, but he is no *mere* embodiment of any

---

[1] Gardiner Stillwell, "Convention and Individuality in Chaucer's *Complaint of Mars*", *PQ*, XXXV (1956), 69-89; and Wolfgang Clemen, *Chaucer's Early Poetry,* trans. C. A. M. Sym (London, 1963), pp. 188-97.

such stale convention. In the Complaint proper as in the whole poem,
Chaucer rocks back and forth between conventions and contradictions
or enrichments of conventions" (p. 74). Stillwell's study enables us to
approach the mutability passage in the *Mars* with more assurance. At
the arrival of Phebus, Venus has been forced to flee to the mansion of
Mercury. This occasions Mars' complaint, the third tern of which is the
following:

> To what fyn made the God that sit so hye,
> Benethen him, love other companye,
> And streyneth folk to love, malgre her hed?
> And then her joy, for oght I can espye,
> Ne lasteth not the twynkelyng of an ye,
> And somme han never joy til they be ded.
> What meneth this? What is this mystihed
> Wherto constreyneth he his folk so faste
> Thing to desyre, but hit shulde laste?
>
> And thogh he made a lover love a thing,
> And maketh his seme stedfast and during,
> Yet putteth he in hyt such mysaventure
> That reste nys ther non in his yeving.
> And that is wonder, that so juste a kyng
> Doth such hardnesse to his creature.
> Thus, whether love breke or elles dure,
> Algates he that hath with love to done
> Hath ofter wo then changed ys the mone.
>
> Hit semeth he hath to lovers enmyte,
> And lyk a fissher, as men alday may se,
> Baiteth hys angle-hok with som plesaunce,
> Til many a fissh ys wod til that he be
> Sesed therwith; and then at erst hath he
> Al his desir, and therwith al myschaunce;
> And thogh the lyne breke, he hath penaunce;
> For with the hok he wounded is so sore
> That he his wages hath for evermore.
>
> (ll. 218-44)

Here as elsewhere in Chaucer's works, the mutability and the mortality
themes are so closely related that one might easily see that the two ideas
were never far apart in the poet's own mind. The significance of this
tern becomes clear when we remember that in the *Mars*, as in the
Knight's Tale, mythology and astrology are inextricably united. Mars
and Venus, as planets, had to come together and they also had to be
caught by Phoebus. It is a question here of fate, just as in the *Troilus*

and in the *Knight's Tale*. Mars and Venus were destined to be together only a very short time and were also destined to be separated. The two ideas which blend here then are the joy which "ne lasteth not the twynkelyng of an ye", and man's inability to control his own sorry situation. About this and the following terns Stillwell says: "In tern III and in tern IV (the brooch of Thebes) Chaucer abandons all pretense of writing a typical love-complaint, and introduces philosophical probing of the most general possible import" (p. 86). Mars' philosophical statements are much like those of Criseyde, in books II and III of the *Troilus,* where she says: "For either joies comen nought yfeere,/ Or elles no wight hath hem alwey here" (III, 818-19), and in love always "som cloude is over that sonne" (II, 781). But Mars probes much deeper than does Criseyde: he even questions the providence of God. Like Troilus, Mars is aware that he is constrained to love; in the *Troilus* in fact Chaucer clearly states that to love is a law of nature (I, 219 ff.). Why then, says Mars, did God make love so transitory? Even when it *seems* "stedfast and during", it is nevertheless full of vicissitude.

This philosophical generalization in tern III becomes exemplified in the story of the brooch of Thebes in tern IV (from the *Thebaid* of Statius, ii, 265 ff.). This brooch, exquisitely wrought and extremely desirable, made its coveter sorrowful until he possessed it; when he possessed it he was haunted with constant dread; and when he had lost it, "Then had he double wo and passioun/ For he so feir a tresor had forgo" (ll. 255-56). This was not due to the brooch, but to the cunning maker who contrived that all who possessed it should suffer. Thus, says Mars:

> So fareth hyt by lovers and by me;
> For thogh my lady have so gret beaute
> That I was mad til I had gete her grace,
> She was not cause of myn adversite,
> But he that wroghte her, also mot I the,
> That putte such a beaute in her face,
> That made me coveyten and purchace
> Myn oune deth; him wite I that I dye,
> And myn unwit, that ever I clamb so hye.
>
> (ll. 263-71)

Skeat glosses lines 270-71 as, "For my death I blame Him, and my own folly for being so ambitious" (I, p. 504). At no other time in his works does Chaucer allow one of his characters to speak so directly in questioning – indeed to deny – the justice of God. Troilus blames Fortune constantly and Criseyde questions Jove in regard to the suffering of the innocent (III, 1016-22), but Mars blasphemes.[2] Certainly then such reasoning on the part of Mars, inserted by Chaucer in the middle of a love-complaint, betrays Chaucer's deep interest in the mutability theme. Stillwell points this out in the conclusion to his article:

To his Valentine's Day audience, then, the unpredictable Chaucer expresses an attitude toward young lovers very much like that of the *Knight's Tale* or the *Troilus*: it is now joy, now sorrow, always fascination to see their *busynesse*, and at the same time they are amusing or pathetic or both together in basing their lives on so unstable a foundation. This attitude Chaucer expresses with remarkable felicity. The astrologized and moralized Ovid (if involved), the aubade, the complaint, the Valentine-tradition, and the conventions of courtly love form an interesting background against which the poet's personality has its intensely individual being. (Pp. 88-89)

Stillwell's study convincingly explores Chaucer's interest in the mutability of love, an interest in fact which found its expression in philosophical speculation that actually reversed the purpose of the very conventions he was using.

Another of Chaucer's shorter poems which evidences this interest in mutability is his *balade, Fortune*, which actually consists of three *balades* and an envoy, and which some of the manuscripts entitle, *Balades de vilage* (no doubt an error for *visage*) *sanz peinture* (referring to "the *face of Fortune*, or else the *face of a supposed friend*", Skeat, I, 543). In the first *balade*, Le Pleintif (the complainant) states that adversity has taught him "to knowen frend fro fo in thy [Fortune's] mirour", and he recognizes that Fortune has no power over "him that over himself hath the maystrye". The refrain of each of the three stanzas is: "For fynally, Fortune, I thee defye!" In the second *balade*, Fortune responds to the Pleintif: "No man is wrecched, but himself it wene,/ And he that hath himself hath suffisaunce." Why should you complain about me, says Fortune; have I not shown you "that were in ignoraunce" the difference between "Frend of effect, and frend of countenaunce"? "Thou born art in my regne of variaunce", continues the fickle goddess, and "Aboute the wheel with other most thou dryve." Your anchor still holds, she says, "and yit thou mayst arryve/ Ther bountee berth the keye of my substaunce". My teachings, in fact, are much more valuable than the price of your suffering from my hands. "And eek thou hast thy beste

---

[2]   Blasphemy, according to St. Thomas Aquinas, occurs first, "when something unfitting is affirmed of God; second ... when something fitting is denied of him; and ... third, when something proper to God is ascribed to a creature". *Summa Theologica of St. Thomas Aquinas*, translated by the Fathers of the English Dominican Province (New York, 1947), *Secundae Partis*, Q. 13, A.1.

frend alyve" is the refrain to this *balade*. In the final *balade,* the poet
and Fortune each speak; the gist of the argument is that what we "blinde
bestes" call Fortune is really the righteous will of God:

> Lo, th'execucion of the majestee
> That al purveyeth of his rightwysnesse,
> That same thing "Fortune" clepen ye,
> Ye blinde bestes, ful of lewednesse!
> The hevene hath propretee of sikernesse,
> This world hath ever resteles travayle;
> Thy laste day is ende of myn intresse:
> In general, this reule may nat fayle.
>
> (ll. 65-72)

In the envoy, Fortune asks the Princes to relieve the complainant of his
pain or "Preyeth his beste frend, of his noblesse,/ That to som beter
estat he may atteyne."

The specific occasion or date of this *balade* need not concern us here.
What I should like to point out in this poem is the particular way in
which Chaucer handles the mutability theme and the originality or
degree of conviction with which he handles it. B. L. Jefferson remarks
that Chaucer "in the main was interested in the picturesque side of
Fortune and in similes descriptive of her mutability" (p. 56). This poem,
however, says Jefferson, combines (1) the complaint against Fortune,
(2) the defense of Fortune by herself, and (3) the deeper significance of
Fortune (p. 57). The first two of these elements are obvious in the above
outline of the poem. What I should like to emphasize in this study,
however, is the extent to which mutability had become a part of
Chaucer's sensibility; in this regard, Jefferson's statements about the
deeper significance of Fortune in the *balade* are apropos:

The poem, in its deeper significance, would seem to indicate a thorough
assimilation of the Boethian Philosophy. The resemblances to the *Consolation* are not verbal. They, rather, are conclusions which would result from
a thoughtful reading of that work. . . . Sentiments akin to those found in the
passages above [see lines 11-15; 17-20; 26; 65-71 in the poem] are found in
the *Consolation* and the *Roman*. But the point to be noted is that Chaucer's
expression of them is largely his own. They had become a part of him, as
the familiarity and dexterity with which he uses them serve to show. . . . In
a nutshell, it contains much of the teaching of the *Consolation*, the turmoil
of the world, the serenity of heaven, and the opportunity of men to escape
from one to the other. (Pp. 58-60)

R. K. Root also recognizes Chaucer's sincerity in this poem: "The
thoughts expressed in *Fortune* are noble thoughts; and they are nobly

spoken forth, not only with art, but with conviction." [3] The more one reads the poem, the more striking is the validity of these critics' statements. Chaucer recognizes and accepts in this poem what he recognizes and accepts in all of his poetry: the transitoriness and the vicissitudes of this world, and that element in man which time and vicissitude may not touch. Just as Troilus looked down from the eighth sphere, beyond the reach of Fortune, and "fully gan despise/ This wrecched world", the Pleintif in this poem, still within Fortune's "regne of variaunce", begins his complaint:

> This wrecched worldes transmutacioun,
> As wele or wo, now povre and now honour,
> Withouten ordre or wys discrecioun
> Governed is by Fortunes errour.
>
> (ll. 1-4)

The arguments and imagery which Fortune uses in her defense are so convincing and commonplace that she leaves the poet little room to deny that she is usurping her rights (it is substantially the same argument that Spenser was later to have his Mutability use in her own defense):

> Thou pinchest at my mutabilitee,
> For I thee lente a drope of my richesse,
> And now me lyketh to withdrawe me,
> Why sholdestow my realtee oppresse?
> The see may ebbe and flowen more or lesse;
> The welkne hath might to shyne, reyne, or
>   hayle;
> Right so mot I kythen my brotelnesse:
> In general, this reule may nat fayle.
>
> (ll. 57-64) [4]

"Swich is this world, whoso it kan byholde", the poet says in the *Troilus* (V, 1748). In the last stanza of the third *balade* (quoted, p. 82), Fortune's language is unmistakably Chaucer's own. "This world hath ever restles travayle", she says. This recalls Chaucer's line in the *Troilus,* "In ech estat is litel hertes reste" (V, 1749); and in *Truth*, "Gret reste stant in litel besinesse" (l. 10); again, the same expression occurs in the *Mars:* If God grants love which seems steadfast and enduring, "Yet putteth he in hyt such mysaventure/ That reste nys ther non in his

---

[3]   *The Poetry of Chaucer*, revised ed. (Gloucester, Mass., 1957), p. 71.
[4]   See Skeat's note to this passage, I, p. 546, for a suggestion of how thoroughly Chaucer had assimilated the philosophy of Boethius. Skeat transposes and rearranges extracts from the *Consolation* to reproduce a passage strikingly similar to Chaucer's.

yeving" (ll. 229-30). "Ye blinde bestes, ful of lewednesse" recalls, furthermore, the line in *Truth*, "Forth, pilgrim, forth! Forth, beste, out of thy stal!" (l. 18); finally, in the *Troilus*, Chaucer writes a passage somewhat similar to this passage under consideration in *Fortune*:

> But O Fortune, executrice of wyrdes,
> O influences of thise hevenes hye!
> Soth is, that under God ye ben oure hierdes,
> Though to us bestes ben the causes wrie.
>
> (III, 617-20)

Not only is the expression in this stanza of *Fortune* (ll. 65-72) Chaucer's own, but the idea of this stanza and of the whole poem penetrates his thought and ramifies throughout all his works.

Man, however, can defy Fortune and escape her mutability and vicissitudes. Socrates defied Fortune, for he "knewe wel the deceit of hir colour", and he therefore stood serene amidst vicissitude. Chaucer himself in this poem defies Fortune and knows that Fortune has no control over "him that over himself hath the maystrye" (l. 14). As has been pointed out, in the second *balade* Fortune responds to the Pleintif:

> Now seestow cleer, that were in ignoraunce.
> Yit halt thyn ancre, and yit thou mayst arryve
> Ther bountee berth the keye of my substaunce.
>
> (ll. 37-39)

In the *Consolation*, Lady Philosophy tells Boethius: " 'And forthy drye thi teeris, for yit nys nat every fortune al hateful to the-ward, ne over-greet tempest hath nat yit fallen upon the, whan that thyne ancres clyven faste, that neither wolen suffren the counfort of this tyme present ne the hope of tyme comyng to passen ne to faylen' " (II, pr. 4, 51-57). This advice of Lady Philosophy might be glossed thus: "You can escape Fortune and put yourself out of her reach if you will not give yourself to the pleasures of the present time or allow the hope of the future to disappoint you." In a word, Lady Philosophy recognizes, as does Fortune in this poem, that to concentrate on virtue and to ignore Time, its pleasures as well as its vicissitudes, is to conquer Fortune in this world. This is, in fact, to bring eternity to earth. The last stanza of the third ballad is an appropriate climax to the entire poem:

> The hevene hath propretee of sikernesse
>
> . . . .
> Thy laste day is ende of myn intresse.
>
> (ll. 69, 71)

One can escape Fortune in this world only through virtue; one can escape Fortune entirely only in eternity, only beyond the sphere of the moon. Chaucer's incidental, perhaps even unconscious, allusion to the *Consolation* in the expression, "Yit halt thyn ancre", indicates the extent to which the philosophy of Boethius had penetrated his thought. The influence of other authors is certainly apparent in the poem,[5] but this influence is general and indirect. J. L. Lowes best describes Chaucer's *Fortune* in relation to his sources:

Jean de Meun, Boethius, and Dante (in that case Deschamps too! . . .) are present – the heart of their teaching grasped and assimilated in Chauser's own thought, and fused in a new and individual expression by his ripened art. There is here no question of originality. Few passages in Chaucer – unless it be the Fortune *balade* itself – show with greater clearness his consummate gift of gathering together and embodying in a new unity the *disjecta membra* of the dominant beliefs and opinions of his day. To overlook that in any study of external influences on Chaucer is to take the chaff and leave the corn.[6]

To these words of Professor Lowes I can only add: What is received is received after the manner of the receiver, and Chaucer's *Fortune* is integrated artistically, perhaps, because it is the work of an integrated conviction. Certainly this poem and *Truth* are the closest that Chaucer ever comes in his works to speaking *in propria persona*.

Truth or *Balade de Bon Conseyl* is similar to *Fortune*: in the latter poem Chaucer defies Fortune and her mutability; in the former he counsels a certain Vache to flee from the world, which is controlled by Fortune and is therefore full of vicissitudes. Like *Fortune*, too, *Truth* has no specific source; the influence of Boethius is everywhere apparent, but the poem does not follow any particular passages of the *Consolation* very closely.[7] R. K. Root represents most of the critics in his high regard for this poem and in his recognition of its originality: "The balade of

---

[5] See B. L. Jefferson, pp. 57-60, 134-35; for the possible influence of a double *balade* of Deschamps, Aage Brusendorff, *The Chaucer Tradition*, pp. 242-44; for the possible influence of Dante, H. R. Patch, "Chaucer and Lady Fortune", *MLR*, XXII (1927), 377-88; and for the influence of the *Roman*, see Skeat's notes to *Fortune*, I, 543-47.

[6] "Chaucer and Dante's 'Convivio' ", *MP*, XIII (1915), 27.

[7] "No stronger evidence of the lasting influence of the *Consolation of Philosophy* upon Chaucer could be shown than that it is the dominating influence of this poem. It shows that the *Consolation* had entered into the very fibre of his thought. The *Consolation* is not a source of the poem in the usual sense. Chaucer went to no particular passage or passages of the *Consolation* for the immediate purpose of its composition." Jefferson, pp. 108-09. Certainly there are also biblical influences in the poem. Also, Aage Brusendorff, pp. 251-52, prints two other *balades* of the type, one in English and one in French, the latter resembling

Truth is the best answer one may give to the charge that Chaucer was incapable of 'high seriousness'. Though suggested in part by Boethius, the poem is essentially original, and expresses, I think, the substance of Chaucer's criticism of life." [8] The poem is addressed to a would-be reformer, but it has universal significance in that throughout the entire poem Chaucer stresses this dichotomy: the tranquility of soul which comes from the knowledge of truth and the practice of virtue on the one hand, and a worldliness which necessarily places one under the rule of Fortune and subject therefore to her vicissitudes on the other. The poem is a plea for detachment and the contemplative life.

Chaucer begins the poem, "Flee fro the prees, and dwelle with soth-fastnesse." B. L. Jefferson explains *prees* as "an expressive word implying the hoarding, hating, envy, vain struggle for position, failure, lack of steadfastness – in brief all the false felicity which enthralls men and makes them beasts" (p. 108).[9] As the poem brings out, in fact, the *prees* is everything which is not *sothfastnesse*. Ambition is subject to mutability, "climbing [hath] tikelnesse", and good-fortune always deceives, "wele blent overal". Therefore, the poet writes, "Suffyce unto thy good, though it be smal"; and then: "Reule wel thyself, that other folk canst rede;/ And trouthe thee shal delivere, it is no drede" (ll. 6-7). Skeat glosses line 6 as: "Thou who canst advise others, rule thyself" (I, 551). It is reasonable to suppose that Chaucer was influenced here by the following text in the *Consolation*: "Yif it so be that thow art myghty over thyself (*that is to seyn, by tranquillite of thi soule*), than hastow thyng in thi power that thow noldest nevere leesen, ne Fortune may nat bynymen it the" (II, pr. 4, 134-38). Certainly this idea is at the very heart of the poem. The poet, in fact, tells Vache:

> Tempest thee noght al croked to redresse,
> *In trust of hir that turneth as a bal:*
> *Gret reste stant in litel besinesse.*
> (ll. 8-10; italics my own)

Chaucer's poem in some of its phrases. But from this no conclusions can be reached in regard to this poem as a source.

[8] *The Poetry of Chaucer*, p. 73. B. L. Jefferson, p. 108, says that "the poem has always been regarded as unusual. Shirley, with no other evidence apparently than its unusualness, decided that it must have been written by Chaucer on his death bed, and in this conclusion he was followed by no less a scholar than ten Brink." Brusendorff, *The Chaucer Tradition*, pp. 249-51, 274, seems still to uphold Shirley's statement, the findings of Miss Rickert in regard to Sir Philip la Vache notwithstanding.

[9] Cf. Robinson's note on *prees*, where he points out that the word is probably used here in reference "to the ambitious throng of the Court".

Agitating oneself even in the work of reformation is subjecting oneself to the mutability of Fortune. We have seen (p. 83) how Chaucer contrasts "reste" and vicissitude and how often he uses the word in connection with Fortune.[10] Worldly activity, whether it be for the common or one's personal good, is subject to Fortune: "This world hath ever resteles travayle", says Fortune to the Pleintif. In short, the only way to overcome the world is to condemn the world. In the third stanza of the poem, Chaucer writes:

> That thee is sent, receyve in buxumnesse;
> The wrastling for this world axeth a fal.
> Her is non hoom, her nis but wildernesse:
> Forth, pilgrim, forth! Forth, beste, out of thy stal!
> Know thy contree, look up, thank God of al;
> Hold the heye wey, and lat thy gost thee lede;
> And trouthe thee shal delivere, it is no drede.
>
> (ll. 15-21)

This is detachment from the world, the *De Contemptu Mundi* theme pure and simple. Jefferson is right when he observes that "*Truth* sums up in a nut shell the teaching of the first three books of the *Consolation*" (p. 109). But the poem *Truth* is unmistakably Christian: "trouthe" is virtue, surely, but it is also a personal, loving God. The poem concludes:

> Therfore, thou Vache, leve thyn old wrecchednesse;
> Unto the world leve now to be thral;
> Crye him mercy, that of his hy goodnesse
> Made thee of noght, and in especial
> Draw unto him, and pray in general
> For thee, and eek for other, hevenlich mede,
> And trouthe thee shal delivere, it is no drede.
>
> (ll. 22-28)

Here, just as in the epilogue to the *Troilus*, is the idea that only in God can man find permanence and escape the mutability of this world. Just as Troilus' "lighte goost" escaped Fortune by ascending to the eighth sphere, so Vache can escape Fortune in so far as he ceases to be a "thral" to the world. The dichotomy between the mutability of this world and the permanence of the spiritual world permeates this entire poem. In this dichotomy which constitutes the basic theme of the poem, *Truth* is in fact similar to *Fortune*.

[10] The terms "rest" and "quiet" occur frequently during the Middle Ages to express permanence and stability (very often found in virtue) as opposed to vicissitude and mutability. See, for example, Chaucer's "vertuous quyete", *MerchT*, E 1395. The concept and the terms are of course Stoical, Plotinian, and Christian (cf. "Eternal Rest").

The fourth poem which evidences Chaucer's interest in mutability is *Lak of Stedfastnesse*, the companion piece to *Truth*. It is also akin to *The Former Age* in that it indirectly touches upon another mutability theme, the Golden Age. In the first stanza, Chaucer writes:

> Somtyme the world was so stedfast and stable
> That mannes word was obligacioun:
> And now it is so fals and deceivable
> That word and deed, as in conclusioun,
> Ben nothing lyk, for turned up-so-doun
> Is al this world for mede and wilfulnesse,
> That al is lost for lak of stedfastnesse.
>
> (ll. 1-7)

The Golden Age theme, however, is not emphasized; the focal point of the poem is the imperfect state of affairs, brought about chiefly by man's covetousness, during the reign of King Richard. The envoy, in fact, is addressed to the king.

In the first stanza, then, Chaucer recognizes that the world is no longer "stedfast and stable", that it is "turned up-so-doun". In the next stanza, he asks: "What maketh this world to be so variable/ But lust that folk have in dissensioun?" In short the world is changeable and unstable because of man's "wilful wrecchednesse". During the present age, continues the poet in the third stanza,

> Trouthe is put doun, resoun is holden fable;
> Vertu hath now no dominacioun;
> Pitee exyled, no man is merciable;
> Through covetyse is blent discrecioun.
> The world hath mad a permutacioun
> Fro right to wrong, fro trouthe to fikelnesse,
> That al is lost for lak of stedfastnesse.
>
> (ll. 15-21)

Mars had lamented the transitoriness of love and of happiness and the many vicissitudes which attend love even if it "seme stedfast and during". In *Fortune*, the Pleintif recognizes that he is under Fortune's "regne of variaunce", but knows also that he can overcome the fickle goddess if he "over himself hath the maystrye!" In brief, virtue conquers Fortune in this world; and in the next world Fortune has no reign whatever since her influence stops beyond the sphere of the moon. The same ideas are found in *Truth*, but expressed more fully and directly. One escapes the mutability and vicissitudes of the world in so far as he condemns the world and recognizes that his true home is not here but in heaven. *Lak of Stedfastnesse* expresses essentially the same idea. To the questions that Mars had asked *Fortune, Truth* and *Lak of Stedfast-nesse* supply the answer.

The basic theme of *Stedfastnesse* is the contrast between the "stedfast and stable" Golden Age and the "variable" world, a world of "fikel-nesse", under Richard II. At the basis of this decline from the Golden Age is man's refusal to follow truth, reason, and virtue: "Trouthe is put doun, resoun is holden fable;/ Vertu hath now no dominacioun." For Chaucer, as for Boethius, virtue and reason are simply other aspects of truth, and these concepts are inseparable from God. Chaucer closes his Envoy to Richard: "Dred God, do law, love trouthe and worthinesse,/ And wed thy folk agein to stedfastnesse" (ll. 27-28). In *Fortune* and *Truth* the poet is concerned primarily with the individual and his relation to Fortune and to the mutable world: "Flee fro the prees", he tells Vache. In *Stedfastnesse* Chaucer looks at the "prees" and identifies it with the world. The "wilful wrecchednesse" of men, their refusal to follow truth (the only escape from Fortune), has brought about this deterioration in the world itself, Chaucer seems to say. In each of his three stanzas, he refers to the world: "Somtyme the world was so stedfast and stable"; "What maketh this world to be so variable/ But lust that folk have in dissensioun?"; "The world hath mad a permutacioun/ Fro right to wrong, fro trouthe to fikelnesse." The fact that Chaucer ex-pressed the contemporary state of affairs in terms of "trouthe" and "fikelnesse", in terms of a decline of a Golden Age, reveals his lasting interest in mutability. The refrain to this poem might rightly characterize Chaucer's thought generally: in the absence of truth and virtue, "al is lost for lak of stedfastnesse".

Stedfastnesse is, I think, essentially original. Skeat and Jefferson assert that the general idea for the poem was taken from the *Consolation,* Book II, Metre 8, the well-known metre about the bond of love. Haldeen Braddy is right, however, when he sees little in common between the poem and the Boethian passage: "Both do discuss mutability, but this is about all. Besides, the examples of mutability are not the same, and there are no verbal parallels between the two." [11] Braddy, on the other hand, follows Brusendorff in seeing Deschamps as the most likely

---

[11] "The Date of Chaucer's *Lak of Stedfastnesse*", *JEGP*, XXXVI (1937), 482. Braddy points out that Root and Robinson doubt the close resemblance of *Stedfastnesse* to the *Consolation* and that French "scouted the whole theory", p. 482. Root thinks that the poem is "essentially original". *The Poetry of Chaucer*, p. 75.

source for the poem.[12] Brusendorff singles out three of Deschamps' *balades* as similar to Chaucer's poem.[13] Especially striking, he notes, is the refrain of *balade* 234 (*Oeuvres* II, 63 f., on Prudent Economy): "*Tout se destruit et par defaut de garde.*" Braddy's study on this point is even more detailed than that of Brusendorff; he points out that "all three poems by Deschamps not only discuss evil conditions at court but also enumerate the characteristics of an unsteadfast age" (p. 483), and that, like Chaucer's poem, *balade* 234 is also addressed to the sovereign (Charles VI of France). All this is true and most probably Chaucer knew these poems.[14] The fact is, however, that while Deschamps' poems and Chaucer's *Stedfastnesse* are similar in their broad outlines, the actual content and detail of the poems are vastly different. Of Deschamps' three *balades*, perhaps the following passage affords the closest parallel to Chaucer's poem. Deschamps is speaking about the governance of unwise lords:

> Je voy a tout changer condicion,
> Et que chascuns de sa regle se part.
> Li sers viennent en dominacion,
> Seignourie des seigneurs se depart,
> Lasche hardi, et li hardi couart,
> Li saige foul, et li foul se font saige,
> Et li donneur veulent tout mettre a part:
> Dont puet venir au jour d'ui tel usaige?
>
> (ll. 1-8)

From this passage it is clear that Deschamps is concerned with the social and economic conditions of the times; Chaucer's concern is primarily a moral one. Suffice it to say that in the three *balades* of Deschamps, neither the Golden Age nor man's word as obligation, truth, reason, virtue, or pity is ever mentioned. The relationship between Chaucer's and Deschamps' poems is, in short, as Braddy says: "No one of these

---

[12] Braddy, in fact, calls attention to another poem of Deschamps (*Œuvres complètes*, SATF [Paris, 1893], VIII, 77-78) which might also be considered a source for Chaucer's poem (p. 484). Admittedly, parts of this poem are closer to Chaucer's than the three poems pointed out as a source by Brusendorff, but there is no question of mutability in the poem. In his book, *Chaucer and the French Poet Graunson* (Baton Rouge, 1947), pp. 67 ff., Braddy points out that the authorship of this poem (*Balade de Sens*) is now attributed to Graunson. Braddy's position about this poem as a source for *Stedfastnesse* is substantially the same as he had expressed earlier.

[13] No. 31 (*Contre le temps present*); no. 209 (*Comment tout change sa condicion*); and no. 234 (*Tout se perd par défaut de soins*), *Œuvres*, I, 113 f.; II, 31 f.; II, 63 f., respectively. See Brusendorff, p. 487.

[14] See Braddy's article, pp. 486-87, and Brusendorff, pp. 489 ff.

French balades affords an exact model, but each contains suggestive parallels" (p. 485). It seems to me, however, that these parallels are such that Deschamps' poems might not seriously be considered as sources for Chaucer's poem. One thing, however, is clear: Chaucer's poem is original (and Boethian) in so far as he contrasts truth, reason, and virtue on the one hand, and mutability, "permutacioun", and "fikelnesse" on the other. In this the poem is essentially similar to *Truth*. These four poems, then, *Mars, Fortune, Truth* and *Stedfastnesse,* of all the shorter poems, constitute the most substantial evidence of Chaucer's interest in mutability. A few passages are scattered throughout some of the other shorter poems.[15]

Brusendorff accurately describes *The Former Age* (in the Hh MS. the poem concludes: "*Finit Etas prima*: Chaucers.") when he says: "In its present stage the piece is little more than a cento of echoes from the descriptions of the primeval state of human innocence in Ovid, Boethius,

---

[15] In *Lenvoy de Chaucer a Scogan,* for example, we find: "But al shal passe that men prose or ryme;/ Take every man hys turn, as for his tyme" (ll. 41-42). In *Anelida and Arcite* (which is mentioned here since I shall not find occasion to deal with it in the following chapter, "The Minor Poems") the poet refers to an old story,

That elde, which that al can frete and bite,
As hit hath freten mony a noble storie,
Hath nygh devoured out of oure memorie.
(ll. 12-14)

For a similar expression, see *Troilus,* II, 22-28, and H. M. Ayers' comment (on the latter passage), *RR,* X (1919), pp. 13-14, where he compares these lines to Seneca's *Epistles,* 114, 13; 36, 7, and says: "Chaucer obviously is not copying these passages; he is not repeating commonplaces; he is giving artistic expression to a point of view, not the ordinary point of view of the Middle Ages, to which he has thought out his way" (p. 14).

Furthermore, not only are truth and steadfastness contrasted with Fortune and vicissitude, as we have seen, but truth and steadfastness are often contrasted with human deception, to indicate a changeable or fickle heart. In *Womanly Noblesse* (ll. 2, 32) and *The Complaint of Venus* (l. 5), for example, truth and steadfast-ness represent a virtuous fidelity as opposed to a fickle heart (in the latter, l. 5 is Chaucer's addition to his source). For this same contrast, see also *Lenvoy de Chaucer a Bukton; Against Women Unconstant* (especially l. 15, "Ye might be shryned, for your *brotelnesse*"; the italicized word is one of Chaucer's favorite words to indicate transitoriness); and *Anelida and Arcite,* esp. ll. 310-14, where God (Truth) and truth of man are associated (see Jefferson, pp. 104 ff., for a discussion of this and similar passages). Admittedly, some of these passages are merely conventional and others are not in a serious context, e.g., the lines from Scogan. But there does emerge from the frequency and consistency with which Chaucer uses these concepts a definite and clear pattern, which unmistakably indicates his interest in mutability. See further, *Anelida and Arcite,* ll. 238-46, for the destiny motif.

and Jean de Meun." [16] The poem recalls the peaceable, sweet, and "blisful lyf" of the Golden Age, when man's food grew without his labor and he was well-satisfied with what he ate; when flesh was not eaten and no one as yet knew how to distinguish true from false coins; when ships did not yet sail and merchants could not fetch "outlandish ware"; when, indeed, there were no wars for, "Ther lay no profit, ther was no richesse." Tyrants go after money, not poverty. People were of one heart in the Golden Age, and "everich of hem his feith to other kepte". People, furthermore, were "lambish", had no vices, and lived together in perfect harmony. At that time, there were "no pryde, non envye, non avaryce,/ no lord, no taylage by no tyrannye", and "Humblesse and pees" filled the earth. But the present age is far from the Golden Age:

> Allas, allas! now may men wepe and crye!
> For in oure dayes nis but covetyse,
> Doublenesse, and tresoun, and envye,
> Poyson, manslauhtre, and mordre in sondry wyse.
>   (ll. 60-63)

The tendency is to dismiss *The Former Age* as a mere adaptation of Boethius and other sources; to dismiss it as a conglomeration of conventional notions culled from much of the Golden Age-literature that Chaucer knew. This, I think, should not be the case. It is therefore useful to remind ourselves of B. L. Jefferson's remarks in indicating Chaucer's interest in *The Former Age*. First, Chaucer filled in the outline of the poem, taken from Boethius, "with details gathered from a surprisingly large number of sources, some of them also describing the primitive age" (p. 90; see also note 16 on this page). Second, Chaucer attempted "to modernize it by his various additions, and hence to make it more applicable in his own day" (p. 91). Third – certainly the most important – "the point most emphasized, the lack of faith in men, corresponds to the chief point of a very serious poem of Chaucer, *Lack of Steadfastness*, a poem of counsel addressed to King Richard II" (p. 91). Furthermore, Chaucer's particularity and detail in the last twelve lines of the poem serve to emphasize his special interest, definitely

---

[16] For a detailed account of Chaucer's sources for this poem, see Skeat, I, 539-42; B. L. Jefferson, p. 134. As Jefferson himself notes (p. 90), the sources for this poem are surprisingly numerous. Boethius, of course, is the principal source: approximately 20 of the poem's 63 lines are a free verse translation of Book II, Metre 5, of the *Consolation*. With this metre as an outline, Chaucer filled in the details from Ovid's *Metamorphoses*, the *Roman de la Rose*, John of Salisbury's *Policraticus* or St. Jerome's *Epistle against Jovinian*, and very probably from the Fourth *Eclogue* of Virgil.

evident in this poem when compared with his sources, in man's relationship to man. "*Lack of Steadfastness*", says Jefferson, "is an expansion
of just this theme"; the two poems are "the same in spirit' (p. 92). I
might add that perhaps it is a bit pedantic to insist that Chaucer was
merely indulging in literary exercise at a time when Langland was
agonizing over this troubled age.[17]

This study of the shorter poems has made clear Chaucer's interest in
mutability. The long philosophical digression in the *Mars* reveals his
abiding preoccupation with the transitoriness of human love and happiness. In *Fortune*, Chaucer uses a poetical figment to symbolize the misfortunes and vicissitudes which man is always subject to in this world.
In *Truth*, on the other hand, he emphasizes the realm over which Fortune has no control: in personal virtue or truth in this world and in
man's union with Divine Truth in the next. The opposition of mutability
and of permanence is the theme of these two poems as it is, in fact, of
Stedfastnesse. *Truth*, however, introduces another mutability motif into
the works of Chaucer: the *De Contemptu Mundi* theme. In this poem,
Chaucer tells Vache that this world "nis but wildernesse"; "Flee fro the
prees", he counsels him, "Know thy contree." In *Stedfastnesse* Chaucer
introduces another mutability motif, the decay of the world. The theme
is implied but it constitutes the background for the entire poem. In *The
Former Age,* the theme is treated directly: Chaucer depicts in great
detail the perfect and harmonious state of the Golden Age, and then
laments the conditions of his own age, "Allas, allas! now may men wepe
and crye!" It is not enough to say that these ideas were "conventional"
or "commonplace"; to Chaucer they were also intensely personal and he
expressed them with sincerity and conviction. Exactly half of the shorter
poems (eleven of the twenty-two including *Anelida and Arcite*) contain
a suggestion of, if indeed their themes are not substantially concerned
with, mutability.

[17] See Frederick J. Furnivall, *Trial-Forewords To My "Parallel-Text Edition of
Chaucer's Minor Poems"*, Chaucer Soc., 2nd Ser., No. 6 (London, 1871), p. 97,
who cites lines 60-63 of this poem, compares them with the corresponding lines
in the *Consolation*, and takes them to indicate "Chaucer's bad opinion of his
own time".

IV

THE MINOR POEMS

THE BOOK OF THE DUCHESS

Chaucer's interest in mutability and mortality is evident even in his youth. It is surprising that his first original work of any length, *The Book of the Duchess* (1369), should so fully evidence a sensibility of the mortal condition of man and a resignation to this mortality.

The Book of the Duchess is an elegy, written for John of Gaunt upon the occasion of the death of his first wife, Blanche. As such, the Ceyx and Alcione episode with which Chaucer prefaces the elegy proper is very appropriate. Alcione's sorrow for the sudden loss of her husband is a fitting counterpart of the sorrow of the duke for the unexpected loss of his wife. Chaucer's sources for this episode are Ovid's *Metamorphoses* (Book XI) and Guillaume de Machaut's *Dit de la Fontaine Amoureuse,* the latter of which he followed rather closely. Chaucer makes a significant addition to these sources, however, and one which is profitable to this study in showing the poet's interest in the transitoriness of life and of happiness.

In the story, Alcione prays the goddess Juno to let her know in a dream whether Ceyx is alive or dead. Juno answers her prayers: Morpheus takes the form of the drowned body of Ceyx and appears to Alcione in her dream. The following excerpts will make Chaucer's source-changes immediately evident. Ovid's account runs thus:

"Do you recognize your Ceyx, O most wretched wife? or is my face changed in death? Look on me! You will know me then and find in place of husband your husband's shade. No help, Alcyone, have your prayers brought to me. For stormy Auster caught my ship on the Aegean sea and, tossing her in his fierce blasts, wrecked her there. My lips, calling vainly upon your name, drank in the waves. And this tale no uncertain messenger brings to you, nor do you hear it in the words of vague report; but I myself, wrecked as you see me, tell you of my fate. Get you up, then, and weep for me; put on your mourning garments and let me not go unlamented to the cheerless land of shades." [1]

The following is Machaut's version, based on Ovid's:

"Dear companion, see here Ceys, for whom thou hast so lost joy and delight that nothing pleases thee (t'abellit). See how I have no colour, joy, or spirit that accompanies me. Look on me, and call me to thy mind. Think not, fair one, that I complain in vain: look at my hair, look at my grizzled beard; look at my dress, which shows true signs of my death." [2]

Chaucer omits many of the details of these versions; his Ceyx is, in fact, concerned primarily with Alcione's resignation and acceptance of his own death.

> "My swete wyf,
> Awake! let be your sorwful lyf!
> For in your sorwe there lyth no red.
> For, certes, swete, I nam but ded;
> Ye shul me never on lyve yse.
> But, goode swete herte, that ye
> Bury my body, for such a tyde
> Ye mowe hyt fynde the see besyde;
> And farewel, swete, *my worldes blysse!*
> *I praye God youre sorwe lysse.*
> *To lytel while oure blysse lasteth!*"
>
> (ll. 201-11)

The italicized lines are obviously Chaucer's own. These lines occasioned Kittredge's well-known remarks with regard to Chaucer's awareness of mortality even when young (*Chaucer and His Poetry,* pp. 71-72). Furthermore, in comparing Chaucer's version of this passage with the versions of Ovid and Machaut, we find that his intentions are clear. There is no self-pity in Chaucer's Ceyx. He tells Alcione to abandon her sorrow: there is no remedy for it, for he is already dead. Ovid's Ceyx, on the other hand, tells his wife to weep for him, to put on her mourning garments and not to let his death go unlamented. Machaut's Ceyx exudes self-pity and goes into much detail in order to convince Alcione of his death. Chaucer's Ceyx is matter-of-fact, has completely accepted his own death and prays that God will help Alcione to do the same. This realization of the evanescence of life and of happiness and the acceptance of this fact of mortality are not only parts of Chaucer's basic outlook generally, but are operative, subtly and indirectly, throughout the poem.

---

[1] *Metamorphoses,* trans. Frank Justus Miller, in *The Loeb Classical Library* (New York, 1926), II, 653-64.
[2] Translated by Furnivall, in *Trial-Forewords,* p. 45.

In the elegy proper, the Dreamer happens upon the Man in Black, who tells him, "Y am sorwe, and sorwe ys y" (l. 597), and then enumerates at great length how Fortune's mutability has affected him:

> My song ys turned to pleynynge,
> And al my laughtre to wepynge,
> My glade thoghtes to hevynesse;
> In travayle ys myn ydelnesse
> And eke my reste; my wele is woo,
> My good ys harm, and evermoo
> In wrathe ys turned my pleynge
> And my delyt into sorwynge.
> Myn hele ys turned into seknesse,
> In drede ys al my sykernesse;
> To derke ys turned al my lyght,
> My wyt ys foly, my day ys nyght,
> My love ys hate, my slep wakynge,
> My myrthe and meles ys fastynge,
> My countenaunce ys nycete,
> And al abaved, where so I be;
> My pees, in pledynge and in werre.
> Allas! how myghte I fare werre?
> My boldnesse ys turned to shame.
> For fals Fortune hath pleyd a game
> Atte ches with me, allas the while!

(ll. 599-619)

This passage might have been suggested by a similar passage in Machaut's *Le Jugement Dou Roy De Behaingne*, which in turn might have been based on Reason's description of the mixed nature of love to the lover in the *Romance of the Rose*.[3] The significant points that I should like to make, however, are these: first, Chaucer's use of Fortune and the chess game at precisely this point, amid the long enumeration of the contrary effects of the Knight's loss, clearly indicates the poet's intention to portray the mutability of love and of happiness.[4] Second, this fact is substantiated by a similar idea which Chaucer used in the *Troilus*. In Troilus' letter to Criseyde, he writes:

> Myn eyen two, in veyn with which I se,

[3] See Robinson's note to these lines. While the influences cited by Robinson might have suggested these contraries to Chaucer, his lines (ll. 599-619) are nevertheless to a great extent original.

[4] Lines 618-86 are taken up with the Man in Black's tirade against Fortune: see Robinson's notes to these lines for Chaucer's sources at this point. Machaut does not combine the Fortune-motif with the contraries at lines 177-87 of his *Le Jugement Dou Roy De Behaingne*. This combination is original with Chaucer here.

Of sorwful teris salte arn woxen welles;
My song, in pleynte of myn adversitee;
My good, in harm; myn ese ek woxen helle is;
My joie, in wo; I kan sey yow naught ellis,
But torned is, for which my lif I warie,
Everich joie or ese in his contrarie.
                                        (V, 1373-79)

Chaucer's comment on this letter to Criseyde is: "But Troilus, thow
maist now, est or west,/ Pipe in an ivy lef, if that the lest!/ Thus goth
the world" (V, 1432-34); Troilus is an *exemplum* of Fortune's mutability. These enumerations in both poems are meant to intensify the
transitoriness of earthly love and happiness.

    This fact is made even more explicit in the long tirade of the Man in
Black against Fortune (ll. 618-86), which occupies the exact center of
the poem. Coming as it does at this point the abstract discussion of
Fortune connects, at least tenuously, the mutability theme of the Ceyx-
Alcione episode and the Man in Black's final and explicit revelation to
the Dreamer of the loss of his lady by death. The Knight's tirade is
composed chiefly of most of the conventional ideas regarding Fortune
found in the literature of the period. It is significant to note the numerous
sources that Chaucer used for this passage and that this interest in
Fortune is prior to his translation of, perhaps even his reading of,
Boethius' *Consolation of Philosophy*.[5] I might suggest, parenthetically,
that the sense of mutability which Chaucer betrays in this poem is
perhaps what finally led him to translate the *Consolation*. At any rate, it
can not be maintained that Chaucer's reliance upon various sources for
this tirade of the Man in Black detracts from his interest in Fortune and
in the subject of mutability generally. Chaucer's use of this tirade is, in
fact, ingenious; artistically, this passage not only emphasizes the mutability theme but also furthers the resignation-motif, established at the
beginning of the poem by the dead Ceyx's words to his wife Alcione.

    In attempting to solve the apparent inconsistencies in the Dreamer's
knowledge of the lady's death, Kittredge has pointed out that the
Dreamer knows all along that the lady is dead but that he wishes "to
afford the knight the only help in his power – the comfort of pouring
his sad story into compassionate ears" (p. 52).[6] Whether or not this is
true (the facts do seem to support this interpretation), certainly the Man

[5]   See Robinson's note to this passage; also B. L. Jefferson, pp. 55-57 and 133.
[6]   Kemp Malone does not agree with Kittredge, but thinks that "here Chaucer
deliberately sacrificed the virtue of consistency to gain the greater virtue of
dramatic irony". *Chapters on Chaucer* (Baltimore, 1951), pp. 38 f.

in Black does achieve some sort of resignation by speaking out his
sorrow, especially in his tirade against Fortune. More than this, however,
the tirade itself functions as a poetical resolution to the losses expressed
throughout the poem.

At this point Fortune is portrayed, as she is elsewhere in the works of
Chaucer, as the force of mutability in this world: "That ys broght up,
she set al doun." Here, however, Fortune does not have the cosmic
dimensions which are apparent in some of Chaucer's later works, such
as in the *Troilus*, for example. Clearly the philosophical implications of
Boethius' Fortune have not yet influenced Chaucer. In this poem, the
emphasis is more on the physical appearance and on the traitorous
nature of the goddess: "ever laughynge/ With oon eye, and that other
wepynge", or she is as a "scorpioun", and is a "false thef". From this
portrait also emerges Fortune's inevitability, as when the Man in Black
says:

> "I shulde have pleyd the bet at ches,
> and kept my fers the bet therby.
> And thogh wherto? for trewely
> I holde that wyssh nat worth a stree!
> Hyt had be never the bet for me."
>
> (ll. 668-72)

And for a moment, at least, the Knight seems almost reconciled to
Fortune's action:

> "And eke she ys the lasse to blame;
> Myself I wolde have do the same,
> Before God, hadde I ben as she;
> She oghte the more excused be."
>
> (ll. 675-78)

The Knight's very recognition of the mutability and power of Fortune is,
finally, an explanation for if not a partial resignation to his loss. The
image of Fortune-at-chess helps to relieve the pathos of the Knight's
sorrow. After this point of the poem, he begins to recall his youthful
devotion to Love and temporarily forgets his loss in the vivid description
of the virtues and excellence of his lady. The poem ends rather abruptly
with the unmistakable revelation of his loss: " 'She ys ded!' 'Nay!' 'Yis,
be my trouthe!'/ 'Is that youre los? Be God, hyt is routhe!' " (ll. 1309-
10).

What, indeed, remains to be said? The poet had said it in the Ceyx-
Alcione episode, in the rhetorical elaboration of contraries which
exemplified Fortune's mutability, in the Knight's long tirade against

Fortune; finally he has said it in the prolonged portrait of the Knight's sorrow: "To little whil oure blisse lasteth." What can be said now but, in effect, "What a pity, such is mortality." Kittredge finds in the mood of the poem a "vaguely troubled pensiveness". "The mind is purged", he says, "not by the tragedy of life, with its pity and terror, but by a sense of the sadness which pervades its beauty and joy. Ours is a pleasant world of birds and flowers and green trees and running streams, and life in such a world is gracious and desirable, and nothing is so good as tender and faithful love, which is its own reward. But the glory of it all is for a moment" (p. 71).[7] Critics who feel that the poem ends too abruptly perhaps overlook the fact that this very abruptness expresses the inevitability which has been implied throughout the poem: the inevitability of death, of loss, of sorrow. What remains for a man of Chaucer's sensibility to say but, "Be God, hyt ys routhe!"?

THE HOUSE OF FAME

Of all Chaucer's poems, *The House of Fame* presents perhaps the most dramatic evidence of his interest in "fikelnesse" and "brotelnesse". For this poem purports to be about love and love's tidings, yet approximately one-third of it is about Fame, the fickle goddess of renown. At least three critics think that the motivation of the poem is the subject of fame,[8] but W. O. Sypherd probably comes closer to revealing the true nature of the poem: "The motive of the dream – that is, the motive of the poem, – is ... that of a journey to the House of Fame, where

[7] For similar studies of mutability in this poem, see Bertrand H. Bronson, "*The Book of the Duchess* Re-opened", *PMLA*, LXVII (1952), 863-81, especially pp. 880-81; I am greatly indebted to Bronson for the idea of resignation which I have found very prevalent in this poem. Dorothy Bethurum, "Chaucer's Point of View as Narrator in the Love Poems", *PMLA*, LXXIV (1959), 513; this discussion is brief but excellent and illuminates Chaucer's sensibility regarding mutability and mortality generally.

[8] See the articles of Paull F. Baum, "Chaucer's 'The House of Fame' ", *ELH*, VIII (1941), 248-56; Paul G. Ruggiers, "The Unity of Chaucer's *House of Fame*", *SP*, L (1953), 16-29; and Gardiner Stillwell, "Chaucer's 'O Sentence' in the *Hous of Fame*", *English Studies*, XXXVII (1956), 149-57. Benjamin G. Koonce, Jr., in his unpublished doctoral dissertation, "Chaucer and the Tradition of Fame: A Study of the Symbolism in *The House of Fame*", Princeton, 1959, presents some interesting information regarding the mutability of fame, Fortune, and some other symbols in the poem; but his thesis that the poem explores and develops the contrast between earthly and heavenly fame on the level of allegory is, it seems to me, quite untenable.

56115

Chaucer may learn about Love – it is the reward which a love-poet is to receive for his services to Love and to Love's servants." [9] In the first book the poet dreams that he is "withyn a temple ymad of glas". Most of this book is taken up with an outline of the earlier portion of Virgil's *Aeneid*. Book Two is concerned with the journey to the House of Fame. Even in this poem Chaucer shows a fascination for the geographical limitation of this world in which we live. About his view from the air while in the claws of the eagle, the poet writes:

> But thus sone in a while he
> Was flowen fro the ground so hye
> That al the world, as to myn yë,
> No more semed than a prikke.
>
> (ll. 904-907) [10]

In Book Three Chaucer describes Fame's abode, "a feble fundament/ To bilden on a place hye". The mutability of fame is suggested in the poet's description of the southern side of this rock of ice:

> Tho sawgh I al the half ygrave
> With famous folkes names fele,
> That had iben in mochel wele,
> And her fames wide yblowe.
> But wel unnethes koude I knowe
> Any lettres for to rede
> Hir names by; for, out of drede,
> They were almost ofthowed so
> That of the lettres oon or two
> Was molte away of every name,
> So unfamous was woxe hir fame.
> But men seyn, "What may ever laste?"
>
> (ll. 1136-47)

On the northern side of the hill of ice, the names were preserved as if they had just been written there, for this side was shaded by the castle which stood atop the hill. This image is an apt symbol of fame's transitoriness and the accidental manner in which one's fame is often preserved; and is significant since Chaucer apparently had no specific source for it.[11]

[9] *Studies in Chaucer's Hous of Fame.* Chaucer Society, 2nd Series, No. 39 (London, 1907), p. 15. To substantiate this statement, Sypherd cites lines 606-98; 1885-89; 2131-54; and *Prologue to the Legend*, ll. 415-17, B version.
[10] Cf. Boethius, II, pr. 7, 17; *Troilus*, V, 1814-16; and *Parliament of Fowls*, ll. 57-58; see A. L. Kellogg, "On the Tradition of Troilus's Vision of the Little Earth", *Mediaeval Studies*, XXII (1960), 204-13.
[11] See Sypherd, pp. 118 ff., where he connects the rock of ice with the goddess of Fortune, and says that "the material itself probably goes back to *La Panthere*

Next Chaucer describes the exterior of the House of Fame ("Al was of ston of beryle,/ Bothe the castel and the tour ... Wythouten peces or joynynges.") and the vast crowd of musicians, jugglers, sorcerers, and magicians in the niches round about the castle.[12] In describing Fame's house, Chaucer is consistent with the nature of Fame herself: he muses long on the walls of beryl,

> That schoone ful lyghter than a glas
> And made wel more than hit was
> To semen every thing, ywis,
> As kynde thyng of Fames is. . . . .
>   (ll. 1289-92)

Likewise, the castle-gate, so well carved that there is no other like it, "was be aventure/ Iwrought, as often as be cure." He then enters the castle and hears the heralds of the goddess Fame. The inside of the castle, he says, "was plated half a foote thikke/ Of gold," and set with gems. Then he describes the goddess Fame ("But, Lord! the perry and the richesse/ I saugh sittyng on this godesse!") and the various inhabitants of her dwelling: Josephus, Homer, Lollius, Virgil, Ovid, Lucan, Claudian – indeed, "What shulde y more telle of this?" he exclaims, and then proceeds to tell of the nine companies who come to plead their cases before the goddess of Fame.

Without presenting a detailed enumeration of Chaucer's portrayal of these nine companies before the goddess, suffice it to say that he spends 357 lines, approximately one-seventh of the entire poem, to show that

---

d'Amours of Nicole de Margival"; the connection comes from "a strong influence on Chaucer's whole portrayal of the goddess of Fame and her 'place' from the qualities and attributes which had become attached to the goddess of Fortune". Also, A. C. Garrett, "Studies on Chaucer's *Hous of Fame*", *Harvard Studies and Notes*, V (1897), 157 ff. Garrett thinks that the ultimate source for Chaucer's hill of ice is the "Glasberg" of German folk-lore.

[12] In the process of this enumeration, Chaucer says:
> There saugh I sitte in other seës,
> Pleyinge upon sondry gleës,
> Whiche that I kan not nevene,
> Moo than sterres ben in hevene,
> Of whiche I nyl as now not ryme,
> For ese of yow, and los of tyme,
> *For tyme ylost, this knowen ye,*
> *Be no way may recovered be.*
>   (ll. 1251-58; italics my own)

These lines (italics) are conventional and proverbial; but the fact that it was a ready tag for Chaucer is at least to be considered. Cf. *Troilus*, II, 1739; IV, 1283; and for a similar expression, III, 615; *Knight's Tale*, ll. 2636; Intro. to *MLT*, ll. 20-32.

Fame is just as arbitrary and purposeless with the distribution of her gifts as is Fortune: "Ryght as her suster, dame Fortune,/ Ys wont to serven in comune" (ll. 1547-48). About this scene Kittredge says that: "Chaucer's plan is a model of schematic precision. All men have some request to make of Fame, and the whole world comes to her throne, in nine separate companies. The treatment they receive exhausts the possibilities of arbitrary freakishness." [13]

When Chaucer had seen this spectacle, he met a bystander who asked him if he had "come hider to han fame?" Chaucer's answer is significant because it shows that this long digression on Fame as renown has not obscured the purpose of his journey:

> "Nay, for sothe, frend", quod y;
> "I cam noght hyder, graunt mercy,
> For no such cause, by my hed! . . .
> I wot myself best how y stonde. . . .
>   That wyl y tellen the,
> The cause why y stonde here:
> Somme newe tydynges for to lere,
> Somme newe thinges, y not what,
> Tydynges, other this or that,
> Of love, or such thynges glade."
>   (ll. 1873-75; 1878; 1884-89)

The poet expressly says that the tidings which he had learned at the House of Fame are not the tidings which he had come to hear (ll. 1897-1900). With this, the guide takes the poet to the House of Rumor. This large wicker cage, sixty miles in length, is the gathering house for all the rumors in the world. In fact, Chaucer spends seventeen lines classifying them. The house itself is built of

> tymber of no strengthe,
> Yet hit is founded to endure
> While that hit lyst to Aventure,
> That is the moder of tydynges. . . .
>   (ll. 1980-83)

Once in the house, the poet is astonished at the huge collection of people, roaming in and out. He sees tidings go from mouth to mouth, "encresing ever moo,/ As fyr ys wont to quyke and go/ From a spark spronge amys", and he also sees true and false tidings compounded to make "oo tydynge". From the House of Rumor, these tidings go to Fame to receive their destiny:

[13] *Chaucer and His Poetry*, pp. 94-95. The sister-relationship of Fortune and Fame is apparently Chaucer's own.

> Thus out at holes gunne wringe
> Every tydynge streght to Fame,
> And she gan yeven ech hys name,
> After hir disposicioun.
> And yaf hem eke duracioun,
> Somme to wexe and wane sone,
> As doth the faire white mone,
> And let hem goon.

(ll. 2110-17)

At the end of the poem Chaucer hears a great noise in the corner of the hall, where men are talking of love-tidings. Everyone runs there, crying out, "What thing is that?" They step on each other's heels trying to find out what is going on. Then the poet says:

> Atte laste y saugh a man,
> Which that y [nevene] nat ne kan;
> But he semed for to be
> A man of gret auctorite. . . .

(ll. 2155-58)

And thus the poem ends. This outline serves to point up two things: (1) Chaucer's detailed description of Fame and her abode and, (2) the disproportionately large amount of space given over to the goddess and her abode (777 of the poem's 2158 lines) in a poem obviously meant to be about love.

W. O. Sypherd has amply shown that Chaucer's Fame and her abode is "so composite that one naturally despairs of finding an actual source or sources for this imaginative portrayal".[14] Three influences, he says, are seen in Chaucer's composition of Fame and her abode. The rock of ice with its two sides is due to the influence of Fortune, as is of course the capriciousness with which Fame distributes her gifts. The aspect of Fame as an enthroned goddess deciding the fate of suppliants betrays the influence of the goddess Love (p. 128). The final influence is that of Boethius: the close connection in the *Consolation* between fame (worldly

---

[14] *Studies in Chaucer's Hous of Fame*, p. 117. The general idea of the poem was suggested by Virgil (*Aeneid*, iv, 173-97) and Ovid (*Metamorphoses*, xii, 39-63). Chaucer is indebted to Ovid chiefly for the House of Rumor, the account of which he follows very closely; the position of Fame's abode (ll. 713-15); and the place of Fame's dwelling on a high mountain-top. To Virgil he is indebted chiefly for Fame's changing size (ll. 1368-76) and her hideous appearance (ll. 1381-92). To both he is indebted for his conception of Fame as rumor, but to his classical sources, he adds the idea of Fame as renown and Ovid's Palace of Fame becomes subordinate to the goddess of Chaucer's invention. For the influence of Dante, see the articles cited by Robinson, particularly that of A. Rambeau, "Chaucer's 'House of Fame' in Seinem Verhältniss zu Dante's 'Divina Commedia'", *Englische Studien*, III (1880), 209-68.

renown) and the vicissitudes of Fortune is present throughout Chaucer's handling of the Fame material (p. 122). The study of H. R. Patch, furthermore, confirms these influences on Chaucer's conception of his goddess Fame.[15] Especially pertinent to the study of Chaucer's interest in the mutability theme, however, is Sypherd's observation (now rather obvious but partly because of his thorough study) that: "For Chaucer, the goddess of Fame evidently had a much greater interest than for other mediaeval poets. . . . [he] atoned for their neglect by creating in this goddess of Fame one of the most powerful deities of this fanciful realm of gods and goddesses" (p. 105). It is, finally, Chaucer's fascination with Fame and the consequent digression devoted to the goddess and her abode which constitutes a major source (not to mention the unfinished state of the poem) of the disparate interpretations of *The House of Fame*.

Much could be said about the many and various interpretations of this poem.[16] Two, however, are especially relevant to this study: those of Paull F. Baum and Paul G. Ruggiers. These critics see the subject of fame as the initial motivation of the poem. Baum thinks that Chaucer began "with the idea of a poem on Fame, in the manner of the French love-vision handled lightly, not to say facetiously" (p. 252). Chaucer's choice of the *Aeneid*, which he summarizes in the first book of the poem as a love story, supplied him with Virgil's description of Fame and the Dido episode supplied him with the example of a false lover. The poem is in order, continues Baum, to line 778, but here Chaucer was obliged to digress because Fame has two aspects, that of renown and that of rumor. Thus the disproportion and the length of Chaucer's "lytel laste book". In spite of this lack of proportion, however, Baum sees "sufficient unity" in the poem. Chaucer, he thinks, had reached his climax in the poem and, having proved his point, perhaps did not feel the need to go further; for,

---

[15] *The Goddess Fortuna in Mediaeval Literature* (Cambridge, Mass., 1927), pp. 96 and 112.
[16] For an excellent survey of the important scholarship on *The House of Fame* to 1934, see Bertrand H. Bronson, "Chaucer's *Hous of Fame*: Another Hypothesis", *University of California Publications in English*, III, No. 4 (1934), 171-92. Bronson himself argues, from the internal evidence of the poem as he sees it, that the only possible tidings that the man of authority might tell would be adverse tidings; that some false lover would be implicated. Because he is surely to be prominent, Chaucer finished the poem (of this Bronson has not the slightest doubt) but did not circulate the conclusion. This interpretation, he says, is in keeping with the ironic spirit of the poem. I present this as just one example of the various interpretations of the poem now under consideration.

he represents at the outset that he is in search of news – news of the actual quotidian affairs of love such as are not to be found in his books. He goes to the place where all of the news of the world is concentrated. He finds all fame a travesty, renown fickle, and rumor a mockery. The ultimate tidings of love from the man of authority would have inevitably been a similar disappointment and disillusion. He returns to his books, with the conclusion that in love, if not in all life, the poetic dream is preferable to the earthly reality. This was his *lore* and his *prow*. ... (Pp. 255-56)

For Ruggiers, the unity of *The House of Fame* is founded on the fact that the functions of Fame, Fortune, and Venus are so similar that there results "a conflation of their activities and the effects of their power over men" (p. 18). Thus he is able to show an organic connection between Books I and III of the poem:

There is in Chaucer's epitome of the *Aeneid*, with its emphasis upon the story of Dido and Aeneas a sufficient foreshadowing of his theme to warrant the long so-called digression of the third book where Chaucer relates the method by which Fame distributes her dubious favors. For his purpose the unhappy catastrophe of love is the work of a divinity whose name might easily be Fortune, or Fame, or Venus; their roles are interdependent; they operate in similar circumstances. (P. 20).

The long account of Fame's caprice throughout the third book, then, is not to be considered a digression but the central theme of the poem, if we consider that Dido and Aeneas are part of the human condition and that their relationship is at the mercy of the composite activities of Love, Fame, and Fortune. Thus, Ruggiers emphasizes: "It is my persuasion that the third book says what Chaucer intends it to say, that Fame and her influence, like that of her sister Fortune, is ever present as a conditioning factor in men's lives, and that men should fasten their hopes on something more stable, over and above this capricious power" (p. 25). In Book III, then, Chaucer absorbs the love elements into the total framework of the poem, enhances Fame by subjecting rumor to her caprice and, throughout, while attempting to stay within the scope of the love-vision, broadens it "to include more direct observation, more invention and detail' (p. 27). Ruggiers thinks that in this poem, as in the *Knight's Tale*, Boethius might have supplied Chaucer's man of authority with a suitable ending, "incorporating the theme of the untrustworthy fortunes of love into the larger picture of the instability of fame in general, a pronouncement voicing the conviction that only disillusion must result from an abuse of the passions and folly of trusting the inconstant goddess" (p. 28).

Ruggiers' interpretation is well-knit but a bit ingenious. The meaning which he sees in the poem is not likely to be the meaning which the reader experiences from the poem, for these reasons: Dido's complaint, directed against wicked Fame (ll. 345-62), constitutes but a small portion of the entire episode; furthermore, it is Fame as rumor, rather than as reputation, which is stressed. Second, while it is certain that the goddess of Love influenced Chaucer's conception of Fame, there is no indication in Chaucer's third book, especially in Fame's actions toward her suppliants (or in the suppliants' requests), that she retains the qualities of Venus; [17] in a word the love elements are insignificant, if in fact they do not disappear entirely at this point of the poem. The interpretation of Baum, on the other hand, is largely conjectural. These interpretations must nevertheless be taken into account in any study which attempts to discuss the function of the mutability theme in Chaucer's poetry; at least they seriously recognize this element in Chaucer's poetic sensibility. If, however, Baum's interpretation is largely conjectural, he does with Sypherd contend that the Fame-as-renown material is a disproportionate digression. And in view of the fact that the final interpretation of *The House of Fame* will never be written, since it is unfinished, this is perhaps all that can with certainty be said about it. This digression, to be sure, and the vivid detail which Chaucer employs to portray Fame and her abode is significantly indicative of his interest in mutability. For even if the mutability of love, of fortune, and of fame is not artistically unified in this poem (as Ruggiers would have it), it is nevertheless present.

THE PARLIAMENT OF FOWLS

The mutability theme in the first part of *The Parliament of Fowls* has provoked most of the recent criticism on the poem. The problem has been to reconcile "Tullyus of the Drem of Scipioun", which Chaucer summarizes in forty-nine lines (ll. 36-84), with the dream-vision which follows, specifically the Garden of Love and the debate. Some attention to the ways in which the critics have attempted to reconcile these two parts of the poem and to their comments regarding Chaucer and mutability generally will, I think, very effectually illuminate Chaucer's use of the theme, not only in this poem, but in his other works.

Chaucer begins the poem with a *sententia* which he adapted from the *Aphorisms* (I, i) of Hippocrates:

---

[17]   Only two companies of the petitioners, the sixth and seventh, mention love at all, and they desire fame "as wel of love as other thyng" (l. 1739).

The lyf so short, the craft so long to lerne,
Th'assay so hard, so sharp the conquerynge,
The dredful joye, alwey that slit so yerne:
Al this mene I by Love. . . .

(ll. 1-4)

"A very un-Hippocratic" use of the aphorism, as Kemp Malone notes; [18] without attaching too much significance to this passage, I do think it exemplifies how ready to hand the mutability theme was for Chaucer. Here he applies the aphorism very deftly to love, by way of introduction to denying any knowledge about Love.

"Nat yoore agon", however, it happened that he read a book, "a certeyn thing to lerne", presumably about love; this book was entitled "Tullyus of the Drem of Scipioun", and thus he begins to "seyn the greete": Africanus the Elder appeared to his grandson, Africanus the Younger, in a dream. Among the stars, high over Carthage, the old man told the younger that only he who loved the "commune profyt" would come into the blissful place, "there joye is that last withouten ende". He told him that "oure present worldes lyves space/ Nis but a maner deth", and that the righteous folk will go to heaven after they die. Then the elder man showed his grandson "the lytel erthe that here is,/ At regard of the hevenes quantite"; and bade him "syn erthe was so lyte,/ And ful of torment and of harde grace,/ That he ne shulde hym in the world delyte". After the Platonic year is up, in fact, "al shulde out of mynde/ That in this world is don of al mankynde". Then Africanus the Younger asked the elder man how he might come to this eternal blessedness. He was told to recognize, first of all, his own immortality and always to work and instruct busily for the "commune profit"; then he might come into this state of perfect bliss. "But brekers of the lawe", says the elder man, "and likerous folk" shall whirl about the earth in pain after their death until they are forgiven; only then may they enter paradise.

It is the *Contemptus Mundi* which is expressed throughout Chaucer's entire summary of the Dream. This is apparent, for example, in the elder's words to the younger that "he ne shulde hym in the world delyte" (Chaucer emphasizes this point by adding to his source that this little world is "ful of torment and of harde grace").[19] Those critics who wish to see a thematic unity in the *Parliament* must attempt to reconcile this contempt of the world prologue with a poem written in honor of St. Valentine.

[18]   *Chapters on Chaucer*, p. 66.
[19]   For a somewhat similar idea, when Chaucer again refers to the sorrows of mortality, cf. *House of Fame*, ll. 406-407.

Bertrand H. Bronson was the first to argue significantly for an artistic unity in the poem.[20] The solution, he says, is in Chaucer's ironic attitude toward his subject of love, a "slyly humorous attitude" (p. 204) which he has assumed from the very beginning of the poem. The connections between the two parts of the poem are many but subtle: Chaucer ironically professes to know nothing about love except what he has learned out of books; then in the *Somnium* follows "a devastating criticism of the lover's philosophy" (p. 204); he makes Africanus "his dubious guide to the realms of love through the portals which recall the gates of Hell" (p. 204); at the gates of the Garden of Love Chaucer again denies his affinity for love; in the invocation to Cytherea, Chaucer has "his tongue in his cheek when he calls on Venus as his inspiration and aid" (p. 205; Bronson interprets *north-north-west* to mean "hardly at all"). In fact, he states, "the beginning of the *Parlement of Foules* is, indisputably, far from being conceived under the inspiration of the goddess of love" (p. 208).

As for the Garden of Love, Bronson compares Chaucer's with his source, the *Teseida*, and finds that Chaucer's Venus is much less sensual than Boccaccio's. Chaucer "has, in fact, nearly stripped her of her glamour" (p. 209). The argument of the birds is a double-edged satire against the unreality of the idealists of courtly love, and the sometimes-contemptible realists who make up the rest of the parliament. "But, Chaucer (a great master of irony) seems to say, let us be as sane as we can. But, again, it is joy to see downright madness!" (p. 219). Then the vision ends and Chaucer goes to other books so that someday he might "read something that will cause him to dream a really profitable dream, not one of these things in which all is left at sixes and sevens and nothing is decided. . . . the wheel has come round to its starting point, and the poem is done" (p. 220). Thus, for Bronson, Chaucer's irony flickers throughout the poem from beginning to end, so that while the poem is ostensibly written in praise of Venus and Love, it is, in reality, qualified throughout by the awareness of the more somber mood of *Scipio's Dream*:

The dilemma here curiously adumbrates the epilogue of the *Troilus and Criseyde*, suggesting a connection more than casual between the two poems. . . . The deeper parallel, in both, lies in the juxtaposition of the same two apparently irreconcilable attitudes. The difference is merely one of pitch and of consequent modification of artistic treatment. In the more serious work,

[20] "In Appreciation of Chaucer's *Parlement of Foules*", *University of California Publications in English*, III (1935), 193-224.

such value and meaning have been given to the human attitude that the poem will easily bear the full weight of the contrasting moral. In the lighter piece, the contrast can only be suggested. In either, no one can doubt that the dualism was real enough in Chaucer's thought, and that he saw no facile resolution of it. (Pp. 199-202)

R. C. Goffin's study is based only upon an analysis of the first ninety-one lines of the poem.[21] Chaucer, he thinks, following upon the hint in the beginning of the *Roman de la Rose*, looked into Macrobius' *Commentary* to find an appropriate opening for his dream-vision (*a certeyn thing to lerne* simply means, he says, "literary material"): "He will examine (or has examined 'not yore agon') its pertinence to his story – one of love, and of very earthly love" (p. 495). But Chaucer did not find what he was looking for and, having given an epitome of the *Somnium,* says:

> And to my bed I gan me for to dresse,
> Fulfyld of thought and busy hevynesse;
> For bothe I hadde thyng which that I nolde,
> And ek I nadde that thyng that I wolde.
>   (ll. 88-91)

Surely the meaning is clear, says Goffin; Chaucer had discovered the true paradise of bliss but not the earthly paradise for which he looked: "He has still to find that 'thing' which is to prefigure his poem of worldly vanity" (p. 496). This antithesis, however, is "peculiarly apposite" at this part of the poem: Not only did Chaucer fail to find what he was looking for in the *Somnium,* but the high vision of perfection which he found there subsequently makes all love poetry "mere earthly 'delight' ... if not 'lechery'" (p. 497). Thus Chaucer, as a love poet, must forever stand frustrated before this high vision of perfection. Goffin does not attempt, as does Bronson, to reconcile the two parts of the poem. He reasonably concludes that there is no resolution in the *Parliament,* but that the "final resolution of this antithesis, so strikingly pictured in its opposing outlines in the *Parlement,* abstract moral theory on the one hand and vital human art on the other, though it was presaged in the *Troilus,* was never fully achieved in Chaucer's mind till he came to write the *Canterbury Tales*" (p. 499).

Accepting Goffin's interpretation (of the first ninety-one lines of the poem) that Chaucer had found in Macrobius only that "thing" which he did not want and had not found the "thing" which he had sought, R. M.

---

[21] "Heaven and Earth in the 'Parlement of Foules'", *MLR*, XXXI (1936), 493-99.

Lumiansky analyzes the whole poem and concludes that the unifying theme is "Chaucer's unsuccessful search for a way of reconciling true and false felicity." [22] He suggests that the "newe science" in Chaucer's lines ("Out of olde bokes . . . Cometh al this newe science that men lere") refers to the new emphasis which the Lollards were placing on the instability of worldly pleasures; and that Chaucer, perhaps, went to the old book of Macrobius in search of a counter-argument to defend his writings on love. Lumiansky argues, from lines 109-12 of the poem, that Chaucer expects Africanus to point out a means of reconciliation of his dilemma during the dream. The theme of Chaucer's unsuccessful search is seen, furthermore, in his doubts before the gates of the park; in his momentary abandonment to the beauty of the park but his sudden recall of his search upon encountering the allegorical creatures who represent earthly joys; and in "his failure to accord the love poet's usual high and detailed praise to Venus; and his rapidity in turning from Venus to Nature, the recognized agent of God" (p. 87). Finally, he says, the formel's request for a year's respite is definitely not a compliment to Venus; in fact, her unwillingness to serve "Venus ne Cupid" might well represent Chaucer's own point of view. Thus the dilemma of salvation and of writing love poetry, or true and false felicity, is not solved; Chaucer therefore goes back to his books, hoping some day to find the answer. But, says Lumiansky, he never did. In fact, continues Lumiansky, "the philosophical content of the *Parlement* indicates an earlier undecided state of the attitude later more decisively presented in the *Retracciouns*. . . . One might suggest also that the epilogue to *Troilus and Criseyde* should be considered as an expression of a similar attitude" (pp. 88-89).

The most elaborate interpretation yet attempted of this poem, however, is that of J. A. W. Bennett,[23] whose arguments are essentially these: The *Somnium* establishes "the implied dichotomy between passionate

[22] "Chaucer's *Parlement of Foules:* A Philosophical Interpretation", *RES*, XXIV (1948), 81-89.
[23] *The Parlement of Foules: An Interpretation* (Oxford, 1957). Bennett deals primarily in terms of literary *topoi*; he attempts to illumine certain passages in the *Parliament* by the light of other passages in the works of Chaucer; he "fills in" certain lines and passages with meanings which "must have been" in Chaucer's associative memory at the time he wrote the poem, loosely related scenes or passages from *De Planctu Naturae* or the *Divina Commedia*, for example. He does not see a definable meaning taking form throughout the poem; rather, he sees the meaning taking shape in reverberating suggestions, associations, and in "the ambiguity we have found in this poem at every turn" (cf. pages 27, 66, 72, 79, 98, and 103, for Bennett's insistence on the ambiguity in the poem).

love and the common weal" (p. 34); "likerous folk" in the *Somnium* should be interpreted in accordance with Alain's *De Planctu Naturae,* as those who hinder "the perpetuation of the species and the operation of the principle of plenitude" (p. 42); the double inscriptions on the gate, furthermore, emphasize this dichotomy found in the *Somnium*. Bennett argues that Chaucer contrasts the Garden of Love and the allegorical personifications, especially in the Temple of Venus. In the Garden Chaucer is depicting Nature "at her loveliest" (p. 72), and in her "abundance" (p. 74), in short as "a Christian Elysium" (p. 78). Having compared Chaucer's personifications with those of Boccaccio, Bennett, in complete opposition to Bronson, finds Chaucer's depiction "more sultry, more sinister, and at the same time more voluptuous" (p. 92). The conclusion is, then, that the Garden is identified with Nature, who as the viceregent of God presides over the parliament, the richly various scale of creatures, and counsels them to choose their mates; and that the basic contrast in the poem is between the principle of plenitude, which leads to chaste love in marriage, and Venus-worship, which does not, but which brings "swich peyne and wo as Loves folk endure" (p. 105). Chaucer's acceptance of this doctrine of plenitude, moreover, is "the only possible way of putting in its proper place the view of the body as the prison of the soul, to which Cicero's *Somnium* gives classic expression" (p. 13). And, thus, in *The Parliament of Fowls,* Chaucer "moves almost imperceptibly towards a position that comes nearest to being explicit in Theseus' noble conclusion to the *Knight's Tale,* and in the firmly measured exordium of the Franklin's" (p. 13).

These various attitudes toward Chaucer's use of the *Somnium*, exemplified in resumés of four interpretations of *The Parliament of Fowls*,[24]

---

[24]   See Robert E. Thackaberry, "Chaucer's *The Parlement of Foules*: A Re-Interpretation", an unpublished thesis (Ph.D.), State University of Iowa (1937), who argues for an artistic unity of the poem. He emphasizes the "common profit" as stated in the *Somnium*, and the contrasting warring classes as depicted in the debate, "in which no one was concerned for the good of all" (p. 39; see this and the following page for an excellent summary of Thackaberry's thesis). Thackaberry's thesis is thinly documented but excellent for his close analysis of the poem; Charles A. Owen, Jr., "The Role of the Narrator in the 'Parlement of Foules'", *College English*, XIV (1953), 264-69. Owen's interpretation is not convincing: The dream vision is Chaucer's sub-conscious indulgence or "release" from the idealism of the *Somnium*, "the victory of impulse and passion, frustrated though they be, over the idealism suggested by his reading" (p. 267). Owen's criticism makes good reading until he speaks of the Garden of Love as "wish fulfilment" (p. 266); Charles O. McDonald, "An Interpretation of Chaucer's *Parlement of Foules*", *Speculum*, XXX (1955), 444-57. With the exception of Bronson's, perhaps this article is most worthy of attention. McDonald's thesis,

speak strongly to suggest the need of a clearer understanding of
Chaucer's use of the mutability theme; indeed the attempts of these
critics to relate this poem with others in the works of Chaucer (as the
excerpts at the end of each resumé have indicated) suggest the need for
a total assessment of the mutability theme in Chaucer's works generally.
For certainly these interpretations of *The Parliament of Fowls* distort, if
they do not wholly misrepresent, the poem. Without attempting here to
refute these interpretations in detail,[25] suffice it to say that all but one
(Goffin does not attempt to interpret the dream-vision) must completely
distort the nature and purpose of the Garden of Love in the poem to
make their interpretations convincing. So too must they misrepresent the
bird-parliament; thus Lumiansky sees in the formel's unwillingness to
serve "Venus ne Cupid" for the nonce a reflection of Chaucer's own
point of view. Bronson, in speaking of Chaucer and the love vision, even
says that "it is clear enough that the subject and the *genre* were radically
uncongenial to his temperament" (p. 197). It is time to reconsider
Chaucer's poem.

Dorothy Bethurum, I think, of all the critics considered here most
accurately indicates the emphasis of the *Parliament*:

It is essentially a love poem, and it is about fertility and generation. It is a
Valentine, not only adorned with, but written about, doves, cupids, and
flowers. And being so centered, it is the most voluptuous poem Chaucer ever

---

the same which Bennett develops with multifarious and dubious detail, is that
the "common profit" mentioned in the *Somnium* is connected to the dream
vision in the "ironic humor and mild satire of courtly love" (p. 450); and he
finds the poem's meaning in Nature's holding all lovers, "courtly and otherwise,
to 'common profit', that is, to marriage and to multiplication of the race" (p. 454).
[25] The main points with which I disagree in Bronson's interpretation have been
touched upon in the text. Goffin's interpretation is interesting but highly conjectural: lines 90-91, upon which he bases so much of his argument, do not
necessarily refer to the poet's reading. As for Chaucer's looking into the *Commentary* for "literary material", this seems a bit doubtful. Both Chaucer and his
Valentine audience knew the *Commentary*, and certainly his audience would not
be convinced by Chaucer's looking to Macrobius for love material, unless, of
course, Chaucer meant to be ironical; which Goffin does not mention as a possibility. The weakness of Lumiansky's thesis might best be seen in his arguments
regarding the dreamer in the Garden of Love and the Temple of Venus. The
dreamer's temporary forgetting of his search at the sight of the Garden and his
sudden remembrance of it at the sight of the allegorical figures (who represent
worldly pleasures) is hardly convincing. Lumiansky is least convincing when he
says that Chaucer is uncomfortable in the Temple of Venus, because he has
love poems on his conscience; and having completed his tour of the park,
Chaucer "feels a bit ashamed for having to some extent enjoyed such sights.
Therefore he walks a short distance for the purpose 'myselven to solace' "
(p. 88).

wrote. . . . If the piece is a love poem, then the Garden of Love is its very center, for the Garden supplies not merely a geographical but a psychological setting, as was its purpose in the *Roman de la Rose* and in all its numerous progeny. . . . The Garden of Love condenses, as is the useful virtue of allegory, the whole amorous experience into a few stanzas. . . . Furthermore, the Garden gives the *significatio* of the poem, and this theme is developed by debate in the Parliament that follows.[26]

These statements of Professor Bethurum reflect the experience which the reader most probably receives from the poem. Nor is the reader even slightly aware that Chaucer's Venus is "nearly stripped . . . of her glamour".[27] This study has suggested that there neither is, nor is there likely to be, a reconciliation of the *Somnium* with the Garden of Love and the debate.[28]

The *Contemptus Mundi* expression and courtly love are irrevocably incompatible; the attitudes are obviously contradictory. Bronson recognizes this when he says that "the deeper parallel, in both [the *Parliament* and the *Troilus*] lies in the juxtaposition of the same two apparently

[26] Dorothy Bethurum, "The Center of the *Parlement of Foules*", in *Essays in Honor of Walter Clyde Curry* (Nashville, 1954), pp. 40-41. Cf. Robert Worth Frank, Jr., "Structure and Meaning in the 'Parlement of Foules' ", *PMLA*, LXXI (1956), 530-39, who sees three separate sections to the *Parliament*, each expressing three different attitudes toward love: the moralistic, the literary, and the realistic, in the *Somnium*, the garden, and the debate, respectively. While Frank over-emphasizes the "realism" at the expense of courtly love in the bird parliament, his study is especially useful in showing that the *Somnium* is in no way related to the rest of the poem. Cf. Dorothy Everett, *Essays on Middle English Literature*, ed. Patricia Kean (Oxford, 1959), pp. 97-114, for an excellently balanced discussion of *PF*.

[27] Bronson's argument from Chaucer's source is hardly valid. Chaucer's audience did not interpret the *Parliament* against his source, and Bronson in fact does not show that Chaucer's Venus is asensual. Robert Pratt says about Chaucer's translation of the *Teseida* at this juncture: "To sum up, the slight changes from the *Teseida* seem mostly a perfunctory by-product of the process of transferring to the *Parliament* the pictorial and sensuous beauty of Boccaccio's description." "Chaucer's Use of the *Teseida*", *PMLA*, LXII (1947), 607.

[28] Wolfgang Clemen, *Chaucer's Early Poetry*, trans. C. A. M. Sym (London, 1963), points out that "even a close study of Chaucer's version of the *Somnium* cannot begin to answer the question why this sort of general view of the world should be placed at the beginning of a poem dealing with love. For it reflects, in an acute form, the medieval Christian-ascetic contempt for this world; there is no room in this conception either for love or for the appreciation of the beauty of this world as God's handiwork. . . . the whole of man's endeavour is fixed solely upon the next world" (p. 134). He states that, "Medieval poetry could pass more easily from what was serious to comedy, from a gloomy to a serene and light-hearted view of life" (p. 136). For a similar statement, cf. Bethurum, pp. 48-49; Kittredge, p. 60; and W. O. Sypherd, *Studies in Chaucer's Hous of Fame*, p. 23 ("It is merely the book which interests Chaucer at the time and which he is eager to tell about").

irreconcilable attitudes" (*supra*). Perhaps this is the reason for his insistence on Chaucer's irony rather than upon the philosophical content
of the *Somnium*, unlike Lumiansky and Bennett. Nevertheless, Bronson
does call the *Somnium* "a devastating criticism of the lover's philosophy"
(*supra*) and one cannot but suspect that this had no small bearing upon
his distortion of the Garden of Love.[29] As will be seen in the study of
the *Troilus*, the *Contemptus Mundi* theme of the epilogue, wherein
Chaucer expressly tells the "yonge, fresshe folkes" to avoid worldly love
and to love God, is in direct contradiction to his praise of love and of
love's power throughout the poem. In short, the *Somnium* and the
Garden of Love (and the debate) were separate and contradictory realms
in the mediaeval mind; and since a reconciliation of the two was impossible, the mediaeval man did not look upon their "resolution" as a
possibility, and *a fortiori* he did not view this irresolution with discomfort. Thus the ultimate value in recognizing the *Somnium* for what
it is, a *Contemptus Mundi* expression, and the Garden of Love (with
the debate) for what it is, a descendant of the *Roman de la Rose,* and in
recognizing their irrevocable dichotomy. Such is not the case in *The
Book of the Duchess*, where the transitory theme of the introductory
episode which, if not organically incorporated into the structure of the
dream vision, is at least consonant with the Man in Black's tirade against
Fortune and finally with the loss of his lady. This is so because the
primary focus of the poem is the elegy, the loss; and the transitory theme
is always compatible with the courtly love theme, whereas the *Contemptus Mundi* is not. The one may stem from a natural point of view,
the other, almost invariably from the supernatural. But while the critics
must fumble somewhat with the attempt to unite the *lore* and the *lust* of
the *Parliament*, they are correct in pointing out the similarities of
Chaucer's dual vision in this poem and in the *Troilus*. Bronson's and
Lumiansky's remarks are particularly significant when they point up a
conflict of attitudes within Chaucer's own mind and temperament; as are
Goffin's when he suggests that this conflict will not finally be resolved
until the *Canterbury Tales*. In the *Troilus*, presently to be examined,
Chaucer utilizes the transitory motif of the *Duchess* and of *Fame,* and

---

[29]   Bronson later revises his opinion somewhat in regard to the *Somnium*'s use
in the *Parliament*. See "The *Parlement of Foules* Revisited", *ELH*, XV (1948),
258, where he says, "It seems undeniable that Chaucer was exhibiting the *tours
de force* of a virtuoso, utilizing whatever lay nearest to hand, compelling it into
service." He says also that the *Somnium* might even be a product of revision of
the poem (p. 259); and in his lectures, *In Search of Chaucer* (Toronto, 1963),
the poem "is too nimble for criticism, which always hops behind" (p. 46).

also the *Contemptus Mundi* motif of the *Parliament*. Here it becomes clear that he is using these motifs with conscious precision, and the materials and art of the *Troilus* are enhanced rather than diminished by this conflict of the natural and supernatural visions.

V

TROILUS AND CRISEYDE

The mutability theme of the *Troilus* has long been recognized. In his
Troy Book, John Lydgate writes:

> And in this wise Troylus first be-gan
> To be a seruaunt, my maister telleth thus,
> Til he was holpe aftir of Pandarus,
> Thorugh whos comforte & mediacioun
> (As in his boke is maked mencioun)
> With great labour firste he cam to grace.
> And so contunneth by certeyn yeres space,
> Til Fortune gan up-on hym frowne,
> That she from hym mvst goon oute of towne
> Al sodeynly, and neuer hym after se.
> Lo! here the ende of worldly brotilnes,
> Of fleshy lust, lo! here thunstabilnes,
> Lo! here the double variacioun
> Of wor[l]dly blisse and transmvtacioun:
> This day in myrthe & in wo to-morwe!
> For ay the fyn, allas! of Ioie is sorwe.[1]

R. C. Goffin says that "the whole of the *Troilus* may . . . be justifiably
viewed as an epic tragedy of the essential transitoriness of earthly love".[2]
Neville Coghill writes, "One might say, using fourteenth-century termi-
nology, that Chaucer saw in Boccaccio's tale of Troilus an *exemplum*
of the Boethian philosophies of tragedy and free will." [3] Root thinks
that "in the fickleness and falsehood of Criseyde, a woman so lovely, so
sweet and gracious, so much to be desired, he [Chaucer] sees the type
of mutability, of the transitoriness and fallacy of earthly happiness".[4] Of
all the critics who have dealt with this subject, however, only two have

[1] Ed. Henry Bergen, EETSES, 97, 103, 106, 126 (1906-35), Book III, lines
4214-30.
[2] "Heaven and Earth in the *PF*", p. 498.
[3] *The Poet Chaucer* (Oxford, 1955), p. 69.
[4] R. K. Root, *The Book of Troilus and Criseyde by Geoffrey Chaucer* (Princeton, 1926), p. xlviii.

done so with any degree of thoroughness, B. L. Jefferson and Willard Farnham. Having pointed out the themes of fortuné and transitoriness in the poem, and having indicated all the passages relative to these themes, Jefferson concludes: "Indeed so philosophical a poem is *Troilus,* so much does it abound in Boethian passages, so much does it illustrate the truth of the Boethian teaching, that it is possible even to suppose that Chaucer translated the *Consolation* for the express purpose that *Troilus* might be the better interpreted; at any rate, the two works go hand in hand." [5] Farnham views the *Troilus* as a *De Casu* tragedy, with all the mediaeval machinery common to the *De Casibus* type; Criseyde is "simply a worldly possession of Troilus'. Like wealth or a crown she takes wings and leaves him." [6] In the hands of Chaucer, he says, "the business of courtly love ... has its aspect of sad vanity which can be viewed with truly detached spirit" (p. 140).

It would be difficult to add materially to the studies of Jefferson and Farnham, for after all one of the basic facts about the *Troilus* is its Boethian philosophy. I should like, however, in this chapter to review this criticism and to add some of my own; I hope thereby to clarify the various themes of mutability which run throughout the poem and to show how conscious Chaucer was of the mutability theme in it.

Kittredge was the first to point out the significance of Chaucer's changes from Boccaccio to implicate his tragic lovers in the doom of Troy. He saw that the fate of the lovers was inextricably interwoven and intensified by the impending doom of Troy. "They are, in fact, caught in the wheels of that resistless mechanism which the gods have set in motion for the ruin of the Trojan race." [7] It is unnecessary to go into all of Chaucer's source-changes to prove this point. One example, however, will be useful to show how closely Chaucer meant to involve Troy and Fortune. Boccaccio simply says: "Things went on between the Trojans and Greeks ever and anon as in time of war. At times the Trojans came forth from their city doughtily against the Greeks and oftentimes, if the story erreth not, the Greeks advanced valiantly even to the moats,

---

[5] *Chaucer and the Consolation,* p. 130.
[6] *Medieval Heritage,* p. 145. B. L. Jefferson says that the poem "may be considered a monk's tale, told with minute attention to human psychology and wrought into infinitely better poetry" (p. 125). It was left for Farnham, however, to develop this idea. Cf. D. W. Robertson, Jr., "Chaucerian Tragedy", *ELH,* XIX (1952), 1-37. Robertson sees in Troilus, in an extreme form, "the tragedy of every mortal sinner" (p. 36); and *A Preface to Chaucer* (Princeton, 1962), pp. 476-502.
[7] *Chaucer and His Poetry,* p. 117.

pillaging on every side, firing and destroying castles and towns." [8]
Chaucer, on the other hand, leaves no doubt about the element of
Fortune in this war:

> The thynges fellen, as they don of werre,
> Bitwixen hem of Troie and Grekes ofte;
> For som day boughten they of Troie it derre,
> And eft the Grekes founden nothing softe
> The folk of Troie; and thus Fortune on lofte,
> And under eft, gan hem to whielen bothe
> Aftir hir cours, ay whil that thei were wrothe.
> (I, 134-40)

The treason of Antenor (IV, 197-210) and the death of Hector (V,
1541-54), neither of which appears in *Il Filostrato,* also occasion
Chaucer's apostrophizing the fate of Troy.[9] Into this background Chaucer
has woven his *De Casu* tragedy.

Chaucer states his theme in the very beginning of the poem:

> The double sorwe of Troilus to tellen,
> That was the kyng Priamus sone of Troye,
> In lovynge, how his aventures fellen
> Fro wo to wele, and after out of joie,
> My purpos is.   (I, 1-5)

Whereas Boccaccio makes nothing of Troilus' being a king's son,
Chaucer makes much of it (Farnham, p. 142). Just before Troilo is to
fall in love with Cressida, Boccaccio writes: "O blindness of mundane
minds! How often follow effects all contrary to our intentions! Troilus
now raileth at the weaknesses and anxious loves of other people without
a thought of what heaven hasteneth to bring upon him, whom Love
transfixed more than any other before he left the temple" (I, 25).
Chaucer turns this one stanza of Boccaccio's into three, and in the first
he inserts the image of a fall:

> O blynde world, O blynde entencioun!
> How often falleth al the effect contraire
> Of surquidrie and foul presumpcioun;
> For kaught is proud, and kaught is debonaire.
> This Troilus is clomben on the staire,
> And litel weneth that he moot descenden;
> But alday faileth thing that fooles wenden.
> (I, 211-17)

---

[8] N. E. Griffin and A. B. Myrick, *The Filostrato of Giovanni Boccaccio: A
Translation with Parallel Text* (Philadelphia, 1929), I, 16. All references to the
Filostrato are from this text.
[9] For further instances of destiny, cf. Kittredge, pp. 117-21.

Then follows the image of proud Bayard who realizes that he is but a horse after all and must endure "horses lawe". Troilus too, therefore, must endure "the lawe of kynde"; "So ferde it by this fierse and proud knyght." Chaucer is here doing no more than speaking of Troilus' being made subject to love, but, says Farnham, "We know from the beginning of the poem the more serious fall that is in store for Troilus, and now we may guess that his pride in princely rank and his ignorance of the world's power over all mankind will soften that fall no more than this" (p. 143). He says, furthermore:

So Troilus falls into his first woe and proceeds out of it to his greatest joy. Like many of the more carefully plotted stories in the *De Casibus*, Chaucer's *Troilus* has a peak of good fortune very near the middle of the action, marked with moralizing upon Fortune's mutability. Here, in some degree, Chaucer follows the *Filostrato*, which, even though it was not written especially to expose and anatomize the mutability of the world, yet as a love poem could rail at Fortune with plenty of precedent. (P. 143)

In the *Filostrato*, Cressida, after the most superficial and conventional objections (II, 134-43), finally succumbs to Pandaro's request that Troilo come secretly to her home at night. Chaucer handles this affair quite differently. He has Criseyde come to Pandarus' house for dinner (III, 604 ff.), unaware of, if not completely unsuspecting, Troilus' presence there. As she is about to leave with her retinue, there comes a cloudburst which forces her to spend the night with her uncle. At this point, Chaucer says:

> But O Fortune, executrice of wyrdes,
> O influences of thise hevenes hye!
> Soth is, that under God ye ben oure hierdes,
> Though to us bestes ben the causes wrie.
> This mene I now, for she gan homward hye,
> But execut was al bisyde hire leve
> The goddes wil; for which she moste bleve.
>   (III, 617-23)

Troilus and Criseyde consummate their love and spend many more nights together. At the end of this third book Boccaccio says simply: "But for a short time lasted this happiness, thanks to envious fortune, which in this world remaineth not stable. It turned toward him its bitter face, by a new chance, as it happeneth, and turning everything upside down, took from him the sweet fruits of Cressida, and changed his happy love into woeful mourning" (III, 94).

This single stanza from *Il Filostrato*, Chaucer spins into a *prohemium* for his fourth book, not only giving the idea much more importance but also setting the tone for what is to follow in the entire book:

> But al to litel, weylaway the whyle,
> Lasteth swich joie, ythonked be Fortune,
> That semeth trewest whan she wol bygyle,
> And kan to fooles so hire song entune,
> That she hem hent and blent, traitour commune!
> And whan a wight is from hire whiel ythrowe,
> Than laugheth she, and maketh hym the mowe.
>
> From Troilus she gan hire brighte face
> Awey to writhe, and tok of hym non heede,
> But caste hym clene out of his lady grace,
> And on hire whiel she sette up Diomede;
> For which right now myn herte gynneth blede,
> And now my penne, allas! with which I write,
> Quaketh for drede of that I moste endite.
>
> (IV, 1-14)

The poet then invokes Mars and the Furies to help him show fully Troilus' loss of love and of life. In this book, Chaucer inserts the long passage of Troilus concerning fate and free will, which, incidentally, does not appear in the first draft of the poem. In his despair, Troilus concludes that there is no such thing as free will and that he is the victim of fate. Shortly thereafter, Criseyde departs for the Greek camp, never to return. In the final book, Chaucer inserts a passage not found in *Il Filostrato*:

> Fortune, which that permutacioun
> Of thynges hath, as it is hire comitted
> Thorugh purveyaunce and disposicioun
> Of heighe Jove, as regnes shal be flitted
> Fro folk in folk, or when they shal be smytted,
> Gan pulle awey the fetheres brighte of Troie
> Fro day to day, til they ben bare of joie.
>
> (V, 1541-47)

What Willard Farnham says about this passage sums up, in brief, much of his criticism of the *Troilus*: This stanza typifies both the conventional treatment of Fortune in the *De Casibus* tragedies, and at the same time shows Chaucer's unique setting for this conventional situation. The stanza begins with the conventional Fortune of the *De Casibus*, but "into this picture of Fate in all its epic grandeur the poet casts the figure of Troy being plucked of its gay feathers like any barnyard fowl. . . .

Probably nothing in small compass could better represent the almost indescribable mingling of sad sooth and smiling irony, of heroic elevation and homely shrewdness, which is the seriocomic spirit of the *Troilus*" (p. 151). To be sure, the *Troilus* is a *De Casu* tragedy. It is not necessary, for this study, to go into the problem of free will and determinism in the poem. Jefferson and Curry have pointed out all the relevant passages which evidence the attitude of Troilus, but arrive at different conclusions.[10] Suffice it to say here that Troilus, in a moment of despair (IV, 54), arrives at his conclusion of determinism; his railings at Fortune throughout the poem are conventional and do not necessarily reflect Chaucer's philosophy of life; much of the problem, in fact, has to do with the conventions of courtly love: Troilus, as a courtly lover, was unable to resist the divine influence of love.[11] Troilus, in actuality, acts as though he has free will, and the other characters in the poem never even question the fact that man lacks it. (Regardless of what attitude one takes toward the problem, however, he must reckon with a passage such as this. Before Troilus is to meet with Criseyde, he says: " 'O fatal sustren, which, er any cloth/ Me shapen was, my destine me sponne,/ So helpeth to this werk that is bygonne!' " [III, 733-35]) To see the heart of the *Troilus* and also Chaucer's vision in the poem, one must pierce through the Fortune machinery of the conventional *De Casibus* tragedy. If one does this, he will find, I think, that Chaucer's main preoccupation in the *Troilus* was with the problem of mutability; that Troilus' fall resulted from his complete and irrevocable attachment to Criseyde, ultimately, as Root and Farnham say, just "another worldly possession",[12] who, as we learn from the epilogue, has turned Troilus away from the only stable happiness, Jesus Christ.

The "bedroom scene", which I shall call it for lack of a better phrase, foreshadows this idea in the epilogue. If one compares the bedroom scene of *Il Filostrato* (III, 27-52) with that of the *Troilus* (III, 1191-1533), he will find that Chaucer heightens the happiness of the lovers considerably; in fact, he equates it with the perfect happiness of heaven. Boccaccio says: "Long would it be to recount the joy and impossible to tell the delight they took together when they came there. ... O sweet and much-desired night, what wert thou to the two joyful lovers! If the

[10] Cf. W. C. Curry, *Chaucer and the Mediaeval Sciences* (New York, 1960), pp. 241 ff.; and B. L. Jefferson, p. 122 ff.

[11] See T. A. Kirby, *Chaucer's Troilus: A Study in Courtly Love* (Baton Rouge, 1940), p. 262.

[12] Root, *The Book of Troilus and Criseyde*, p. xlviii; Farnham, *Med. Heritage*, p. 145.

knowledge that all the poets once possessed were given me, I should be
unable to describe it. Let him who was ever before so much favored by
Love as they, take thought of it, and he will know in part their delight"
(III, 31, 33). Chaucer writes:

> Of hire delit, or joies oon the leeste,
> Were impossible to my wit to seye;
> But juggeth ye that han ben at the feste
> Of swich gladnesse, if that hem liste pleye!
> I kan namore, but thus thise ilke tweye,
> That nyght, bitwixen drede and sikernesse,
> Felten in love the grete worthynesse.
>
> O blisful nyght, of hem so longe isought,
> How blithe unto hem bothe two thow weere!
> Why nad I swich oon with my soule ybought,
> Ye, or the leeste joie that was theere?
> Awey, thow foule daunger and thow feere,
> *And lat hem in this hevene blisse dwelle,*
> *That is so heigh that al ne kan I telle!*
>   (III, 1310-23) [13]

It is significant that in these two lines (italicized) Chaucer actually
refers to the joy of the lovers as "hevene blisse", and that he remarks
that their joy is so high that he cannot even tell of it. In the lines which
follow (1338-65), Chaucer adheres very closely to *Il Filostrato;* in the
works of both authors the lovers cannot believe that their experience is
real: "lo, this was hir mooste feere,/ That al this thyng but nyce dremes
were"; furthermore, Troilus says:

> "O deere herte, may it be
> That it be soth, that ye ben in this place?"
> "Yee, herte myn, God thank I of his grace,"
> Quod tho Criseyde, and therwithal hym kiste,
> *That where his spirit was, for joie he nyste.*
>   (III, 1347-51)

This line (italicized) is Chaucer's addition to *Il Filostrato* and, I
think, a possible allusion to Second Corinthians, where St. Paul, in
ecstasy, is brought up into paradise.[14] Chaucer's inability to tell of the

---

[13]   Italics my own, as are all the italic passages from Chaucer's works in this
chapter.

[14]   "I know a man in Christ above fourteen years ago (whether in the body, I
know not, or out of the body, I know not; God knoweth), such a one caught up
to the third heaven. And I know such a man (whether in the body, or out of the
body, I know not: God knoweth): That he was caught up into paradise and heard
secret words, which it is not granted to man to utter" (xii, 2-4). From the

lovers' perfect joy parallels St. Paul's inability to utter the secrets of
paradise. Chaucer's whole presentation of this love scene, where neither
of the lovers is able to comprehend the reality of their presence together,
has the ring of ecstasy about it; Chaucer's biblical allusion here is appropriate to the context and consistent with his emphasis upon the
lovers' "celestial" happiness throughout the love scenes generally. He
continues this image-pattern in his references to the lovers' joy, after
Criseyde's address to "rakle nyght" and Troilus' "aube".

In *Il Filostrato* (III, 42), the lovers hear the cocks crow and are
sorrowful because of their impending separation. Boccaccio then writes
the following: "When Cressida heard them crow she said in sorrow: 'O
my love now is it time to arise, if we wish to conceal our desire. But I
wish to embrace thee a little, my love, before thou arisest, that I may
feel less grief at thy departure. Do thou embrace me, my sweet life'"
(III, 43). Chaucer incorporates this idea into a single stanza and then
adds, without a hint from Boccaccio, Criseyde's address to swift Night:

> "Myn hertes lif, my trist, and my plesaunce,
> That I was born, allas, what me is wo,
> That day of us moot make disseveraunce!
> For tyme it is to ryse and hennes go,
> Or ellis I am lost for evere mo!
> O nyght, allas! why nyltow over us hove,
> As longe as whan Almena lay by Jove?
>
> "O blake nyght, as folk in bokes rede,
> That shapen art by God this world to hide
> At certeyn tymes wyth thi derke wede,
> That under that men myghte in reste abide,
> Wel oughten bestes pleyne, and folk the chide,
> That there as day wyth labour wolde us breste,
> That thow thus fleest, and deynest us nought
>   reste.
>
> "Thow doost, allas, to shortly thyn office,
> Thow rakle nyght, ther God, maker of kynde,
> The, for thyn haste and thyn unkynde vice,
> So faste ay to oure hemysperie bynde,
> That nevere more under the ground thow wynde!
> For now, for thow so hiest out of Troie,
> Have I forgon thus hastili my joie!"
>   (III, 1422-42)

Rheims version. Without doubt this passage from Second Corinthians was ready
to hand for Chaucer: In *HF*, when the eagle carries him beyond the clouds toward the Galaxie, Chaucer says: "Y wot wel y am here;/ But wher in body or
in gost/ I not, ywys; but God, thou wost!" (ll. 980-82).

Criseyde's address to Night particularly and, to a certain extent, Troilus'
dawn-song (ll. 1450-70), merely suggested by Boccaccio, serve not only
to intensify the sorrow of the lovers' parting, but these lengthy additions
of Chaucer serve also to point up (1) the illusory nature of this "heavenly
bliss", which they themselves were unable to comprehend fully, and (2)
the transitoriness of such "perfit joie" (l. 1379). Indeed, Chaucer's
emphasis on the harsh reality of the dawn, which forces the lovers apart,
is a brilliant contrast to the ecstasy which the Night had granted them.
Chaucer then returns to his celestial imagery to describe the joy of the
lovers.

In *Il Filostrato*, Troilo tells Pandaro about his meeting with Cressida:
"I burn more than ever, but this new fire that I feel is of another quality
than what I felt before" (III, 62). From this suggestion, Chaucer writes:

> "I not myself naught wisly what it is;
> But now I feele a newe qualitee,
> Yee, al another than I dide er this."
>
> > (ll. 1653-55)

Pandarus' answer to Troilus' statement is not in *Il Filostrato*:

> *"he*
> *That ones may in hevene blisse be,*
> He feleth other weyes, dar I leye,
> Than thilke tyme he first herde of it seye."
>
> > (ll. 1656-59)

Thus Pandarus uses this imagery as well as the narrator himself. Again,
Troilus and Criseyde have another rendezvous. About this event,
Chaucer writes (an addition to his source):

> Nought nedeth it to you, syn they ben met,
> To axe at me if that they blithe were;
> For if it erst was wel, tho was it bet
> A thousand fold; this nedeth nought enquere.
> Agon was every sorwe and every feere;
> And bothe, ywis, they hadde, and so they
>   wende,
> As muche joie as herte may comprende.
>
> This is no litel thyng of for to seye;
> This passeth every wit for to devyse;
> For ech of hem gan otheres lust obeye.
> *Felicite, which that thise clerkes wise*
> *Comenden so, ne may nought here suffise;*
> This joie may nought writen be with inke;
> This passeth al that herte may bythynke.
>
> > (III, 1681-94)

In these lines (italicized), Chaucer can be talking about nothing short of the happiness of heaven.[15] It is clear, therefore, that unlike Boccaccio's rendering of these love scenes, Chaucer's account both implicitly and explicitly equates the happiness of the lovers with the happiness of heaven. While Boccaccio's account sometimes achieves the effects of ecstasy, only once is the comparison of the two types of happiness mentioned (or even suggested). In Troilo's recounting to Pandaro the experience of the first night with Cressida, he says: "Thou hast, my friend, taken me from hell to usher me into paradise, as sure as I do live" (III, 56). This expression, however, is highly conventional in the language of courtly love and is also appropriate to Troilo's typified characterization throughout the entire *Filostrato*. Boccaccio's account, in fact, is extremely sensuous, even gross; [16] Chaucer's elimination of these elements is not only consonant with his usual habit of avoiding the

[15] It seems almost certain that "Felicite, which that thise clerkes wise/ Comenden so" refers to any form of earthly happiness whatever. In the *Consolation*, III, pr. 2, 25 ff., Lady Philosophy enumerates all the theories in regard to what constitutes happiness that wise clerks have advanced or might possibly advance. These she rejects and later concludes that "we han establissched that the sovereyne good is verry blisfulnesse. Thanne moot it nedis be that verray blisfulnesse is set in sovereyn God" (III, pr. 10, 59-62). Clearly the inference is that the happiness of the lovers is a heavenly happiness. Note, incidentally, the general similarity between Chaucer's lines (1687, 1689, 1693-94) and First Corinthians, ii, 9: "*That eye hath not seen, nor ear heard, neither hath it entered into the heart of man, what things God hath prepared for them that love him*" (here St. Paul quotes Isaias, lxiv, 2). Chaucer's ironical use of similar (celestial) imagery in the *Merchant's Tale* should not be overlooked in interpreting his use of this same imagery here.

The idea which I am developing here, that Chaucer through sustained celestial imagery is consciously portraying a reversal of values on the part of the lovers, particularly Troilus, and that he is deliberately heightening the happiness of the lovers to point up the mutability of their happiness, was hinted at by B. L. Jefferson, who quotes lines 1691-94 and remarks that the lovers "are enjoying the very essence of bliss" (p. 128). Cf. D. W. Robertson, Jr., "Chaucerian Tragedy", and *A Preface to Chaucer*. Robertson develops the thesis that the tragedy of Troilus is a perversity of reason in that he chooses Criseyde as his Highest Good rather than God (Robertson modifies somewhat his original argument in his book), and points out the abundant religious imagery in the third book of the poem. Here I am merely filling in the details and pointing out the celestial imagery more thoroughly than does Professor Robertson in order to emphasize the "brotilnesse" of the lovers' happiness. For other treatments of the religious imagery in the third and fourth books of the *Troilus*, cf. Sister Anne Barbara Gill, *Paradoxical Patterns in Chaucer's Troilus: An Explanation of the Palinode* (Washington, D. C., 1960), pp. 80 and 85; and Siegfried Wenzel, "Chaucer's Troilus of Book IV", *PMLA*, LXXXIX (1964), 546-47.

[16] *Il Filostrato*, III, especially stanzas 31-32, 42, 62, 65-69, and 71.

sensual, but it also enables him to sustain the imagery and theme of heavenly bliss.

What, finally, is the significance of this imagery in relation to the whole poem, and especially the epilogue? At the risk of laboring the obvious, it must be recognized that this celestial imagery does not invalidate the fact that Chaucer's love poetry at this point is "some of the greatest erotic poetry of the world".[17] On the contrary, what could be more erotic than to celebrate the flesh in terms of the beatific vision, if it is artistically successful? My point is simply this: to the mediaeval mind, of which Boethius is the archetype, the action of Troilus (and of Criseyde) would be *complete* attachment to a worldly possession and, consequently, *complete* abandonment of God. Thus Chaucer, in the epilogue, says: "Swich fyn hath, lo, this Troilus for love!" and thus Troilus, from the eighth sphere, could condemn all our work that follows after the "blynde lust". As is evident, therefore, in this section under consideration, could Chaucer better have been, at one and the same time, the poet of courtly love and also the mediaeval man thoroughly saturated with the philosophy of Boethius? [18]

That Chaucer actually intended this heavenly imagery throughout the love scenes as an implied criticism or commentary of the lovers' actions is impossible to prove. Since Troilus is not a Christian and since he is the courtly lover par excellence, it is difficult to conclude with Professor Robertson that the tragedy of Troilus is essentially what is involved in that of every mortal sinner. But, on the other hand, in Chaucer's heightening the joy of the lovers to that of celestial joy, it is equally difficult to assume that such a possibility escaped his ironic and wary perception. It is clear from what follows in the poem, that Troilus is at the highest point on the wheel of Fortune. Troilus had abandoned himself to Fortune from the very beginning of the poem. In the love scenes, however, Chaucer spares nothing to tell the reader that Troilus' abandonment has become complete, irrevocable, and indeed highly precarious. Precisely at this point in a *De Casu* tragedy begins the fall.

In *Il Filostrato*, when Troilo comes back to Pandaro to report his success with Cressida, Pandaro simply counsels him to be prudent and wise in order not to lose the joy which he had gained. In the *Troilus*, Pandarus gives the same advice, but adds:

[17]   C. S. Lewis, *The Allegory of Love*, p. 196.
[18]   See A. J. Denomy, "The Two Moralities of Chaucer's *Troilus and Criseyde*", *Trans. of the Royal Society of Canada*, sec. 2, vol. 44 (1950), 35-46.

"For of fortunes sharpe adversitee
The worste kynde of infortune is this,
A man to han ben in prosperitee,
And it remembren, whan it passed is.
Th'art wis ynough, forthi do nat amys:
Be naught to rakel, theigh thow sitte warme;
For if thow be, certeyn, it wol the harme.

"Thow art at ese, and hold the wel therinne;
For also seur as reed is every fir,
As gret a craft is kepe wel as wynne.
Bridle alwey wel thi speche and thi desir,
For worldly joie halt nought but by a wir.
That preveth wel it brest al day so ofte;
Forthi nede is to werken with it softe."
(III, 1625-38)

Proverbial as much of this advice is, it does function as a choric comment on the action which is to come and draws attention to the mutability theme as it operates throughout the poem. That this Boethian
concept occurs just at this point is indicative of the way in which
Chaucer fashioned the *Troilus* to the *De Casu* tradition; it is to be
noted, certainly, that this advice about fortune comes from the same
Pandarus who regards fortune so slightly throughout the rest of the poem
(e.g., I, 841-47; IV, 600-602).

Just before the poet tells of the lovers' second meeting, he writes:

Soon after this, *for that Fortune it wolde,*
Icomen was the blisful tyme swete
That Troilus was warned that he sholde,
There he was erst, Criseyde his lady mete.
(III, 1667-70)

After he describes this second meeting in all the terms of "perfect
felicite", he says:

And many a nyght they wroughte in this
 manere,
And thus Fortune a tyme ledde in joie
Criseyde, and ek this kynges sone of Troie.
(III, 1713-15)

These two passages are also Chaucer's addition to *Il Filostrato*. He
added these passages, following upon the love scene, and removed
Boccaccio's final stanza of Book III to the *prohemium* of his own fourth
book. These additions not only serve to point up the *De Casu* theme,
but they also emphasize the illusory nature of the lovers' "heavenly

blisse". For the lovers' "heavenly blisse" is but transitory, and this too points to the epilogue.

The *De Casu* theme, then, is one theme of mutability which prevails in the *Troilus*. In its broadest outlines, the *Troilus* fits the *De Casibus* tradition accurately. A king's son, at the point of his highest pleasure, suddenly falls a victim of Fortune. It must be remembered, however, that Chaucer is portraying this theme dramatically. By combining the courtly love conventions (specifically the irresistibility of the God of Love) with Fortune, Chaucer achieves the same effects, but dramatically, as if he were simply relating, *de casu*, the arbitrary rise and fall of a great man on the wheel of Fortune. Troilus himself sees his life as ruled by Fortune, and the numerous Fortune passages in the poem make it abundantly clear that it is. "Have I the nought honoured al my lyve,/ As thow wel woost, above the goddes alle?" (IV, 267-68), he asks Fortune. This is indeed the very source of his fall. Regardless of the evidence which one might gather to support the fact that Chaucer intended to portray in Troilus a character thoroughly determined in his actions, the whole meaning and drift of the poem is against this conclusion. It must be admitted that Chaucer is teetering between the conventional *De Casibus* tragedy, wherein character has no relation to the fall, and the type of tragedy, perfected in Greek and Shakespearean drama, which grows out of character. This gives the poem a certain amount of complexity, and, it must be admitted, of confusion also. But as long as one is able to identify the confusing elements in this complicated poem, he is on the right track. The elements briefly are, first, the mediaeval *De Casibus* made up of Fortune and the rise-and-fall of a nobleman; and second, perhaps an *implied* criticism of Troilus which is made explicit in the epilogue. I have shown I think that Troilus, when he was highest on the wheel of Fortune, abandoned himself completely to Love. Chaucer describes this abandonment in terms of celestial ecstasy which, in the mediaeval framework, and certainly in the mind of a poet so thoroughly saturated with the philosophy of Boethius, implies a perversion of values. Given these facts, it seems to me, certainly, that Chaucer is working toward the tragedy that issues from character. Farnham says that Chaucer "refines the telling of *De Casibus* tragedy by showing at length the pitiful grasp which a man can keep upon this world of illusion even after convincing demonstration of its vanity has been given him" (p. 149).

Another mutability theme in the *Troilus* is the transitoriness of earthly happiness, expressed chiefly in the speeches of Criseyde. One of the strokes whereby Chaucer achieves Criseyde's complexity is her abiding sensibility that "every joie of worldly thyng mot flee" (III, 828). Boccaccio's Cressida is the "sophisticated Neapolitan lady of pleasure. . . . she is not seduced but seduces herself" (Myrick and Griffin, p. 106). Only twice does she refer to the transitory-theme, and both times it is with the superficiality suitable to her own characterization. (1) When Pandaro is attempting to persuade her to accept Troilo as her lover he tells her, "Lose no time, consider that old age or death will take away all thy beauty" (II, 54). She replies in a typically commonplace fashion: " 'Alas', said Cressida, 'thou speakest the truth. Thus do the years little by little bear us forward. The greater number die before the path granted by the celestial fire is completed. But let us now stop thinking of this . . .' " (II, 55). Chaucer keeps the words of Pandaro (II, 54) and turns them into a whole stanza (II, 393-99), in which Pandarus recognizes them as proverbial.[19] (2) The other instance occurs in Cressida's argument with herself about accepting Troilo. She says, "Every hour my youth takes flight. Am I to lose it so miserably?" (II, 70) The fact that Chaucer uses neither of these passages from *Il Filostrato* in his portrayal of Criseyde is perhaps indicative of the depth of outlook which he intended for his own heroine.

In *Il Filostrato*, Cressida replies to Pandaro, when he attempts to have her accept Troilo: " 'I would have thought, Pandarus, if I had ever fallen into such folly that Troilus had ever come into my desire, that thou wouldst have beaten me, not merely restrained me, as one who should seek my honor. O God help me! What will others do now that thou strivest to make me follow the precepts of Love?' " (II, 48) At this point Chaucer reveals that Criseyde is easily given to disillusionment. He turns this stanza of Boccaccio's into two stanzas, wherein Criseyde says:

> "Allas, for wo! Why nere I deed?
> For of this world the feyth is al agoon.
> Allas! what sholden straunge to me doon,
> When he, that for my beste frend I wende,
> Ret me to love, and sholde it me defende?
>
> . . . .
> This false world, allas! who may it leve?"
> (II, 409-13, 420)

---

[19] These exhortations of Pandaro and Pandarus are examples of the *carpe diem* theme, a commonplace motif in the literature of the Middle Ages, which most probably finds its source in Ovid's *The Art of Love*, where it is used or proposed frequently for seductive purposes (but not so used in Horace).

Chaucer's changes in his source here are evident and sure. First, these changes establish a point of view which is to characterize Criseyde throughout the entire poem: her inability to view the world or happiness as anything but unstable and transitory. Second, Chaucer's version makes more evident the close and affable relationship which exists between Criseyde and her uncle; he is her best and most trusted friend. That she should use the word "straunge" here seems to imply her complete dependence upon, and her attachment to, her uncle to the exclusion of anyone else. This suggests immediately what is obvious throughout the poem, that Criseyde's ruling passion is fear. C. S. Lewis writes about her thus: "Fortunately Chaucer has so emphasized the ruling passion of his heroine, that we cannot mistake it. It is Fear – fear of loneliness, of old age, of death, of love, and of hostility; of everything, indeed, that can be feared. And from this Fear springs the only positive passion which can be permanent in such a nature; the pitiable longing, more childlike than womanly, for protection, for some strong and stable thing that will hide her away and take the burden from her shoulders" (*Allegory*, p. 185). Lewis' insight into Criseyde is evidenced at every turn in the poem. That she should constantly see the world as false and happiness as transitory is simply another aspect of her ruling passion of fear: her fearful and insecure nature leads her to seek perfect and permanent happiness, but she is forever conscious that "nothing of the world (and she knows nothing else) is abiding" (Jefferson, p. 129).

This close relationship of Criseyde's fearfulness and her consciousness of the transitoriness of all worldly happiness is borne out even more clearly in another episode of the *Troilus*. In *Il Filostrato,* Cressida also debates with herself about loving Troilo. The debate is, of course, quite superficial and is heavily unbalanced by Cressida's vanity and her prospects of sensuous fulfillment. After she thinks over the favorable points for loving Troilo, she turns her thoughts in the opposite direction and muses: " 'What dost thou propose to do, wretched one? Knowest thou not how bad is the life that one liveth with one's lover when passion languisheth, for there must ever be in it continuance of woes, of sighs, and grieving, with jealousy added, which is far worse than wretched death?' " (II, 75) She hesitates further about her love for Troilo because he is of a much higher rank than she, and his love therefore will probably not last. But even if it were to last a long time, she continues, she has no guarantee that their love will be concealed. Once it is discovered she will lose her excellent reputation (II, 76-77).

In the *Troilus*, on the other hand, this scene is handled much more convincingly. From one sentence in Boccaccio Chaucer spins a complete stanza, reminiscent of Boethius:

> But right as when the sonne shyneth brighte
> In March, that chaungeth ofte tyme his face,
> And that a cloude is put with wynd to flighte,
> Which oversprat the sonne as for as space,
> A cloudy thought gan thorugh hire soule pace,
> That overspradde hire brighte thoughtes alle,
> So that for feere almost she gan to falle.
>   (II, 764-70) [20]

Perhaps this stanza more than any other in the entire poem best characterizes Criseyde's complex point of view. All her bright thoughts are forever shadowed by the realization of the mixed nature of earthly happiness and by the fact that it is, finally, transitory. Why should she accept a lover and lose her "sikernesse"? May she not see in other folk who love "hire dredfull joye, hire constreinte, and hire peyne?" She continues to philosophize about love (which Boccaccio's heroine does not do):

> "For love is yet the mooste stormy lyf,
> Right of hymself, that evere was bigonne;
> For evere som mystrust or nice strif
> Ther is in love, som cloude is over that sonne."
>   (II, 778-81) [21]

Her self-interest, furthermore, is mixed with the generalized reflection that men in general are untrue (l. 786), that once their pleasure ceases their love ceases (ll. 787-88). She even questions the very existence of love:

> "How ofte tyme hath it yknowen be,
> The tresoun that to wommen hath ben do!
> To what fyn is swich love I kan not see,
> Or wher bycometh it, whan it is ago.
> Ther is no wight that woot, I trowe so,
> Where it bycometh; lo, no wight on it sporneth:
> That erst was nothing, into nought it torneth."
>   (II, 792-98)

This soliloquy of Criseyde shows the depth and complexity which Chaucer sees in his heroine. The soliloquy begins, as has been seen, with Criseyde's hesitancy to give up her emotional "sikernesse" and to accept the "dredfull joye" of love, where always "som cloude is over that

[20] Cf. Boethius, I, m. 3, 4 ff. for the influence on ll. 766-67.
[21] Cf. IV, 1644-45. "For I am ever agast, forwhy men rede/ That love is thyng ay ful of bisy drede."

sonne". From this, her own personal hesitancy, she then proceeds further with the more general reflection that all men are untrue; and finally she questions the very nature of love itself: it comes from nothing and it returns to nothing; "lo, no wight on it sporneth." Criseyde's doubts have been so philosophical that Chaucer had to insert the Antigone episode (not in *Il Filostrato*) to motivate convincingly her continuing interest in Troilus.

This attitude of Criseyde toward love and happiness is made even more evident in Book III. Pandarus had invited his niece to his home for dinner but the rain made it impossible for her to leave. In an effort to bring Criseyde and Troilus together, Pandarus concocted the accusation of her love for Horaste. Criseyde launches into a long digression (from Boethius) on felicity, just as does Troilus in the following book of the poem on providence and free will. Again, she longs for death: "for now lyve I to longe!" (l. 805) and then:

> "O God!" quod she, "so worldly selynesse,
> Which clerkes callen fals felicitee,
> Imedled is with many a bitternesse!
> Ful angwissous than is, God woot", quod she,
> "Condicioun of veyn prosperitee;
> For either joies comen nought yfeere,
> Or elles no wight hath hem alwey here.
>
> "O brotel wele of mannes joie unstable!
> With what wight so thow be, or how thow
>   pleye,
> Either he woot that thow, joie, art muable,
> Or woot it nought: it mot ben oon of tweye.
> Now if he woot it nought, how may he seye
> That he hath verray joie and selynesse
> That is of ignoraunce ay in darknesse?
>
> "Now if he woot that joie is transitorie,
> As every joie of worldly thyng mot flee,
> Than every tyme he that hath in memorie,
> The drede of lesyng maketh hym that he
> May in no perfit selynesse be;
> And if to lese his joie he sette a myte,
> Then semeth it that joie is worth ful lite.
>
> "Wherfore I wol diffyne in this matere,
> That trewely, for aught I kan espie,
> Ther is no verray weele in this world heere."
>   (III, 813-36)

This soliloquy is comparable to Troilus' soliloquy on free will and providence in Book IV (ll. 958-1085). Both are taken almost entirely from Boethius. Both keep the "clerkish' dialogue, completely out of character for either Troilus or Criseyde. Both give in rather abstract form the predominant philosophical attitudes which are dramatically evident in the rest of the poem: Troilus at every turn of the action considers himself to be in the hands of Fortune,[22] and Criseyde at many crucial points of the action reflects upon the transitoriness of earthly love and happiness. Both might have been omitted without affecting the action of the poem. This leads us to suspect – in fact the evidence is very clear – that Chaucer used these digressions from Boethius not only to characterize Troilus and Criseyde more fully, but also to point up the two main themes which run through the poem: the *De Casu* and the transitory themes, two aspects of the mutability theme.[23]

It might be mentioned at this point that these contrasting speeches of Troilus and Criseyde find a parallel in two other speeches wherein their philosophical attitudes are also revealed in terms of what appears to be clearly reminiscent of the *memento mori* theme. After Troilus finds out that Criseyde is to be exchanged for Antenor, he says in his complaint:

> "O ye loveris, that heigh upon the whiel
> Ben set of Fortune, in good aventure,
> God leve that wye fynde ay love of stiel,
> And longe mote youre lif in joie endure!
> *But whan ye comen by my sepulture,*
> *Remembreth that youre felawe resteth there;*
> *For I loved ek, though ich unworthi were."*
>
> (IV, 323-29) [24]

---

[22] See B. L. Jefferson, pp. 122-23 (note), for references to the numerous passages which contribute to Troilus' fatalism.

[23] One might even be tempted to conjecture, in fact, that this soliloquy of Criseyde suggested Chaucer's insertion of the soliloquy of Troilus into his revised version.

[24] Without going into the *memento mori* tradition, I cite the following as one of many parallels which might be found for this passage: "Respice sepulcra, et vide quis servus, quis dominus, quis pauper, quis dives. Discerne, si potes, victum a rege, fortem a debili, pulchrum a deformi. Memor itaque naturae, non extollaris aliquando. Memor autem eris, si te ipsum respexeris." Saint Prosper of Aquitaine (390?-463?), printed in the works of St. Augustine, Migne, *Pat. Lat.*, t. 45, cols. 1897-98. The theme is perhaps as old as mankind. Cf. *The Greek Anthology*, W. R. Paton, trans., *The Loeb Classical Library* (New York, 1925), II, 175 and 201. For a more detailed study that I am able to present in this chapter of the *memento mori* and *ubi sunt* allusions in the *Troilus*, see my "Further Aspects of Mutability in Chaucer's *Troilus*", *Papers on English Language and Literature*, I (1965), 72-77.

The passage of Criseyde's complaint is not so clearly related to the *memento mori* as is the passage from the complaint of Troilus, but it is, nevertheless, an allusion to it:

> "Endeth thanne love in wo? Ye, or men lieth!
> And alle worldly blisse, as thynketh me.
> The ende of blisse ay sorwe it occupieth;
> *And whoso troweth nat that it so be,*
> *Lat hym upon me, woful wrecche, ysee,*
> That myself hate, and ay my burthe acorse,
> Felyng alwey, fro wikke I go to worse."
>
>   (IV, 834-40)

These echoes of the *memento mori* theme are of course not in *Il Filostrato,* nor is there any suggestion of them. It is significant that in each of these instances the *memento mori* theme is conjoined with the characteristic "themes" of the speakers: in Troilus' case, Fortune, and in Criseyde's, transitoriness.

While it is clear, however, that Criseyde's attitude toward love and happiness as transitory supplements the *De Casu* theme and adds philosophical depth to the tragedy as a whole, it is not precisely evident how this attitude motivates her actions generally. Certainly it lends complexity to her character; certainly she herself is, as she says, the living example that love, indeed all worldly bliss, ends in woe (IV, 834-40). B. L. Jefferson says that Chaucer "conceived her as representative of the class of people described by Boethius who are constantly beset by the fear that joys will fade" (p. 128). This may be true but tells us little; most of what Boethius says on this subject is said by Criseyde in her soliloquy (III, 813-36). That this attitude of Criseyde is the result of her fearful nature, there is little doubt. But the flaw in her nature which Chaucer wishes to emphasize and which is the cause of her betrayal of Troilus is that she is "tendre-herted, slydynge of corage" (V, 825). Had Chaucer not emphasized this flaw in Criseyde's make-up and had he not surrounded her betrayal with so many extenuating circumstances, one might be tempted to suppose that this extreme sensitivity to the "brotelnesse" of human love and happiness might ultimately have accounted for a certain pragmatism on the part of Criseyde, which led her to readily grasp happiness near to hand, namely Diomede. Such, however, is not the case. One indication that Chaucer made nothing of this vision of Criseyde is that only once after she had accepted Diomede does she refer to the transitory theme, and this only in passing. When she writes to Troilus, expressing her regret for what has happened, she ends thus: "But al shal passe; and thus take I my leve" (V, 1085). At this point, Criseyde's reference to the transitory theme is actually incongruous with her regret for having falsed Troilus. She appears in fact almost flippant. The very fact that Chaucer does not incorporate Criseyde's sensibility of the mutability of all things into the action of the poem, that is, the fact that this quality in Criseyde's outlook has nothing to do with the motivation of her actions, perhaps suggests Chaucer's interest in the transitory theme for its own sake.

There is another mutability theme in the *Troilus*, but it appears only incidentally and indirectly: the *ubi sunt* theme. After Troilus had left Criseyde with Diomede and her father at the outer gate of the rampart, he returned in grief to his own palace in Troy. The following is Boccaccio's account of Troilo the night on which he had delivered Cressida to the Greeks:

And as he turned in his bed now here and now there, without finding any resting place, at such times would he in his weeping say to himself: "What a night is this! When I consider the past night, if I read the hour aright, such time as it now is did I kiss the white bosom, the mouth, the eyes, and the lovely face of my lady, and oft embrace her.

"She would kiss me and we took a happy and gracious pleasure in conversing together. Now I find myself alone, alas, and weeping, in doubt whether so joyous a night is ever to come again. Now I keep embracing the pillow, and I feel the flame of love waxing greater, and hope becoming less on account of the grief that overwhelmeth it." (V, 19-20)

Chaucer condenses these two stanzas into one:

> "Wher is myn owene lady, lief and deere?
> Wher is hire white brest? wher is it, where?
> Wher ben hire armes and hire eyen cleere,
> That yesternyght this tyme with me were?
> . . . .
> Save a pilowe, I fynde naught t'enbrace."
> (V, 218-24)

This clearly resembles the many *ubi sunt* poems of the Middle Ages which lament loss by death and the decay of feminine pulchritude. Chaucer's use of the formula here is clearly ironic: Troilus is never to see Criseyde again. Certainly Chaucer's audience, who were very familiar with the *ubi sunt* commonplace, must have immediately caught the implications of Troilus' complaint.

This reminiscence of the *ubi sunt* tradition in the complaint of Troilus foreshadows another *ubi sunt* allusion by Troilus which Chaucer took over practically unchanged from Boccaccio. When Troilus has seen the

brooch which he had given Criseyde on the morning of her departure
from Troy now pinned to Diomede's coat, he is certain of Criseyde's
infidelity. At this point, Boccaccio writes in *Il Filostrato*:

And then he began to say in the midst of his tears: "O Cressida mine, where
now is the faith, where the love, where the desire, where the so pleasing
guerdon given me by thee at thy departure? Diomede possesseth all and I,
who loved thee more, have been left in weeping and distress on account of
thy deceit." (VIII, 12)

Chaucer has Troilus say:

> "O lady myn, Criseyde,
> Where is youre feith, and where is youre biheste?
> Where is youre love? where is youre trouth? . . .
> Of Diomede have ye now al this feeste!"
>
> (V, 1674-77)

A comparison of Boccaccio's and Chaucer's versions of Troilus' complaint at this point will indicate that Chaucer, most probably, deliberately
altered the *Il Filostrato* passage with an eye to the *ubi sunt* convention.
The repetition of "where is" for Boccaccio's "where" (in every instance
but one) makes Chaucer's passage definitely resemble the *ubi sunt*
convention. Chaucer's use of "where is", together with the personal
address to Criseyde in the form of "youre", serve to emphasize the loss
of each of these virtues. These *ubi sunt* complaints of Troilus, coming
as they do at the moments when he realizes his loss most intensely
(his first night away from Criseyde after he had given her over to the
Greeks; and the moment at which he can no longer force himself to
believe in her fidelity) are dramatically appropriate places for Chaucer
and his audience to recall the many *ubi sunt* poems that they must have
known, to express more effectively the transitoriness of Troilus' love.
That the use of the *ubi sunt* to express the transitoriness of love was not
far from Chaucer's mind when he wrote the *Troilus* is shown by a
speech of Pandarus. On the night of the tenth day after Criseyde's
departure, Troilus and Pandarus stand at the gates of the city to await
her return. Troilus is pathetic in his expectation of Criseyde and tells
Pandarus that he is sure, in fact he would wager his life, that Criseyde
will appear. Whereupon Chaucer writes:

> Pandare answerde, "It may be, wel ynough",
> And held with hym of al that evere he seyde.
> But in his herte he thoughte, and softe lough,
> And to hymself ful sobreliche he seyde,
> "From haselwode. there Joly Robyn pleyde,

Shal come al that that thow abidest heere,
Ye, fare wel al the snow of ferne yere!"
(V, 1170-76)

This last line is Chaucer's substitution for the words of Boccaccio's Pandaro: " 'This wretched youth expecteth a wind from Mongibello' " (VII, 10). Clearly Chaucer was familiar with this common mediaeval symbol to express the irrevocable past; Villon, a few years later, was to make it even more familiar by using it as a refrain in his *Ballade des Dames du Temps Jadis.*

These then are the motifs of the mutability theme which might easily be delineated in the *Troilus*: the *De Casu* theme, which involves the mutability of Fortune; the transitoriness theme, the nether aspect of the Fortune theme, which finds its most definite expression in the tragic vision of Criseyde; finally, the *ubi sunt* and the *memento mori* themes, which find expression in the poem more or less indirectly and lend dramatic power to the situations in which they appear and to the mutability theme of the poem as a whole.[25]

There are, finally, two other aspects of the *Troilus* which must be recognized in a study of the poem's mutability themes. These are, first, the element in Chaucer's poetic vision which tends to view the close connection between happiness and sorrow, and second, the element in his vision which is always cognizant of and resigned to the limitations of mortality. These elements in fact help to inform the *Troilus* with its tonal unity, and constitute perhaps the most basic elements in Chaucer's tragic vision.

We have already seen the ideas expressed in the *Troilus* that always "som cloude is over the sonne" (II, 781), that "the ende of blisse ay sorwe it occupieth" (IV, 836), that love is "dredfull joye" (II, 776) and "is thyng ay ful of bisy drede" (IV, 1645). B. L. Jefferson points out that "the entire poem abounds in allusions to the transitory nature of worldly joys, now brightening, now darkening, but ever fading entirely away in the end" (pp. 125-26). This is the over-all tone and the guiding idea of the tragedy. It is my purpose here, however, simply to point out a few of the instances, numerous throughout the poem, in which Chaucer couples the ideas of joy and sorrow. Rarely does Chaucer think of joy except in terms of past sorrows.

In Troilo's and Cressida's love scene Boccaccio writes: "And all this

---

[25] Cf. other expressions of this theme in *I*, 134-40; 211-17; 946-52; *II*, 764-70; *III*, 351-57; 1058-64; 1219-22; 1625-28; 1636-37; 1714; *IV*, 1-11; 269-72; 323-26; 384-92; 421-24; 834-40; *V*, 731-33; 1432-35; 1457-1519; 1541-47.

talk they often interrupted with fervent kissing and abandoning their past suffering, shared delicious joy" (III, 40). Chaucer turns Boccaccio's stanza into two and intensifies more strongly the lovers' joy by connecting it more closely with their past woes:

> but al swich hevynesse,
> I thank it God, was torned to gladnesse.
>
> .   .   .   .
>
> And [they] diden al hire myght, syn they were oon,
> For to recoveren blisse and ben at eise,
> And passed wo with joie contrepeise.
> (III, 1399-1407)

Again Chaucer adds a passage not contained in his source, wherein he juxtaposes "hevynesse" and "gladnesse"; after Criseyde's address to "rakle nyght", in the same scene, Chaucer writes:

> This Troilus, that with tho wordes felte,
> As thoughte hym tho, for piëtous distresse,
> The blody teris from his herte melte,
> *As he that nevere yet swich hevynesse*
> *Assayed hadde, out of so gret gladnesse ...*
> (III, 1443-47)

Again, in the same scene, Chaucer writes: "And now swetnesse semeth more swete,/ That bitternesse assaied was byforn" (III, 1219-20; cf. lines 1212-23, which are not in Chaucer's source and which elaborate this idea at length). Pandarus expresses the same idea to Troilus in the very beginning of the poem:

> "For how myghte evere swetnesse han ben knowe
> To him that nevere tasted bitternesse?
> Ne no man may ben inly glad, I trowe,
> That nevere was in sorwe or som destresse.
> Eke whit by blak, by shame ek worthinesse,
> Ech set by other, more for other semeth,
> As men may se, and so the wyse it demeth."
> (I, 638-44)

The poem abounds with images which intricately connect the ideas of joy and sorrow. Chaucer accepts the fact that in this state of mortality, the one defines the other: "hevynesse" is inevitable; and "gladnesse", when it comes, is but brief and fleeting. The final impression of the tragedy is not that "joie is next the fyn of sorwe" (I, 952); these are the words of Pandarus, always the optimist, whose attitude is fixed to motivate the action. Rather, the theme of the poem is expressed by Troilus when he says:

"But torned is, for which my lif I warie,
Everich joie or ese in his contrarie."
(V, 1378-79)

Second, Chaucer is also well aware of the limitations of man's vision:
"O blynde world, O blynde entencioun!" he says early in the poem. At
the beginning of Book IV, the point at which the action begins to turn,
he writes:

But al to litel, weylaway the whyle,
Lasteth swich joie, ythonked be Fortune,
That semeth trewest whan she wol bygyle,
And kan to fooles so hire song entune,
That she hem hent and blent, traitour comune!
(IV, 1-5)

Fortune's ability to beguile and to blind her victims is well known, but
this trait of Fortune is not mentioned at this point in Chaucer's source.
The Fortune image is of course merely a figure for the limitation of
man's vision.

The mention of Antenor's betrayal is not found in *Il Filostrato*.
Chaucer's addition of the fact lends an irony to the tragedy as a whole
and further emphasizes the blindness of mundane minds. Chaucer
introduces Antenor's betrayal thus:

O Juvenal, lord! trewe is thy sentence,
That litel wyten folk what is to yerne
That they ne fynde in hire desir offence;
For cloude of errour lat hem nat discerne
What best is.
(IV, 197-201)

The limitations of mortality are inseparable from the mutability themes
expressed throughout the poem. The clamor of Troy to exchange
Criseyde for Antenor is an excellent example of this intimate connection
of the mortality and mutability themes. It is in fact the cloud of ignorance inherent in mortal man which was responsible for the fleeting
happiness of Troilus and Criseyde. Chaucer makes the connection himself:

And lo, here ensample as yerne:
This folk desiren now deliveraunce
Of Antenor, that brought hem to meschaunce.

For he was after traitour to the town
Of Troye; allas, they quytte hym out to rathe!

O nyce world, lo, thy discrecioun!
Criseyde, which that nevere dide hem scathe,
Shal now no lenger in hire blisse bathe;
But Antenor, he shal com hom to towne,
And she shal out; thus seyden here and howne.
                                          (IV, 201-10)

So long as man lives under the moon, he is subject to the laws of mutability. This is in reality the meaning of mortality. The following passage
epitomizes the mortality-mutability themes in the *Troilus* and Chaucer's
attitude toward his subject generally. In order to show more clearly
Chaucer's attitude in the poem, I shall quote the corresponding passage
from *Il Filostrato*: "Great were the laments and bitterness but Fortune
still ran her course. She loved Diomede with all her heart and Troilus
wept. Diomede thanked the gods and Troilus, on the contrary, grieved.
Troilus did ever enter the battles and more than others did he seek
Diomede" (VIII, 25). Chaucer renders this:

Gret was the sorwe and pleynte of Troilus;
But forth hire cours Fortune ay gan to holde
Criseyde loveth the sone of Tideüs,
And Troilus moot wepe in cares colde.
Swich is this world, whoso it kan byholde:
In ech estat is litel hertes reste.
God leve us for to take it for the beste!
                                          (V, 1744-50) [26]

This passage of Chaucer's, with his additions to the *Il Filostrato*, em-
bodies and unifies the two main mutability motifs which inform the
entire poem. Fortune is only a poetic figment used to express the misfortunes, vicissitudes, and the transitoriness of this world. Chaucer's
ever-present awareness of, and his complete resignation to, man's mortality, to the world's mortality, is one of the basic sources of his objectivi-
ty toward his subject in this poem; at the same time it is the basic
source perhaps of his sympathy for Criseyde. The following passage
from Chaucer's *balade, Fortune,* might be a comment on the entire
poem. Fortune speaks to the complainant:

Thou pinchest at my mutabilitee,
For I thee lente a drope of my richesse,
And now me lyketh to withdrawe me.
Why sholdestow my realtee oppresse?

[26] For the same expression, "Swich is this world", and a similar one, "Thus
goth the world", cf. *Troilus*, IV, 384-92; and V, 1429-35. These are Chaucer's
additions and are spoken in similar circumstances with the exception that the
former is spoken by Pandarus.

The see may ebb and flowen more or lesse;
The welkne hath might to shyne, reyne, or
     hayle;
Right so mot I kythen my brotelnesse:
In general, this reule may nat fayle.

Lo, th'execucion of the majestee
That al purveyeth of his rightwysnesse,
That same thing "Fortune" clepen ye,
Ye blinde bestes, ful of lewednesse!
The hevene hath propretee of sikernesse,
This world hath ever resteles travayle;
Thy laste day is ende of myn intresse:
In general, this reule may nat fayle.

(ll. 57-72)

This excerpt from *Fortune* expresses abstractly what Chaucer has expressed dramatically in the *Troilus*: Criseyde and Chaucer (as narrator in the poem) have known at every turn that the world, happiness, and love are mutable; and Troilus is the *exemplum* of Fortune's mutability. The very language of Chaucer's descriptions in the love scenes of *Troilus and Criseyde* is so ecstatic that in itself it seems to hint of a final catastrophe. The world is mutable; and the *Troilus* proves it. Here is "resteles travayle" and "litel hertes reste"; only the region beyond the moon does not change, and it is significant that Fortune tells the complainant: "Thy laste day is ende of myn intresse." Thus the significance of Chaucer's epilogue to the *Troilus*.

Far from being inappropriate as some critics maintain, the epilogue evolves naturally from the poem.[27] The epilogues of Chaucer and of Boccaccio differ, in fact, inasmuch as the two poems themselves differ; and these separate epilogues themselves indicate the principal concerns of the two poets in the poems. The epilogue of Boccaccio is in a very real sense a "*Contemptus Feminarum*": "A young woman is fickle and is desirous of many lovers. . . . She hath no feeling for virtue or reason, inconstant ever as leaf in the wind" (VIII, 30). Therefore, pray for Troilo to Love and also for yourself, "that Love may kindly grant you the boon of loving so wisely that ye shall not die in the end for an evil woman" (VIII, 33). The epilogue of Chaucer, on the other hand, gathers together and emphasizes the various mutability themes which are in the poem into the all-inclusive *Contemptus Mundi* theme. Troilus has been

[27] For an excellent discussion of this thesis, see Charles Muscatine, *Chaucer and the French Tradition* (Berkeley, 1957), pp. 161-65. Also Root, *The Book of Troilus and Criseyde*, p. 1 ("Introduction").

slain and his spirit has gone "up to the holughnesse of the eighthe
spere" (V, 1809); Chaucer writes about Troilus:

> And down from thennes faste he gan avyse
> This litel spot of erthe, that with the se
> Embraced is, and fully gan despise
> This wrecched world, and held al vanite
> To respect of the pleyn felicite
> That is in hevene above; and at the laste,
> Ther he was slayn, his lokyng down he caste.
>
> And in hymself he lough right at the wo
> Of hem that wepten for his deth so faste;
> And dampned al oure werk that foloweth so
> The blynde lust, the which that may nat laste,
> And sholden al oure herte on heven caste.
>
> (V, 1814-25) [28]

What is more integral to the *De Contemptu Mundi* theme than that
Troilus should "fully gan despise/ This wrecched world", and that we
"sholden al oure herte on heven caste"? Willard Farnham has pointed
out that this *De Contemptu Mundi* moral of Chaucer is "the climax of
the changes that Chaucer has made throughout the story in order to
accomplish its shading as *De Casibus* tragedy" (p. 151). Chaucer took
from the *Teseida* his device of following Troilus' soul to the eighth
sphere. This enabled him to make explicit what was implicit in the poem
all along. As we have seen, it is as if Chaucer were saying: "Here I am
showing you what does not last"; but in the epilogue, it is as if he were
saying – in fact, he does say – "Here I am telling you what is lasting and,
indeed, the only thing which is lasting." To be sure, if one reads the
epilogue closely, he will find that the *Contemptus Mundi* theme is
subsequent to and is the logical outcome of the theme of transitoriness.
Troilus despised the world and "held al vanite/ To respect of the pleyn
felicite/ That is in hevene above". From the vantage point of the eighth
sphere, beyond the reach of mortality, of chance, of Time, in short, of
Fortune, Troilus sees the "brotelnesse" of worldly felicity, which
Criseyde had seen at every turn of the action and which had inspired
many of Chaucer's changes from *Il Filostrato*. Again, when Troilus
"dampned al oure werk that foloweth so/ The blynde lust", there is no
question of man's sinful endeavors; it is "the which that may nat laste"
that causes Troilus to despise the world. Chaucer makes this clear when

[28] See Alfred L. Kellogg, "On the Tradition of Troilus's Vision of the Little
Earth", *Mediaeval Studies*, XXII (1960), 204-13.

he says: "Swych fyn hath false worldes brotelnesse!" Chaucer's concern, then, is not the sinfulness or the wickedness of the world, as is the concern of Innocent III and most of the *De Contemptu Mundi* writers but the transitoriness of all earthly things:

> Repeyreth hom fro worldly vanyte,
> And of youre herte up casteth the visage
> To thilke God that after his ymage
> Yow made, and thynketh al nys but a faire
> This world, that passeth soone as floures faire.
>
> (V, 1837-41)

It is the transitoriness of this world, a Vanity Fair, and the mutability of Fortune which ultimately turn Chaucer's mind to the only symbol of permanence, "that sothefast Crist" (l. 1860), who "nyl falsen no wight" (l. 1845). If, certainly, the *Troilus* is an *exemplum* of mutability – and in many ways it obviously is – then the epilogue is artistically appropriate to the poem; actually it is but the climax of a *De Casu* tragedy. "What is there more to say?" asks Dorothy Bethurum:

Only what Chaucer does implicitly say: Love is wonderful, the most wonderful thing in the world. I don't have it, but the books say it is, and successful lovers say it is. Troilus and Criseyde both said it often, but at the end of the poem neither has it. The truth is, nobody has it in its perfection – or has it very long. That is what Chaucer always knew. "To litel whil our blisse lasteth." And by putting himself exactly in our position, he has presented the ideal vision and his sober realistic comment on it. ("Chaucer's Point of View", p. 518)

Nor does it invalidate the epilogue to say that Chaucer throughout the whole poem portrayed love as inescapable and ennobling. The most that can be said against the epilogue is said I think by Willard Farnham: "The most glaring inconsistency of which Chaucer is guilty in his own comment is between this final admonition [in the epilogue] not to love in the way of the world and his earlier admonition, when Troilus first sees Cressida, not to scorn love, since the worthiest of mankind have been and always will be conquered and ennobled by it' (p. 156). There is obviously this inconsistency in the poem; and it can be said that Chaucer's convictions were superseding the conventions of courtly love. The mediaeval sensibility was not one characterized by a refined ambivalence toward the world and toward God; rather it was a divided, inconsistent, even a contradictory sensibility. John Speirs is right when he says, "Those of us who find this conclusion not in accordance with the great humane Chaucerian poem as a whole perhaps fall into the error of those who would ignore the context of Dante's Paolo and Francesca episode." [29] In brief, perhaps the people of the Middle Ages could afford intellectual contradictions and divided sympathies simply because they felt dogmatically secure. It is, certainly, ironic that they could give themselves most wholeheartedly to the world because the world, theologically, meant little to them. Thus Chaucer's complete abandonment to the power of love in the poem and his complete insistence that this same love is transitory. He "retracted", as it were, solely because he believed still that only Christ "nyl falsen no wight". His retractions indicate an acceptance of the world in an age which still recognized the reality of heaven. It is this reality, a reality of permanence, expressed in the epilogue, which is perhaps ultimately responsible for the mutability themes in the *Troilus*.

[29] *Chaucer the Maker* (London, 1940), p. 82.

VI

THE CANTERBURY TALES

PART 1: *THE KNIGHT'S TALE*

In the *Canterbury Tales,* the height of Chaucer's narrative art, the
mutability theme is still very apparent. The *Knight's Tale* in fact contains as much mutability material, proportionately, as does the *Troilus;*
but here it is clear that Chaucer is working toward a solution to his
dilemma evidenced in the *Troilus,* that is, the antithesis of the spiritual
and the worldly realms. The remaining tales are the product of this
resolution.

With the exception of the *Troilus*, no single poem by Chaucer has
received so much critical attention as the *Knight's Tale.* E. B. Ham, for
example, entitled his article of 1950 *"Knight's Tale* 38" and called his
title "an egregious understatement".[1] And, indisputably, no single poem
of Chaucer's has caused so much disagreement among the critics with
regard to the poem's purpose and intention. This disagreement, however, does not usually center around the mutability elements in the poem;
these are clear and generally clearly recognized. But even though this is
so, the mutability elements themselves have been the source of various
interpretations in regard to the poem. In 1927, for example, H. N. Fairchild, in defending Chaucer's individuation of Arcite and Palamon, saw
Arcite as representative of the Active Life and Palamon of the Contemplative Life: "Is it better to plunge into the turmoil of practical
affairs . . . or to 'flee from the press' " in order to serve God directly?[2]
This for Fairchild is the issue of the *Knight's Tale.*

Charles Muscatine's interpretation of the poem implies the concept of
mutability, even if it does not directly treat of it. He sees the poem as
essentially expressing a tension between order (the nature of the noble
life lived ideally) and disorder or chaos:

[1] *ELH*, XVII (1950), 252.
[2] "Active Arcite, Contemplative Palamon", *JEGP*, XXVI (1927), 286.

Order, which characterizes the structure of the poem, is also the heart of its meaning. . . . And what gives this conception of life its perspective, its depth and seriousness, is its constant awareness of a formidably antagonistic element – chaos, disorder – which in life is an ever-threatening possibility, even in the moments of supremest assuredness, . . . exemplified in the erratic reversals of the poem's plot, and deeply embedded in the poem's texture.[3]

Muscatine's order-disorder theme is essentially the mutability-permanence theme. This is further suggested when, having pointed out various instances and portrayals of misfortune and disorder in the poem (including the inevitability of death, expressed by Theseus), he concludes that the poem goes even beyond the perspective of social and civil order, "beyond magnificence in any earthly sense, to a perception of the order beyond chaos. . . . true nobility is faith in the ultimate order of all things" (pp. 189-90). In short, a major theme in the *Knight's Tale* is the perspective of the divine simplicity amid the multifarious earthly vicissitudes.

Perhaps one of the more illuminating interpretations of the *Knight's Tale* is that of W. C. Curry,[4] who argues that Chaucer has substituted astrological influences for much of the ancient mythological machinery of the *Teseida* and that "the real conflict behind the surface action is a conflict between the planets, Saturn and Mars" (p. 120). Lycurgus and Emetreus, the heroes' champions, are respectively Saturnalian and Martian men; and Saturn, Arcite's planetary enemy, is ultimately responsible for his death.[5] In short, the two knights in Chaucer's tale are not actors but victims, thereby mirroring artistically the plight of man's mortality. "For the *Knight's Tale*", says Curry, "is fashioned out of vivid life-materials, in which there is mingled much of human joy and distress, hope, grief, tragedy, and death" (p. 154). But Chaucer is not content to leave mankind's pain and woe and the world's misery to "the cold, unsympathetic direction of the stars" (*loc. cit*); Curry ends his study by pointing out the relationship of these astrological forces to Destiny, and to Providence, and by indicating these relationships in the poem.

Another interpretation centered around the mutability theme is that of R. M. Lumiansky,[6] who holds that the approximately 100 lines

---

[3]   *Chaucer and the French Tradition*, p. 181.
[4]   *Chaucer and the Mediaeval Sciences* (New York, 1960), pp. 119-63.
[5]   Cf. J. M. Manly, *Canterbury Tales by Geoffrey Chaucer* (New York, 1928), p. 543, who disagrees with Curry in regard to Saturn as Arcite's planetary enemy. Manly says: "Saturn seems . . . to have acted from no personal enmity, but only to please Venus (cf. I, 2438-78) and to have taken no special interest in the heroes earlier. But Chaucer undoubtedly inserts the early references to the planets to prepare the reader for their later influence."
[6]   *Of Sondry Folk* (Austin, 1955), pp. 29-49.

comprising the speeches of Arcite, Palamon, and Theseus "both motivate the characters and reflect upon the action occurring in the remaining 2,100 lines" of the poem.[7] He notes, moreover, numerous instances in which "the Knight accounts for each event by suggesting that it resulted from an influence outside the individual. ... Providence, Destiny, Fortune, Nature, 'cas', or 'aventure' " (p. 35), all, of course, from the *Consolation*; and concludes that "the Boethian influence is so pervasive as virtually to control the action" of the poem (p. 38). Lumiansky further relates the poem to the *Consolation* by a detailed study of "the philosophical shifts which Palamon and Arcite experience" (p. 38). At the beginning of the poem Arcite accepts his fortune, Palamon does not; thus each resembles Boethius, at the end and at the beginning of the *Consolation,* respectively. Having fallen in love with Emily, however, Arcite changes, gives himself up to Love and Fortune, thereby seeking false felicity. So that, at the end, "he can only make a final effort at a sensible reconciliation by urging Emily to remember Palamon if she ever decides to marry" (p. 47). But with Arcite's death, Palamon becomes "gentil Palamon" (l. 2976), no longer restlessly striving to fulfill his desires; he "has now realized the folly of his blind pursuit of false felicity and has thus reached some understanding of an established benevolent order in the universe" (p. 40). As such, he deserves Emily's hand, and "the Knight takes his leave of this couple in words which suggest that Palamon's happy state results, in part at least, from his realization of his former misconceptions and his present acceptance of the Boethian view" (p. 41).

If Lumiansky's interpretation is perhaps not justified by the text, at least it suggests that the mutability elements in the poem are sufficiently important that the poem might be viewed wholly in these terms. Such for example is the interpretation of R. A. Pratt, in " 'Joye After Wo' in the *Knight's Tale*".[8] As the title indicates, "this tale of Palamon and Arcite begins in sorrow and ends in gladness". The poem opens with the "Theseidic" events, which suggest war and suffering; the prison experiences and speeches of Palamon and Arcite are indeed sad enough. At the end, however, after the tournament and funeral, "Arcite has found 'welfare' (l. 3063) and Palamon has found his 'wele' (l. 3101) living in bliss with Emelye. The end is joy after sadness" (pp. 416-17).

A glance at these five interpretations of the *Knight's Tale* is sufficient, I think, to show the extent and importance of the concept of mutability

[7] P. 34. Arcite, ll. 1251-74; Palamon, ll. 1303-33; Theseus, ll. 2987-3074.
[8] *JEGP*, LXVII (1958), 416-23.

in the poem itself.[9] (1) Were Hoxie N. Fairchild's interpretation valid
(but it is not), this poem would exhibit a situation somewhat similar to
Truth and would therefore depict the *Contemptus Mundi* theme. (2)
Much of Muscatine's study is concerned with "the poem's symmetrically
ordered structure" (p. 187) and the nature of the noble life. Since it
deals primarily with the social order, he is not overly concerned with
the vicissitudes and the other forces of disorder which affect life generally, and which constitute perhaps one of the more important themes of
the *Knight's Tale*. Whatever he does say in this regard, however, is
valuable and will be incorporated into the present study. (3) Curry's
interpretation explains a very important aspect of the mutability theme
in the poem. For him, the poem is a tightly-woven structure held together by the interplay of destinal forces. Man is at the mercy of these
forces; thus the vanity of human wishes or the fruitless efforts of man
to escape the limitations of his own destiny. (4) Lumiansky enlarges
upon Jefferson's study of the Boethian elements in the poem; he attempts
to explain its motivation by these elements. It is true certainly that
fortune, destiny, true and false felicity have large parts in the poem, but
his conclusions are forced. One might take almost any poem and discuss
it in terms of "true" and "false" felicity, if one uses these terms broadly
enough; the action-*vs*-withdrawal theme is found in many literary works.
(5) Finally, Pratt's thesis is "Chaucerian" enough and his findings are
valid, to be sure; but is his interpretation not a little specious when he
speaks of Arcite's "welfare" as "joye after wo"? Yet there is a certain
validity, more or less, in each of these interpretations; and I cannot,
certainly, proffer a "new" interpretation of the *Knight's Tale*.

My purpose in this study, therefore, is twofold: First, to integrate
some of the criticism offered thus far in regard to the mutability elements
in this poem. I shall do this by suggesting that the basic theme of the
poem might conveniently be seen in this dichotomy: between mutability,
expressed most pointedly in the speeches of Arcite and Palamon, but
also in the portrayals of fortune and vicissitude throughout the poem;
and order, the symbol of permanence, expressed in the speeches of
Theseus and Egeus and in the resolution of the poem. Second, by discussing at length the mutability elements contained in this poem, I hope

---

[9]   See H. S. Wilson, "The *Knight's Tale* and the *Teseida* Again", *UTQ*, XVIII
(1949), 131-46, which only remotely touches upon this theme. William Frost,
"An Interpretation of Chaucer's *Knight's Tale*", *RES*, XXV (1949), 300 ff. Only
one-third of Frost's article deals with mutability elements in the poem, but this
is concise and generally excellent.

to provide a somewhat clearer picture of the scope and depth of Chaucer's concern with the many aspects of mutability.

The major speeches in the poem are taken from the *Consolation* of Boethius and are Chaucer's own additions to his source. These are the speeches of Arcite, Palamon, and of Theseus.[10] Arcite's and Palamon's are essentially the same and differ only in so far as their own circumstances are different: both deal with the limitations of mortal man in opposition to an ultimate order which he is unable to comprehend. Arcite, who has just been released from prison at the request of his friend Perotheus, is dismayed that he must leave Athens and will therefore not be able to see Emily again. At this point, he complains:

> "Allas, why pleynen folk so in commune
> On purveiaunce of God, or of Fortune,
> That yeveth hem ful ofte in many a gyse
> Wel bettre than they kan hemself devyse?
> Som man desireth for to han richesse,
> That cause is of his mordre or greet siknesse;
> And som man wolde out of his prisoun fayn,
> That in his hous is of his meynee slayn.
> Infinite harmes been in this mateere.
> We witen nat what thing we preyen heere:
> We faren as he that dronke is as a mous.
> A dronke man woot wel he hath an hous,
> But he noot which the righte wey is thider,
> And to a dronke man the wey is slider.
> And certes, in this world so faren we;
> We seken faste after felicitee,
> But we goon wrong ful often, trewely.
> Thus may we seyen alle, and namely I,
> That wende and hadde a greet opinioun
> That if I myghte escapen from prisoun,
> Thanne hadde I been in joye and perfit heele,
> Ther now I am exiled fro my wele.
> Syn that I may nat seen you, Emelye,
> I nam but deed; ther nys no remedye."
>
> (ll. 1251-74)

These last seven lines explain the circumstances which have determined the attitude of Arcite. Throughout his speech he is concerned with the vanity of human wishes.[11]

[10] For the sources of these speeches in the *Consolation*, see the notes to these lines in the edition of F. N. Robinson, pp. 672 and 682.
[11] This idea of the limitation of man's vision and the consequent irony of his intentions is also expressed in the *Troilus*, IV, 197-203. Germaine Dempster, *Dramatic Irony in Chaucer* (New York, 1959), pages 20 and 89, points out the irony of these passages from the *Troilus* and the *Knight's Tale*.

The imprisoned Palamon, on the other hand, jealous of Arcite's "good fortune", exclaims:

> "O crueel goddes that governe
> This world with byndyng of youre word eterne,
> And writen in the table of atthamaunt
> Youre parlement and youre eterne graunt,
> What is mankynde moore unto you holde
> Than is the sheep that rouketh in the folde?
> For slayn is man right as another beest,
> And dwelleth eek in prison and arreest,
> And hath siknesse and great adversitee,
> And ofte tymes gilteless, pardee.
>   What governance is in this prescience,
> That giltelees tormenteth innocence?
> And yet encresseth this al my penaunce,
> That man is bounden to his observaunce,
> For Goddes sake, to letten of his wille,
> Ther as a beest may al his lust fulfille.
> And whan a beest is deed he hath no peyne;
> But man after his deeth moot wepe and pleyne,
> Though in this world he have care and wo.
> Withouten doute it may stonden so.
> The answere of this lete I to dyvynes,
> But wel I woot that in this world greet pyne ys."
>   (ll. 1303-24)

"Thus", says Pratt, "the two kinsmen find this world a place of woe: Arcite blames man's stupidity; Palamon blames the gods" (p. 418). The point to be made here is that these separate speeches are most probably not meant to characterize the two knights,[12] but that Chaucer added this Boethian material, perhaps, for two reasons: First, these long philosophical reflections, coming as they do in the very beginning of the poem, themselves focus attention upon the mutability theme and its many ramifications throughout the poem. Second, these complaints anticipate Theseus' "solution" at the poem's end.

It is, finally, in these speeches a question of man's mortality, of his inability to control his own destiny. Each of the knights in fact reflects

---

[12] B. L. Jefferson, p. 131, Fairchild, and Lumiansky (both cited above) see a significant differentiation between the characters of Arcite and Palamon. R. K. Root, *The Poetry of Chaucer*, pp. 169-70, denies them subtle characterization, but finds Arcite the man of action and Palamon the dreamer. Germaine Dempster, *Dramatic Irony*, p. 89, and J. R. Hulbert, "What Was Chaucer's Aim in the *Knight's Tale?*", *SP*, XXVI (1929), 375 ff., see little if any differentiation between the two kinsmen. It is doubtful that Arcite's "submissive" attitude here is meant to characterize him; most probably Chaucer is merely interested in injecting these problems into the poem.

his destiny in the very act of moralizing on the human condition. Arcite says: "And som man wolde out of his prisoun fayn,/ That in his hous is of his meynee slayn", an irony somewhat similar to his own situation. Palamon, on the other hand, refers to man's imprisonment as one of the adversities of this world. Arcite compares man to a drunkard, who is completely ignorant of, and irresponsible for, his own actions; to Palamon, men are as sheep, cowering in the fold. Palamon furthermore raises the question of innocent suffering, a question which Criseyde also brings up in the *Troilus*.[13] These and similar problems in regard to the human condition are, as we shall now see, expressed throughout the poem generally.

In the beginning the Theban women, wailing because Creon will not permit them to bury their dead, tell Theseus:

> "Now be we caytyves, as it is wel seene,
> Thanked be Fortune and hire false wheel,
> That noon estaat assureth to be weel."
> (ll. 924-26) [14]

While in prison, Arcite recognizes the helplessness of man, whose destiny is ruled by the stars:

> "Fortune hath yeven us this adversitee.
> Some wikke aspect or disposicioun
> Of Saturne, by som constellacioun,
> Hath yeven us this, although we hadde it sworn;
> So stood the hevene whan that we were born."
> (ll. 1086-90)

Palamon also recognizes the force of destiny upon man's life (ll. 1108-1109). The destiny motif runs throughout the poem.[15] In the *Troilus,* when Criseyde is forced to spend the night at the home of Pandarus because of the terrible storm, Chaucer blames Fortune (III, 617-23); here, too, he relies upon Fortune to explain the chance meeting of Theseus and the two knights, who are fighting in the woods:

> The destinee, ministre general,
> That executeth in the world over al
> The purveiaunce that God hath seyn biforn,
> So strong it is that, though the world had sworn

13 Cf. *Troilus*, III, 1016-22.
14 Cf. *Troilus*, V, 1749, "In ech estat is little hertes reste." The Fortune-image here is not in the *Teseida*. Unless otherwise indicated, all the passages which I quote in connection with the *Knight's Tale* are Chaucer's additions to his source.
15 See, for example, lines 915-16; 1074; 1238-43; 1465-66; 1490; 1507; 1516; 1566; 1841-44; 1861 (perhaps no more than conventional phraseology); 2322-25. Also, Curry, pp. 119-63.

> The contrarie of a thyng by ye or nay,
> Yet sometyme it shal fallen on a day
> That falleth nat eft withinne a thousand yeer.
> For certeinly, oure appetites heer,
> Be it of werre, or pees, or hate, or love,
> Al is this reuled by the sighte above.
>
> (ll. 1663-72)

This passage makes clear that the destiny motif is simply another aspect of the theme of mutability. It is, in fact, the explanation of change, vicissitude, and misfortune in the world.[16] Chaucer calls upon destiny to explain an "accidental" occurrence which might come about only once in a thousand years. So throughout the poem do Arcite and Palamon explain their adverse or agreeable circumstances in terms of destiny, a force which causes whatever "happens" to them. Indeed the cumulative force of all these references to destiny and to fortune serves to portray and to emphasize the limitation of man's own actions and explains in part his subjection to vicissitudes (another instance in the works of Chaucer of the inseparability of the mortality and mutability themes). The speeches of Arcite and Palamon, then, are merely focal points of a theme which persists throughout the *Knight's Tale*.

The mutability theme is also stressed in the vicissitudes which the kinsmen suffer for love. For example, the poet says:

> Whan that Arcite hadde romed al his fille,
> And songen al the roundel lustily,
> Into a studie he fill sodeynly,
> As doon thise loveres in hir queynte geres,
> Now in the crope, now doun in the breres,
> Now up, now doun, as boket in a welle.
> Right as the Friday, soothly for to telle,
> Now it shyneth, now it reyneth faste,
> Right so kan geery Venus overcaste
> The hertes of hir folk; right as hir day
> Is gereful, right so chaungeth she array.
> Selde is the Friday al the wowke ylike.
>
> (ll. 1528-39) [17]

---

[16] Cf. Curry's discussion of Providence, Destiny, and the destinal forces, pp. 154 ff.

[17] See Skeat's note (V, 72) to line 1532, where he points out that "Here up, here doune" in the *De Reg. Princip.* of Occleve refers to the lack of stability in the world. It might be helpful to mention at this point that Skeat glosses "geery" (l. 1536) as "changeable", *loc. cit.* This passage is not in the work of Boccaccio, and I have not seen it cited by critics as an instance of the mutability of love in the poem. One of Boccaccio's favorite motifs is the portrayal of the effects of

The "ups-and-downs", in fact, which Arcite and Palamon suffer for love constitute the plot of this poem: their despair while in prison upon seeing Emily in the garden, the disruption of their own knightly brotherhood, Arcite's hopes upon his release from prison and his subsequent frustrations, the duel in the woods, and finally the tournament itself, all of these result from love's power over them.

The vicissitudes of love are brought out by Chaucer even more clearly in the wall-paintings on the temple of Venus. Here is depicted in great detail, and "ful pitous to biholde":

> The broken slepes, and the sikes colde,
> The sacred teeris, and the waymentynge . . .
> That loves servantz in this lyf enduren . . .
>   and alle the circumstaunces
> Of love, which that I reckned and rekne shal,
>
> . . . .
> And mo than I kan make of mencioun.
>   (ll. 1919-21; 1923; 1932-35)

The sufferings and folly of Narcissus, Solomon, Hercules, and others are also depicted on the wall of the temple; then Chaucer mentions the tyranny of the goddess of Love:

> Thus may ye seen that wysdom ne richesse,
> Beautee ne sleighte, strengthe ne hardynesse,
> Ne may with Venus holde champartie,
> For as hir list the world than may she gye.
> Lo, alle thise folk so caught were in hir las,
> Til they for wo ful ofte seyde "allas!"
>   (ll. 1947-52)

Obviously the goddess of Love is just as "crueel" as are the gods whom Palamon had questioned in his complaint. This same cruelty is implied in Theseus' words about the god of Love:

> "The god of love, a, *benedicite!*
> How myghty and how greet a lord is he!
> Ayeyns his myght ther gayneth none obstacles.
> He may be cleped a god for his myracles;
> For he kan maken, at his owene gyse,
> Of everich herte as that hym list divyse."
>   (ll. 1785-90)

---

abandonment and absence, and the pains and joys of love. See S. Battaglia, "Schemi lirici nell'art del Boccaccio", *Archivum romanicum*, XIX (1935), 61-78. For this information I am indebted to R. A. Pratt, "Chaucer's Use of the *Teseida*", *PMLA*, LXII (1947), 602-603.

The crowning irony of the duel in the woods is of course that Emily "woot namoore of al this hoote fare . . . than woot a cokkow or an hare!" (ll. 1809-10). These two lines, Chaucer's addition to his source, emphasize the "blynde entencioun" of mankind, the very thing that Arcite had complained about in the first part of the poem. In fact, all these quoted passages on love are Chaucer's additions to the *Teseida*. The helplessness of Palamon and Arcite before the god of Love parallels their helplessness before God and the destinal forces. And the ups and downs of love are themselves but a part of the vicissitudes of life generally, as it is portrayed in the poem.

Much of the plot of this tale revolves around vicissitudes: the Theban women have been widowed by civil wars; Thebes has been sacked by Athens, which led to the knights' imprisonment; and Arcite dies of a fall from his horse. It has been pointed out that the poem "abounds in such words of suffering as 'waymentynge', 'criynge', 'youlynge', 'distresse', 'angwissh', 'deeth', 'torment', 'strif', 'adversitee', 'lamentacioun', 'wrecched', 'pitous', 'deedly', 'suffre', 'compleyne', 'sorwe', and 'wo'." [18] To be sure, the poem presents in many and various ways the image of "every worldly soore". In the temple of Mars, for example, is seen:

> the derke ymaginyng
> Of Felonye, and al the compassyng;
> The crueel Ire, reed as any gleede;
> The pykepurs, and eek the pale Drede;
> The smylere with the knyf under the cloke;
> The shepne brennynge with the blake smoke;
> The tresoun of the mordrynge in the bedde;
> The open werre, with woundes al bibledde;
> Contek, with blody knyf and sharp manace.
> Al ful of chirkyng was that sory place.
> The sleere of hymself yet saught I ther, –
> His herte-blood hath bathed al his heer;
> The nayl ydryven in the shode a-nyght;
> The colde deeth, with mouth gaping upright.
> Admyddes of the temple sat Meschaunce,
> With disconfort and sory contenaunce.
>   (ll. 1995-2010) [19]

---

[18] Jack G. Gilbert, "The 'Philosophy Group' in the *Canterbury Tales*: A Study of the *Knight's Tale*, the *Monk's Tale*, and the *Nun's Priest's Tale*", an unpublished thesis (M.A.), Louisiana State University (1959), p. 80. For a survey of the scholarship on the philosophical aspects of the *Knight's Tale* and for a clear statement of the issues involved in the poem, Gilbert's study is very useful.
[19] Frost, p. 301, and Muscatine, p. 189, are right I think in considering these wall-paintings organic rather than merely decorative.

There is not found such a detailed enumeration of vice, villainy, and mischance in all of Chaucer's poetry; it is as if Mars were the source of every possible evil. Almost every catastrophe which might happen to mankind is depicted on the walls of this temple. The walls of the temple of Diana, not found in the *Teseida*, also sustain this theme of "care and wo" (l. 2072).

The climax of all these vicissitudes portrayed in the poem is seen in the death speech of Arcite; here it is also clear that "the theme of love itself is subsumed in the category of all earthly experience" (Muscatine, p. 187):

> "Naught may the woful spirit in myn herte
> Declare o point of alle my sorwes smerte
> To yow, my lady, that I love moost;
> But I biquethe the servyce of my goost
> To yow aboven every creature,
> Syn that my lyf may no lenger dure.
> Allas, the wo! allas, the peynes stronge,
> That I for yow have suffred, and so longe!
> Allas, the deeth! allas, myn Emelye!
> Allas, departynge of oure compaignye!
> Allas, myn hertes queene! allas, my wyf!
> Myn hertes lady, endere of my lyf!
> What is this world? what asketh men to have?
> Now with his love, now in his colde grave
> Allone, withouten any compaignye."
> (ll. 2765-79)

"What is it", says Arcite, "that men want?" The circle has come full-turn: it is the same question which he raised after he had been released from prison – only to find that he was forever a prisoner to mortality; "We faren as he that dronke is as a mous. ... We seken faste after felicitee,/ But we goon wrong ful often, trewely." Arcite had won Emily, but he had also won his death. As if in a momentary flash, Arcite sees the full impact of the limitation of man's vision and of the limitation of man's happiness (by death). His happiness, in fact, lasted "as it were a twynklyng of an ye". And as if Chaucer would not let the point rest here, he writes: " 'Why woldestow be deed', thise wommen crye,/ 'And haddest gold ynough, and Emelye?' " (ll. 2835-36) [20] This is certainly the very moment of irony. These two lines constitute the only dialogue in the scene of mourning just after Arcite's death (ll. 2817-36). It is opportune for Egeus to come on stage at this point:

[20] This passage is not in the *Teseida*; nor are lines 2777-79 of the preceding passage.

> No man myghte gladen Theseus,
> Savynge his olde fader Egeus,
> That knew this worldes transmutacioun,
> As he hadde seyn it chaunge bothe up and down,
> Joye after wo, and wo after gladnesse.
>
> (ll. 2837-41)

Egeus is ostensibly talking about death, but his remarks supply the poem's commentary about life. The intensive questioning of life's meaning in the speeches of Arcite and Palamon, the numerous references to destiny throughout the poem, the many different ways in which Chaucer has portrayed the vicissitudes of love and of life generally, in brief, the mutability of all worldly endeavor: these find their solution at the end of the poem in the speeches of Egeus and Theseus. After Egeus had given Theseus many examples and illustrations (l. 2842) of "this worldes transmutacioun", he tells him:

> "This world nys but a thurghfare ful of wo,
> And we been pilgrymes, passynge to and fro.
> Deeth is an ende of every worldly soore."
>
> (ll. 2847-49)

These lines are more than merely "commonplace".[21] Pratt points out that "in Egeus' words we begin to find an answer to Palamon's complaint" (p. 421); he remarks, moreover, that this speech of Egeus prepares for the long speech of Theseus, who develops the idea of "this worldes transmutacioun" as he speaks of the "Firste Moevere" (p. 421). Besides the dramatic function of Egeus' words, however, it seems to me that his relationship both to what has gone before in the poem and to the speech of Theseus which follows might be viewed in another way. When Egeus says that "this world nys but a thurghfare ful of wo", he is expressing abstractly what has been to this point dramatically portrayed in the poem. He recapitulates as it were a dominant theme of the poem. Furthermore, when Egeus adds to this idea that "we been pilgryms, passynge to and fro", he is giving expression to the *Contemptus*

---

[21]   F. N. Robinson (notes to lines 2837 and 2849, p. 682) calls these sentiments "commonplace". Dale Underwood, "The First of *The Canterbury Tales*", *ELH*, XXVI (1959), 464 n., says: "That the ideas in the Egeus passage are commonplace and even platitudinous has been repeatedly stressed by commentators. So in themselves they are. But they are as close to the *Consolation* as the other three speeches here discussed [the speeches of Arcite, Palamon, and Theseus], for which Boethian correspondences have been generally recognized." See William Frost, p. 300, for a defense of these lines. It might be added here that what, after all, is "commonplace" but a term attached to a pattern of thought of an epoch? The word is sometimes perilous because it implies that the thought does not function in the work in which it appears.

Mundi idea. This idea is not strongly emphasized by Egeus, surely, but the woe of the world has been portrayed constantly throughout the poem, and Theseus himself speaks of "this wrecched world" (l. 2995) and of the "foule prisoun of this lyf" (l. 3061).[22] The speech of Egeus is related to that of Theseus in a manner similar to the way in which the *Contemptus Mundi* expression precedes the answer to it in *Truth* and in the epilogue of the *Troilus*. In *Truth*, it is to be recalled, Chaucer writes:

> The wrastling for this world axeth a fal.
> Her is non hoom, her nis but wildernesse:
> Forth, pilgrim, forth! Forth, beste, out of
>   thy stal!
> Know thy contree, look up, thank God of al;
> Hold the heye wey, and lat thy gost thee lede;
> And trouthe thee shal delivere, it is no drede.
>
> .   .   .   .
>
> Unto the world leve now to be thral;
> Crye him mercy, that of his hy goodnesse
> Made thee of noght, and in especial
> Draw unto him. . . .
>
> (ll. 16-21; 23-26)

The negative aspect of the *Contemptus Mundi* idea is inseparable in Chaucer's mind from its positive aspect: the turning away *from* the world indeed suggests the turning *toward* God. This same pattern is seen in the epilogue of the *Troilus*. Troilus "gan despise/ This wrecched world, and held al vanite/ To respect of the pleyn felicite/ That is in hevene above . . ." (V, 1816-19). He condemned "al oure werk that foloweth so/ The blynde lust, the which that may nat laste . . ." (V, 1823-24). But to this negative expression Chaucer adds his exhortation to the "yonge, fresshe folkes", and counsels them to lay their hearts "al holly" on Christ. Against the *Contemptus Mundi* expression is balanced the goodness and the stability of God. Such too is the pattern which prevails at this point of the *Knight's Tale*. And in this regard it is significant to note two things: First, neither the *Contemptus Mundi* expression of Egeus nor the "Firste Moevere" expression of Theseus are in the *Teseida*. Second, the words of Egeus which immediately precede this *Contemptus Mundi* expression (ll. 2843-46), and from which this expression naturally evolves, were, in the *Teseida,* spoken by Theseus in the last book of the poem.[23]

---

[22]   The importance of the imprisonment symbolism throughout the poem has often been noted. Cf. Frost, p. 302.

[23]   Ll. 2843-46 were spoken by Theseus, *Teseida*, XII, 6, when proposing the

Theseus' speech at the close of the poem occurs a "lengthe of certeyn yeres" (l. 2967) after the death of Arcite. Still saddened by Arcite's death, he summons Emily and Palamon, themselves still grieving. He begins his speech by talking about "the faire cheyne of love", which binds together all things in the universe under the "Firste Moevere". Things do not just "happen", nor is destiny simply a blind force; there is a divine plan operating in the world. When the First Mover made this "faire cheyne of love . . . heigh was his entente./ Wel wiste he why, and what thereof he mente". Theseus' words relate primarily to death and successions, but the concepts of order and stability as against chaos and purposeless mutability underlie everything he says. "That same Prince and that Moevere", he continues:

> "Hath stablissed in this wrecched world adoun
> Certeyne dayes and duracioun
> To al that is engendred in this place,
> Over the whiche day they may nat pace,
>
> . . . .
>
> Thanne may men by this ordre wel discerne
> *That thilke Moevere stable is and eterne.*
> Wel may men knowe, but it be a fool,
> That every part dirryveth from his hool;
> For nature hath nat taken his bigynnyng
> Of no partie or cantel of a thing,
> *But of a thyng that parfit is and stable,*
> Descendynge so til it be corrumpable."
>
> (ll. 2995-98; 3003-10)

From this passage it is clear that Theseus' speech emphasizes two points: First, there is a guiding purpose operating throughout all creation: this supplies the answers to the questionings of Arcite and Palamon and to all the other problems in regard to mutability which are raised in the poem. Second, the dichotomy between the mutable and corruptible world (at the outer edge of the circle from the creator) and the perfect and stable "Firste Moevere" (indicated in the italicized lines) is clearly stated. Twice again does Theseus refer to this order in creation:

> "And therfore, of his wise purveiaunce,
> He hath so wel biset his ordinaunce,
> That speces of thynges and progressiouns
> Shullen enduren by successiouns,
> And nat eterne,
>
> . . . .

---

marriage of Palamon and Emily. Chaucer substitutes the "Firste Moevere" passage in their stead.

> What maketh this but Juppiter, the kyng,
> That is prince and cause of alle thyng,
> Convertynge al unto his propre welle
> From which it is dirryved, sooth to telle?"
>
> (ll. 3011-15; 3035-38)

To rebel against this order is folly (ll. 3045-46). The death of Arcite then is part of the divine plan and should therefore not be lamented. "Why have we hevynesse", he says, since he has departed honorably out of the "foule prisoun of this lyf?" (ll. 3058; 3061) Thus the positive aspects of Egeus' *Contemptus Mundi* speech are seen in the order of the universe and in the perfection and stability of the First Mover.[24] As in *Truth* and in the *Troilus*, Theseus' speech ends on the note of the promise and the hope of eternal immutability; death is, in reality, the conversion of the creature back "unto his propre welle/ From which it is dirryved".[25]

Once this is stated, the way is prepared for the marriage of Emily and Palamon and for the reader's acceptance of these words of Theseus:

> "What may I conclude of this longe serye,
> But after wo I rede us to be merye,
> And thanken Juppiter of al his grace?
> And er that we departen from this place
> I rede that we make of sorwes two
> O perfit joye, lastynge evermo."
>
> (ll. 3067-72)

After the vivid portrayal in the poem of the many vicissitudes of life, Theseus' conclusion here and the Knight's relating that the entire wedded life of Palamon and Emily was spent in perfect bliss are convincing perhaps only because of the preceding speech of Theseus. The world has been "ordered", Palamon and Emily are part of the "faire cheyne of love" and, under these aspects, they can have "O parfit joye, lastynge

[24] In the *Troilus*, Chaucer had already used the device (from the *Teseida*, XI, 1-3) of Troilus' flight after death to the eighth sphere (on the date of the *Knight's Tale*, see J. S. P. Tatlock, *The Development and Chronology of Chaucer's Works*, Chaucer Soc., 2nd Ser., No. 37 [London, 1907], pp. 70-83). In the *Knight's Tale*, therefore, he simply inserts the fact that Arcite's "spirit chaunged hous and went ther,/ As I cam nevere, I kan nat tellen wher" (ll. 2809-10). He then went to the *Consolation* for Theseus' speech on the First Mover and the fair chain of love. This passage, like the epilogue to the *Troilus* and the abstractly stated ending of *Truth*, provides Chaucer's chief commentary on the poem and on life itself.

[25] Cf. Elizabeth Salter, *Chaucer: The Knight's Tale and The Clerk's Tale* (London, 1962), pp. 30-33, for the view that the speech of Theseus is a rhetorical rather than an imaginative resolution or ordering of the crueler actions on the part of the gods in the poem.

evermo." At this point, the philosophy of Boethius and the romance of chivalry blend, become one and indistinguishable.

Part 2: THE REMAINDER OF THE *CANTERBURY TALES*

Of the rest of the *Canterbury Tales*, only the Man of Law's sustains the mutability theme throughout the entire poem. In the beginning of the poem, Chaucer emphasizes the destiny theme and at the end, the transitory theme. In between are references to fortune and to transitoriness. All of the mutability elements in the *Man of Law's Tale* are Chaucer's additions to his source; these effect the high seriousness of the poem and contribute genuine significance and pathos to a plot which in Trivet's work is simply a factual narration of incidents befalling a human victim. The high seriousness of Chaucer's poem consists precisely in the manifestation of Christian perfection, especially the perseverance in the belief in the "sothefast Christ", amid all the forces of mutability and mortality which operate in this world beneath the moon. In the other tales, on the other hand, the mutability theme appears very often to motivate or to explain incidents in the plot, but in no one of the tales is there any attempt made to sustain the theme throughout the entire narrative.

In the *Man of Law's Tale*, the mutability motifs are very distinct: they are the destiny and the transitory motifs. These are also the predominant motifs in the other tales. For this reason I shall examine these tales under the aspects of Chaucer's use of fortune, his employment of the transitory theme, and a few other mutability references which can not properly be placed in either of these categories.[26] It is to be noted here, as has been pointed out in the examination of the *Knight's Tale*, that Chaucer's use of fortune and destiny, from the point of view of mutability, is not essentially different. Theoretically destiny operates of course through fortune. Thus in Chaucer's poetic, destiny is used to explain a "hap" which might just as well have been explained by fortune. For this reason I shall use the two concepts interchangeably except when the context calls for their distinction.

In the *Man of Law's Tale* the Sultan, having heard his merchants describe the nobility of Constance, wanted her for his wife, "to love hire while his lyf may dure". This line, Chaucer's addition, becomes ironical when it is immediately followed by another addition to Trivet's work:

---

[26] Throughout this section I consider only Chaucer's additions to his sources unless otherwise indicated.

Paraventure in thilke large book
Which that men clepe the hevene ywriten was
With sterres, whan that he his birthe took,
That he for love sholde han his deeth, allas!
For in the sterres, clerer than is glas,
Is writen, God woot, whoso koude it rede,
The deeth of every man, withouten drede.

In sterres, many a wynter therbiforn,
Was writen the deeth of Ector, Achilles,
Of Pompei, Julius, er they were born;
The strif of Thebes; and of Ercules,
Of Sampson, Turnus, and of Socrates
The deeth; but mennes wittes ben so dulle
That no wight kan wel rede it atte fulle.
(B¹ 190-203)

The astrological material not only foretells the death of the Sultan but
gives "high seriousness" and universality to the entire story. Chaucer's
lengthy enumeration of great historical personages functions to lend
credibility to the stars' influence upon the lives and deaths of men. In
short, the destiny motif is intended to explain the "mutability" in the
life of the Sultan. As with the Sultan, so too with Constance. "The
woful day fatal is come" for her to leave her father the emperor and to
go to Syria to marry the Mohammedan ruler. Chaucer apostrophizes the
unfavorable astrological conditions which prevail at her departure:

O firste moevyng! crueel firmament,
With thy diurnal sweigh that crowdest ay
And hurlest al from est til occident
That naturelly wolde holde another way,
Thy crowdyng set the hevene in swich array
At the bigynnyng of the fiers viage,
That crueel Mars hath slayn this mariage.

He further observes that both Mars and Luna have passed from the sign
Libra into Scorpio, the darker (night) mansion of Mars. This is a very
unfavorable time for Constance to begin her journey. For this reason,
Chaucer says:

Impudent Emperour of Rome, allas!
Was ther no philosophre in al thy toun?
Is no tyme bet than oother in swich cas?
Of viage is ther noon eleccioun,
Namely to folk of heigh condicioun?
Noght when a roote is of a burthe yknowe?
Allas, we been to lewed or to slowe!
(B¹ 295-315)

Constance's "root of nativity" was already known; it would have been easy to determine the "election" of this particular time but, alas, observes Chaucer, there is the element of man's mortality.[27] Here, as in the lines on the Sultan's death as written in the stars, the poet combines the destiny motif with the limitation of man's vision. These destiny passages in the very beginning of the poem set the tone for the entire work; Constance is forever the victim of forces beyond her control. Chaucer does not, however, maintain the destinal motif throughout the entire poem, as he does in the *Knight's Tale*; from this time on, the transitory theme predominates.

One of Chaucer's favorite rhetorical devices throughout the *Canterbury Tales* is the apostrophe. His use of the fortune-destiny material usually takes this form. Notice the grave tone of the apostrophe just examined and, in contrast, the mock-heroic tone of the following apostrophe in the *Merchant's Tale*. Having satirized January's senile illusion of finding heavenly bliss, "ful deliciously", in the sensuous enjoyment of his young wife May, Chaucer prefaces the old man's ensuing blindness thus:

> O sodeyn hap! o thou Fortune unstable!
> Lyk to the scorpion so deceyvable,
> That flaterest with thyn heed whan thou wolt stynge;
> Thy tayl is deeth, thurgh thyn envenymynge.
> O brotil joye! o sweete venym queynte!
> O monstre, that so subtilly kanst peynte
> Thy yiftes under hewe of stidefastnesse,
> That thou deceyvest bothe moore and lesse!
> Why hastow Januarie thus deceyved,
> That haddest hym for thy fulle freend receyved?
> And now thou hast biraft hym bothe his yen,
> For sorwe of which desireth he to dyen.
>   Allas! this noble Januarie free,
> Amydde his lust and his prosperitee,
> Is woxen blynd, and that al sodeynly.
>   (E 2057-2071)

---

[27] W. C. Curry, *Chaucer and the Med. Sciences*, pp. 175 ff., argues that the horoscope presented here refers to "the conjunction of stars at Constance's birth; this is the 'root of her nativity'". An election was not made therefore since it would have been useless; Constance's marriages were doomed from birth. Curry's argument I think misinterprets the context. Chaucer clearly laments the fact that an election has been overlooked (B[1] 309-15), not disregarded because it would have been useless.

Chaucer obviously is using the fortune material ironically here; it is January who is still being satirized. It is interesting to note that in Chaucer's mock-heroic apostrophe to Fortune the imagery is highly conventional. It is in fact surprisingly similar to that imagery used in the Man in Black's tirade against Fortune in the *Book of the Duchess*. Thus we see the mature Chaucer, now in complete control of his material. This apostrophe, furthermore, prepares for the turn in the plot. From here on, January's fortune constantly becomes worse until finally he is shown to be the complete and utter fool.

A similar use of the destiny-fortune material occurs in the *Nun's Priest's Tale*. After Daun Russell the fox seized Chauntecleer "and on his bak toward the wode hym beer", the poet says:

> O destinee, that mayst nat been eschewed!
> Allas, that Chauntecleer fleigh fro the bemes!
> Allas, his wyf ne roghte nat of dremes!
> And on a Friday fil al this meschaunce.
> (B² 3338-41)

Chaucer then apostrophizes Venus and Geoffrey de Vinsauf (who, in turn, had apostrophized Friday, the day on which Richard I was wounded). It is clear that Chaucer's use of the destiny material here is only another part of his sustaining the mock-heroic style. There remains only one more significant use of fortune in this manner, in the *Franklin's Tale*.

It is to be recalled that Dorigen, the faithful wife of Arveragus, playfully promised to become Aurelius' *amie* if he should remove the dangerously jutting rocks from the coast of Brittany. This with the aid of magic Aurelius did. Dorigen, caught between her love and her devotion to truth, apostrophizes Fortune:

> "Allas", quod she, "on thee, Fortune, I pleyne,
> That unwar wrapped hast me in thy cheyne,
> Fro which t'escape woot I no socour,
> Save oonly deeth or elles dishonour;
> Oon of thise two bihoveth me to chese.
> But nathelees, yet have I levere to lese
> My lif than of my body to have a shame,
> Or knowe myselven fals, or lese my name;
> And with my deth I may be quyt, ywis.
> Hath ther nat many a noble wyf er this,
> And many a mayde, yslayn hirself, allas!
> Rather than with hir body doon trespas?"
> (F 1355-66)

The fortune-motif is obviously not developed. The apostrophe takes the special form of the complaint; Fortune is merely the dramatic pretext for Dorigen's lengthy complaint. Following this passage are nearly one hundred lines of rhetorical *exempla* of famous women who chose death rather than to submit their bodies to dishonor.

These five passages, then, four of which take the form of the rhetorical apostrophe (and one of these the more special form of the complaint) constitute with the exception of the *Monk's Tale* Chaucer's major uses of fortune and destiny in the *Canterbury Tales*. Of these passages two are used to enhance the gravity or seriousness of the plot and two are used for mock-heroic effects. The apostrophes in the *Merchant's* and in the *Nun's Priest's Tales* effect an ironical gravity of relatively insignificant incidents (January's loss of vision is not so serious as is his intellectual blindness). Finally, in Dorigen's complaint Chaucer uses fortune merely to introduce the complaint itself which, with the nearly one hundred lines of *exempla*, serves to emphasize Dorigen's dilemma. Chaucer's use of the fortune-destiny material in these tales is therefore exclusively for dramatic purposes; that is, the extent and presentation of this material are determined by the dramatic effects which he wishes to achieve. Aside from incidental references to fortune or destiny scattered throughout the *Tales*, and of course the *Monk's Tale*, which deals almost entirely with fortune, these instances which I have presented constitute the greater extent of Chaucer's use of fortune in the *Canterbury Tales*.[28]

The *Monk's Tale* was written before the Canterbury period but at least one of the tragedies was added after 1385.[29] Chaucer's use of fortune here follows the conventional mediaeval *De Casibus* scheme. The tale illustrates by seventeen *exempla* the falls of famous persons who had formerly enjoyed great prosperity. Generally the agent in these falls is Fortune, "For certein, whan that Fortune list to flee,/ Ther may no man the cours of hire withholde." The Monk begins by relating the fall of Lucifer but pedantically insists that his fall was not influenced by Fortune, for "Fortune may noon angel dere"; he thereby reminds the pilgrims that Fortune's power does not extend beyond the moon. Throughout the poem in fact the Monk makes thirty references to Fortune.[30]

[28]   See also the *Merchant's Tale*, E 1967-73.
[29]   Robinson's edn., p. 746.
[30]   Cf. Gilbert's classification of these references, p. 99.

E. M. Socola's argument is convenient as a summary glance at the tragedies and Chaucer's presentation of Fortune in the tale. Assuming that the Modern Instances belong between the tragedies of Zenobia and Nero, he sees three successive groupings of the seventeen tragedies, which constitute the following design:

(1) those tragedies in which Fortune is not mentioned or plays no part (Lucifer, Adam, and Samson); (2) those tragedies in which Fortune appears as an abstraction (Hercules, Nebuchadnezzar-Balshazzar, Zenobia, Peter of Spain, Peter of Cyprus, Barnabo, and Ugolino); and (3) those tragedies in which Fortune is a personal and an individualized being (Nero, Holofernes, Antiochus, Caesar, and Croesus).[31]

Socola's argument is convincing and offers internal evidence for the arrangement of the tragedies other than that in the Ellesmere. It must be remembered, however, that throughout Chaucer's poetry generally Fortune is presented both abstractly and allegorically without any perceivable pattern. More pertinent to this study is Chaucer's use of Fortune in the tragedies.

B. L. Jefferson points out that "the *Monk's Tale* is nothing more nor less than a list of illustrations showing the fickleness and emptiness of power so emphasized by Boethius" (p. 85). Willard Farnham, who discusses the *Monk's Tale* in the light of the *De Casibus* tradition, states that the Monk's central theory is that "tragedy is a manifestation of man's powerlessness in an irrational world"; and that "most of the Monk's efforts are open-and-shut tragedies showing how Fortune at her pleasure overthrows the innocent and the wicked alike" (p. 133). Eight of the sixteen victims (Lucifer's fall was beyond the realm of tragedy) are free from any tragic fault whatever; Fortune favored Nero even when he was wicked but suddenly changed and says: "By God! I am to nyce/ To sette a man that is fulfild of vice/ in heigh degree, and emperour hym calle" (B² 3712-14). Thus it is Fortune's whimsicality which is emphasized rather than a causal relationship between Nero's actions and his fall. In the case of Ugolino, furthermore, Chaucer even heightens the pathos of the tragedy. In Dante's *Inferno* Ugolino is guilty of treason and therefore seems to deserve his suffering (even if his children do not). Chaucer leaves Ugolino innocent and thus "shapes the story to fit his main thesis that the world is a realm of causeless misfortune" (Farnham, p. 136). Even when the victims appear more or less

[31] "Chaucer's Development of Fortune in the 'Monk's Tale'", *JEGP*, LXIX (1950), 164.

to deserve their falls, as in the cases of Adam and Antiochus, Chaucer makes no attempt to show a causal connection between the actions of Fortune and of the victims. And in the case of Samson, whose most serious fault is that he trusted a woman – perhaps of all the tragedies the most potentially dramatic for relating the flaw to the fall – Fortune is not even mentioned and Samson's fall is made to occasion the Monk's advice that one should not tell his wife his secret. All of which is to say that if at times Chaucer seems to hint at a connection between man's failings and his fall, he does not do so very clearly or consistently, not nearly so clearly as does Boccaccio. In short a close scrutiny of the tragedies will bear out the truth of Farnham's statement: "One has the feeling that he [the Monk] is never getting far away from his teaching that misfortunes have no rational causes and are expected simply because the world is a vale of tears" (p. 134). At the end of the tragedy of Hercules, the Monk offers a brief moral:

> Lo, who may truste on Fortune any throwe?
> For hym that folweth al this world of prees,
> Er he be war, is ofte yleyd ful lowe.
> Ful wys is he that kan hymselven knowe!
>   (B² 3326-29)

It is the same philosophy as that expressed in *Truth*, where Chaucer tells Vache, "Flee fro the prees, and dwelle with sothfastnesse"; and in *Fortune*, where the Pleintif speaks, "But trewely, no force of thy reddour/ To him that over himself hath the maystrye!" *Fortune*, in fact, might well be Chaucer's commentary on the *Monk's Tale*: "This wrecched worldes transmutacioun,/ As wele or wo, now povre and now honour,/ Withouten ordre or wys discrecioun/ Governed is by Fortunes errour." [32]

Like the fortune motif (in tales other than the Monk's), the transitory theme is generally used dramatically. This theme is most conspicuous in the *Man of Law's Tale*. The Sultan's intention to become a Christian aroused his mother, who plotted to slay him and the Christians (who had come with Constance) alike. Immediately before relating this incident, Chaucer adds to his source the following apostrophe from Innocent III's *De Contemptu Mundi*:

---

[32] Chaucer implies the *de casu* pattern in the *Man of Law's Tale*, B 652-58; and the *Clerk's Tale*, E 810-12. In the latter, he adapts his source to imply this pattern of tragedy.

O sodeyn wo, that evere art successour
To worldly blisse, spreynd with bitternesse!
The ende of the joye of oure worldly labour!
Wo occupieth the fyn of oure gladnesse.
Herke this conseil for thy sikernesse:
Upon thy glade day have in thy mynde
The unwar wo or harm that comth bihynde.
(B¹ 421-27)

This apostrophe sustains the destiny motif introduced in the beginning
of the poem (the impression is that in our state of mortality it is necessary
that woe is ever the successor to worldly bliss) and gives an exalted
significance to the action which is to follow. Granted that this *exclamatio*
is a rhetorical device, it offers an excellent example of Chaucer's ability
to adapt his reading (in this case, part of his translation of *De Contemptu
Mundi*) to his poetry; and the fact that he should recall (even "look up",
since it is a close translation) this passage from the work of Innocent
betrays his interest in the transitory theme generally.

This interest is again evidenced in part of one stanza and all of
another in the *Man of Law's Tale*, both of which are also adapted from
the *De Contemptu Mundi*. Alla and Constance were reunited in Rome,
"And swich a blisse is there bitwix hem two/ That, save the joye that
lasteth evermo,/ Ther is noon lyk that any creature/ Hath seyn or shal,
whil that the world may dure" (B¹ 1075-78; note the seemingly natural
reservation in line 1076, which perhaps betrays Chaucer's ever-present
consciousness of the dichotomy between the mutable and the immutable
worlds). This happiness however lasted but a short time, for before a
year has passed Alla died. Chaucer prepares for the announcement of
his death thus:

But litel while it lasteth, I yow heete,
Joye of this world, for tyme wol nat abyde;
Fro day to nyght it changeth as the tyde.

Who lyved euere in swich delit o day
That hym ne moeved outher conscience,
Or ire, or talent, or som kynnes affray,
Envye, or pride, or passion, or offence?
I ne seye but for this ende this sentence,
That litel while in joye or in plesance
Lasteth the blisse of Alla with Custance.
(B¹ 1132-41)

These lines are another rather close translation of a section of Innocent's
work. The *Man of Law's Tale* was written late in Chaucer's literary
career (most probably about 1390) and it was also around this time

that he translated the *De Contemptu Mundi*.[33] Innocent's work then perhaps relates to the *Man of Law's Tale* as the work of Boethius relates to the *Troilus* and to the *Knight's Tale*, written five to eight years earlier. That Chaucer should almost literally translate essentially the same ideas from both Innocent's and Boethius' works (cf. especially Criseyde's speech, III, 814 ff.) – and interpolate similar ideas of his own into Mars' complaint – certainly indicates a sympathy for the theme. The first chapter of this study has shown how commonplace this theme was throughout the Middle Ages. The idea of the transitoriness of life and of joy was in fact trite. Chaucer's adaptations of this theme, however, from two authorities esteemed by the mediaeval mind lend the theme a gravity, beyond the realm of the trite and the commonplace, which it might not otherwise have had. This fact I think must not be overlooked in determining the extent of Chaucer's fondness for the theme of transitoriness. Finally, at the end of the *Man of Law's Tale* the teller prays: "Now Jhesu Crist, that of his myght may sende/ Joye after wo, governe us in his grace . . ." (B¹ 1160-61). Thus the transitory theme is clearly an intricate part of Chaucer's story of Constance. United with the destiny motif, it turns a bare narrative into one of the finest tales of genuine pathos in all English literature.

The transitory theme is woven into the dramatic texture of the *Merchant's Tale* and is used for ironic effects. And because of its ironic use it provides, perhaps of all Chaucer's works, the clearest expression of his poetical sensibility in regard to the dichotomy between the worlds of mutability and immutability. Most of the marriage material in the first part of the *Merchant's Tale* is taken from the sixth chapter of Deschamps' *Miroir de Mariage*.[34] In this work the description of marriage in its ideal state is suggestive of paradise, but the equation of the two states of bliss is never made. In Chaucer's poem, on the other hand, the equation is made both in the Merchant's conscious irony at the very beginning of the poem and in the unconscious and dramatic irony of January, whose illusion constitutes the main point of the poem.

The Merchant, about to tell the story of January and May, speaks ironically of marriage before he gets very far into his story. Bachelors, he says, "have often peyne and wo;/ On brotel ground they buylde, and brotelnesse/ They fynde, whan they wene sikernesse" (E 1278-80). In fact:

---

[33]   Robinson's edn., p. 692.
[34]   J. L. Lowes, "Chaucer and the *Miroir De Mariage*", *MP*, VIII (1910-11), 165-86. See especially the parallel texts on pp. 170-75.

A wyf is Goddes yifte verraily;
Alle othere manere yiftes hardily,
As londes, rentes, pasture, or commune,
Or moebles, *alle been yiftes of Fortune,*
That passen as a shadwe upon a wal.
But drede nat, if pleynly speke I shal,
A wyf wol laste, and in thyn hous endure,
Wel lenger than thee list, paraventure.
                              (E 1311-18)

The italicized lines of this passage are not found in the *Miroir*. It is significant that Chaucer uses the transitory imagery in the merchant-teller's ironic description of wedlock. A wife, he says, is man's "paradys terrestre" (E 1332); then continues his "ideal" portrayal of wedlock in imagery somewhat reminiscent of that in the love scenes of the *Troilus:*

How myghte a man han any adversitee
That hath a wyf? Certes, I kan nat seye.
The blisse which that is bitwixe hem tweye
Ther may no tonge telle, or herte thynke.
                              (E 1338-41)

The Merchant's "satire not only helps to build up the atmosphere of extreme bitterness that will give the irony of action its unique character, but also allows us to anticipate January's coming troubles more definitely than we could if we were less keenly aware of the teller's real feelings about married life".[35] Before going into January's troubles, however, Chaucer very carefully builds up his illusions of "parfit felicitee" in marriage.

Old January, who is sixty years of age but who feels "nowhere hoor" except on his head, prepares to seek a young and beautiful wife not to exceed twenty years of age. He spurns Justinus' advice that he should choose a wife for her virtue as well as her beauty and then only after long consideration. January finally finds the young and beautiful maiden whom "he wolde han to his wyf,/ To lede in ese and hoolynesse his lyf" (E 1627-28). One thing, however, bothers his conscience; and this he tells to his friends:

"I have", quod he, "herd seyd, ful yoore ago,
Ther may no man han parfite blisses two, –
This is to seye, in erthe and eek in hevene.
For though he kepe hym fro the synnes sevene,
And eek from every branche of thilke tree,
Yet is ther so parfit felicitee

[35] Dempster, *Dramatic Irony*, p. 49.

> And so greet ese and lust in mariage,
> That evere I am agast now in myn age
> That I shal lede now so myrie a lyf,
> So delicat, withouten wo and stryf,
> That I shal have myn hevene in erthe heere.
>
> . . . .
>
> How sholde I thanne, that lyve in swich plesaunce
> As alle wedded men doon with hire wyvys,
> Come to the blisse ther Crist eterne on lyve ys?
>   (E 1637-52)

After January has become blind, the poet says:

> O Januarie, what myghte it thee availle,
> Thogh thou myghte se as fer as shippes saille?
> For as good is blynd deceyved be
> As to be deceyved whan a man may se.
>   (E 2107-10)

Chaucer uses a variation of the transitory theme, namely the perfect felicity and "sikernesse" of marriage as against the imperfect felicity and the vicissitudes of its reality, to portray the foolish January's illusion that marriage is "withouten wo and stryf" and is a "hevene in erthe here". January's folly reaches its climax in the fruit-tree incident.

The *Merchant's Tale* is of course in part a *fabliau* and as such Chaucer's satire against January, while perhaps the bitterest satire he ever wrote, should not be interpreted apart from its particular context. It is primarily January's unrealistic view of marriage which makes him the butt of the satire. Chaucer need not have used the celestial imagery to heighten January's illusion, but he used it to make January's folly appear even more ridiculous and thus to sharpen the point of the *fabliau*.[36] But, parenthetically, the mere fact that he so used this celestial imagery is significant in interpreting the full meaning of this same imagery in the third book of the *Troilus*. The intent and dramatic situations of the two poems are, to be sure, vastly different; but Margaret Schlauch's statement in regard to Chaucer's satire of the courtly lover in Damian is applicable to his uses of the celestial imagery both in the

---

[36] Germaine Dempster (pp. 52-53) thinks that E 1637-54 was inserted by Chaucer to occasion Justinus' advice to January, that a wife may be his "purgatorie" (E 1670), which in turn was dictated by the Wife of Bath's remarks (D 175, 489-90). Regardless of Chaucer's motive for using the heavenly imagery, the irony and satire derive from January's blindness in attributing perfection and perfect stability and happiness to the state of marriage. For another aspect of the transitory theme here, cf. Paul A. Olson, "Chaucer's Merchant and January's 'Heaven in Earthe Heere' ", *ELH*, XXVIII (1961), 208-9.

Troilus and in the *Merchant's Tale*: "The mere act of changing a romantic situation into a *fabliau* implies a critical attitude. The mediaeval *fabliaux* constitute our antidote for the unsubstantial and sugared fare of the romances; they present an antithesis of sharp unconscious criticism, and it is significant that they spring largely from a different class. When the values of one type are permitted to intrude in the other, the result is not only comedy but also social satire, whether deliberate or involuntary." [37] January's visions of perfect bliss in marriage parallel, to some extent, the courtly lover's vision of perfect bliss when he is with his *amie*. Specifically, Chaucer seems to portray this situation in the love scenes of Troilus and Criseyde. If January's illusion of the heavenly bliss of marriage is not an indirect commentary on the illusions of Troilus and Criseyde, is it not at least probable that Chaucer's conscious use of this celestial imagery in the *Merchant's Tale* might indicate his conscious ironical use of this same imagery in the *Troilus*?

The transitory theme has a much less substantial role in the other tales of the Canterbury group. Different aspects of this theme appear scattered throughout and, more often than not, have little or no connection with the plots. In the Introduction to the *Man of Law's Tale*, for example, the Host reminds the company of the late time of the day, which observation occasions the following:

> "Lordynges, the tyme wasteth nyght and day,
> And steleth from us, what pryvely slepynge,
> And what thurgh necligence in oure wakynge,
> As dooth the streem that turneth nevere agayn,
> Descendynge fro the montaigne into playn.
> Wel kan Senec and many a philosophre
> Biwaillen tyme moore than gold in cofre;
> For 'los of catel may recovered be,
> But los of tyme shendeth us', quod he.
> It wol nat come agayn, withouten drede,
> Namoore than wole Malkynes maydenhede,
> Whan she hath lost it in hir wantownesse.
> Lat us nat mowlen thus in ydelnesse."
>
> (B¹ 20-32)

The Host then calls upon the Man of Law to tell his tale. Most of the transitory references which will presently be considered are, like the comment of the Host, digressions of greater or lesser length. The Wife of Bath, for example, refers to the passage of time by interrupting the fond remembrance of her "yowth" and "jolitee" to say: "But age, allas!

---

[37] "Chaucer's 'Merchant's Tale' and Courtly Love", *ELH*, IV (1937), 210.

that al wole envenyme,/ Hath me biraft my beautee and my pith"
(D 474-75). Besides these references to the transitoriness of time one
other group of transitory-references figures significantly in the *Tales,*
those which relate to death.

In the Prologue to the *Clerk's Tale,* the Clerk mentions that he had
learned the tale which he is about to tell from Petrarch. The mention of
Petrarch occasions this digression:

> "Fraunceys Petrak, the lauriat poete,
> Highte this clerk, whos rethorike sweete
> Enlumyned al Ytaille of poetrie,
> As Lynyan dide of philosophie,
> Or lawe, or oother art particuler;
> But deeth, that wol nat suffre us dwellen heer,
> But as it were a twynklyng of an ye,
> Hem bothe hath slayn, and alle shul we dye."
>
>   (E 31-38)

A similar digression on death occurs in the *Reeve's Prologue.* The first
part of the Reeve's "sermonyng" is as it were a portrait of old age
(A 3874-82), but there is no interpretation of old age in terms of the
transitoriness of life, such as that already pointed out in the *Wife of
Bath's Prologue* (D 474-75). A little beyond the middle of his sermon,
however, he says:

> "And yet ik have alwey a coltes tooth,
> As many a yeer as it is passed henne
> Syn that my tappe of lif bigan to renne.
> For sikerly, whan I was bore, anon
> Deeth drough the tappe of lyf and leet it gon;
> And ever sithe hath so the tappe yronne
> Til that almoost al empty is the tonne.
> The streem of lyf now droppeth on the chymbe.
> The sely tonge may wel rynge and chymbe
> Of wrecchednesse that passed is ful yoore;
> With olde folk, save dotage, is namoore!"
>
>   (A 3888-98)

It was seen in Chapter I that the idea of death's beginning at birth goes
back at least to classical times. This image of Death's drawing the tap
from the barrel, however, is so far as I know original with Chaucer.
Tyrwhitt admired line 3895, "The streem of lyf now droppeth on the
chymbe", and said that "the imagery is very exact and beautiful" (Skeat,
V, 114). This figure is one of the most beautiful in all Chaucer's poetry
and the entire image is among the most vivid of his imagery. In view of

Chaucer's general interest in the transitoriness of life, I suspect that the image is not simply conventional or commonplace but that it derived from a sensibility forever alerted to the sound of the drops "on the chymbe".[38]

The final instance of the transitory theme which I shall focus upon occurs in the *Miller's Tale*. In this tale the old "lewed" carpenter is contrasted with the young "hende" Nicholas, clerk, astrologer, trickster, and lover. When Nicholas had determined upon a plan to trick the simple old man, he went to his room and stayed there for two days. Upon learning this, John, thinking Nicholas ill, exclaims:

> "I am adrad, by Seint Thomas,
> It stondeth nat aright with Nicholas.
> God shilde that he deyde sodeynly!
> This world is now ful tikel, sikerly.
> I saugh to-day a cors yborn to chirche
> That now, on Monday last, I saugh hym wirche."
> (A 3425-30)

Chaucer uses this dialogue to characterize the "sely" carpenter: the simplicity of the old carpenter is seen in his immediate association of the ill Nicholas and the corpse; and the extent of his sensibility is revealed in the fact that only six days previously he had seen him "wirche". Perhaps more importantly, however, the revelation of John's primitive sensibility here (and in l. 3450) prepares for his gullibility in believing the story of Nicholas regarding the destruction of the world. In short, the superstitious realization of a "ful tikel" world encompasses even the possibility of a flood which will drown all mankind.

These references to the fortune and to the transitory themes constitute the more important and conspicuous uses of the mutability theme in the *Canterbury Tales*. There are, moreover, many incidental references to these themes which are not so important but which indicate Chaucer's abiding interest in mutability and show the extent to which this concept occupied his poetic sensibility. In the *Merchant's Tale*, for example, we find: "But worldly joye may nat alwey dure/ To Januarie, ne to no creature" (E 2055-56); in the *Nun's Priest's Tale*, "For evere the latter ende of joye is wo./ God woot that worldly joye is soone ago" (B² 4395-96); and in the same tale there are two incidental references to fortune (B² 4189-90, 4593-94). In the *Wife of Bath's Tale*, "gentillesse"

[38] See A. H. MacLaine, "Chaucer's Wine-Cask Image: Word Play in *The Reeve's Prologue*", *Medium Aevum*, XXXI (1962), 129-31; and for the old age tradition, George R. Coffman, "Old Age from Horace to Chaucer. Some Literary Affinities and Adventures of an Idea", *Speculum*, IX (1934), 249-77.

is opposed to "temporel thyng, that man may hurte and mayme" (D 1132); when the "riotoures thre" of the *Pardoner's Tale* find the treasure, they immediately exclaim, "This tresor hath Fortune unto us yiven" (C 779); even the falcon in the *Squire's Tale* tells Canacee, about her mate: "But finally, thus atte laste it stood,/ That Fortune wolde that he moste twynne/ Out of that place which that I was inne" (F 576-78); and the moral which the Host draws from the sad story of the beautiful Virginia, in the *Physician's Tale,* is "that yiftes of Fortune and of Nature/ Been cause of deeth to many a creature" (C 295-96). Again, in the *Miller's Tale* we find, "A man woot litel what hym shal bityde" (A 3450); in the *Physician's Tale,* "Beth war, for no man woot whom God wol smyte/ In no degree . . ." (C 278-79); and in the *Shipman's Tale,* salutations and gestures accorded to feminine beauty and personality "passen as dooth a shadwe upon the wal" (B² 1199). In one of Chaucer's few additions to Petrarch's Griselda story, he has the more serious folk of the town apostrophize the inconstancy of the mob: " 'O stormy peple! unsad and evere untrewe!/ Ay undiscreet and chaungynge as a fane!/ Delitynge evere in rumbul that is newe,/ For lyk the moone ay wexe ye and wane!' " (E 995-98) [39] Twice again Chaucer refers to inconstancy, both times to that of men: for the Manciple, "Flessh is so newefangel, with meschaunce,/ That we ne konne in nothyng han plesaunce/ That sowneth into vertu any while" (H 193-95); and for the falcon in the *Squire's Tale,* "Men loven of propre kynde newefangelnesse,/ As briddes doon that men in cages fede." If one of these birds escapes he "wol spurne adoun his cuppe,/ And to the wode he wole, and wormes ete" (F 610-11, 616-17). Finally, in the same tale, Canacee's question to the suffering falcon epitomizes the mutability theme as it appears in the *Canterbury Tales*: " 'Is this for sorwe of deeth or los of love?/ For, as I trowe, thise been causes two/ That causen moost a gentil herte wo;/ Of oother harm it nedeth nat to speke' " (F 450-53). In seventeen of the twenty-three tales which have been considered here, some aspect of the mutability theme appears, at least incidentally (and while the theme does not occur in the *Reeve's Tale,* it does appear in his *Prologue*).[40]

Now to consider Chaucer's use of the other mutability themes in the *Tales*. In the *Canterbury Tales* (other than in the *Knight's Tale*),

[39] See S. K. Heninger, Jr., "The Concept of Order in Chaucer's *Clerk's Tale*", *JEGP,* LVI (1957), 382-95. Heninger's discussion of the mutability elements in *The Clerk's Tale* in their relation to order (*passim*) is thorough and illuminating.
[40] See the following lines for other fortune and transitory references: B² 2640-50, 3972; C 22-23; I 470-74, 1068, 1076-80.

Chaucer makes little use of those mutability themes which are not properly speaking identifiable with the transitory theme. His only use of the decay of the world theme, for example, occurs in the *Clerk's Tale* and is his own addition to his source. At the end of his narrative the Clerk speaks the following about Walter's son:

> His sone succedeth in his heritage
> In reste and pees, after his fader day,
> And fortunate was eek in mariage,
> Al putte he nat his wyf in greet assay.
> *This world is nat so strong, it is no nay,*
> *As it hath been in olde tymes yoore.* ....
>
> (E 1135-40)

The *ubi sunt* formula in the *Parson's Tale* has no known source: "Where been thanne the gaye robes, and the softe shetes, and the smale shertes?" (I 197). It is probable that this formula is not Chaucer's own but its occurrence in the *Tales* is nevertheless significant.

The final motif in this category is the same as that expressed by Palamon in his prison-speech: how can an all-good God permit evil? In the *Man of Law's Tale*, the motif takes the form of innocent-suffering. When the constable receives the counterfeit letter from Alla's mother, wherein he is told to exile Constance, he exclaims:

> "O myghty God, if that it be thy wille,
> Sith thou art rightful juge, how may it be
> That thou wolt suffren innocentz to spille,
> And wikked folk regne in prosperitee?"
>
> (B¹ 813-16)

Similarly in Dorigen's complaint the problem is why should an all-wise and "stable" God create something which apparently serves no purpose and which is the means whereby men lose their lives?

> "Eterne God, that thurgh thy purveiaunce
> Ledest the world by certein governaunce,
> In ydel, as men seyn, ye no thyng make.
> But, Lord, thise grisly feendly rokkes blake,
> That semen rather a foul confusion
> Of werk than any fair creacion
> Of swich a parfit wys God and a stable,
> Why han ye wroght this werk unresonable?
> For by this werk, south, north, ne west, ne eest,
> Ther nys yfostred man, ne bryd, ne beest;
> It dooth no good, to my wit, but anoyeth.
> Se ye nat, Lord, how mankynde it destroyeth?

An hundred thousand bodyes of mankynde
Han rokkes slayn, al be they nat in mynde,
Which mankynde is so fair part of thy werk
That thou it madest lyk to thyn owene merk.
Thanne semed it ye hadde a greet chiertee
Toward mankynde; but how thanne may it bee
That ye swiche meenes make it to destroyen?
Whiche meenes do no good, but evere anoyen?"

(F 865-84)

While this complaint of Dorigen makes for a rather long digression, it is in fact motivated dramatically: her fear of "thise grisly feendly rokkes blake" for her husband's life ultimately brings about her spontaneous and playful promise to Aurelius. These, then, are the only mutability motifs other than those of fortune and transitoriness which are to be found in the tales presently under consideration.

The *Canterbury Tales* represent Chaucer's most complete development as an artist. There are many reasons for this. First, Chaucer's narrative technique found its fullest expression in the world of observation and experience, as in the *Canterbury Tales*. Second, the dramatic framework of a pilgrimage offered him an opportunity to display a great variety of characters, moods, situations, and social classes; through this dramatic interplay of characters, he was able to reveal the universality of character through the particularity of the individual. Not the least important element of Chaucer's artistic success in the *Canterbury Tales*, however, is his "final resolution" of the antithesis expressed in his earlier works, "abstract moral theory on the one hand and vital human art on the other" (p. 109, *supra*). Specifically, as Chaucer accepted the world of experience for his artistic scope he concomitantly abandoned, but never completely, the *De Contemptu Mundi* idea. This may seem obvious and in fact a logical necessity, but the full implications of Chaucer's final resolution of this antithesis can be seen only in the light of his earlier works.

The only two pre-Canterbury period poems which pose serious problems are the *Parliament of Fowls* and the *Troilus*. The reason for this is that the *De Contemptu Mundi* idea is juxtaposed with the exaltation of courtly love. It is significant that outside of the shorter poems (especially *Truth*) the clearly defined *De Contemptu Mundi* occurs only in these two poems. Perhaps this fact, plus Chaucer's rejection of courtly love in the *Tales*, led Bronson to conclude that the subject of courtly love was radically incompatible with Chaucer's temperament (p. 112 *supra*) and then to proceed with his interpretation of the

Parliament accordingly. While this statement is no doubt true in view of Chaucer's subsequent poetry (and the Retraction), it cannot be justified by the *Parliament* itself. At the time Chaucer wrote the *Parliament*, it might just as validly be said that the *De Contemptu Mundi* idea was incompatible with his temperament! In short there is a perceivable, progressive interplay between Chaucer's art and his "moral theory". The pattern, as I see it, is this: in the *Parliament*, Chaucer's sensibility was indeed divided. It was perfectly allowable in the mediaeval poetic to contrapoise lore and lust, the spirtual and the sensuous, the *Somnium* and the Garden of Love.[41] This Chaucer did and in this sense he was typically mediaeval. The *Parliament* itself offers absolutely no evidence that Chaucer was seeking or even thought about a final resolution of these antithetical ideas. At this point, then, Chaucer was still working within the framework of the mediaeval convention and poetic. The *Troilus*, however, constitutes an intermediate stage in Chaucer's intellectual development. It is true that Chaucer praises courtly love in the texture of the poem and that he denies the courtly love ideal in the epilogue. There is, however, a genuine, integrated ambivalence in the *Troilus* itself. Here Chaucer, by converting Boccaccio's tale into a *de casu* tragedy and by implicitly criticizing the courtly love ideal in his use of the celestial imagery at the very height of the poem (or at least by pointing up its illusory and transitory nature), is working away from the convention of courtly love and toward the world of reality which will eventually be portrayed in the *Canterbury Tales*. The predominant motif in the epilogue is the transitoriness of all earthly love and it is this motif which is woven throughout the poem at every turn.

In the *Knight's Tale* there is further progression. There is, certainly, no deliberate idealization of courtly love in the *Knight's Tale*; here Chaucer maintains the courtly love conventions, but only in so far as these conventions are equated with the noble life. Unlike his use of these conventions in the *Troilus*, they are the vehicle of the poem's underlying meaning rather than ends in themselves. The main problem of the poem, I think, is order *versus* disorder or immutability *versus* mutability: Chaucer is seeking, actually, an order or pattern whereby he may interpret the mutable world of experience. This he finds in the

---

[41] Wolfgang Clemen, *Der Junge Chaucer*, Kölner Anglistische Arbeiten (Bochum-Langendreer, 1938), pp. 168-72, argues from mediaeval literary convention that the *Somnium* provides the *lore* mingled with the *lust* of the poem, and that it provides a serious contrast before the gay play begins. The transition is indeed abrupt, he says, but not for the Middle Ages.

speech of Theseus, which is the positive answer to the *De Contemptu
Mundi* expression of Egeus. Chaucer's mutable and immutable worlds
are finally reconciled; it is even possible to see in this final affirmation
of order in the universe a foreshadowing of the Renaissance's insistence
upon this same order. It is the beginning of the end of the *De Contemptu
Mundi* idea. It was the chaotic, contaminating matter of this world, as
was pointed out earlier in this study, which introduced the *De Contemptu
Mundi* idea into Plato's philosophy. The ending of the *Knight's Tale*
then is significant for two reasons: the expression of a final affirmation
of order in the world in the speech of Theseus and the rejection of the
courtly love code in the marriage of Emily and Palamon.[42] Thus the
way is open for the portrayal of the world of experience in the remaining
tales.

In the *Canterbury Tales* Chaucer's acceptance of the world was never
complete. The "final resolution" of which Goffin speaks was tilted
heavily on the side of the immutable world. Chaucer's rejection of
courtly love (he satirizes it in the *Merchant's* and in the *Nun's Priest's
Tales*) seems to have obviated the necessity for the out-and-out *De
Contemptu Mundi* expressions. But while there is no definite, strong
expression of repudiation of the world in the *Tales* (with the exception
of the Retraction), such as is found in the epilogue to the *Troilus*, it has
been pointed out that the transitory theme plays a very substantial part
throughout. Its importance and function in fact have been too often
overlooked. From youth through maturity, the transitoriness of all earthly things is the most abiding aspect of Chaucer's poetry. With the exception of the theme of love no other is more predominant; yet, in almost
every instance, it is the transitoriness of love which finally occupies
Chaucer's attention. The mature Chaucer generally used the theme more
dramatically than he did in his earlier works; if it is not incorporated
into the plot, as are the complaints of Dorigen, for example, it is more
often than not incorporated into a rhetorical device which has a direct
bearing on the tale itself. Chaucer's interest in the theme never waned;
the artist merely waxed and so learned better to control his interest. One
might even, incidentally, view Chaucer's development as an artist in
terms of his use of the mutability theme. As his artistic scope became
more and more oriented toward the world of experience, so did the
transitory motif become more predominant and the *De Contemptu*

[42]   Cf. Gervase Mathew, "Marriage and *Amour Courtois* in Late Fourteenth-
Century England", *Essays Presented to Charles Williams* (Oxford, 1947), pp.
128-35.

Mundi motif tend to disappear. If the *De Contemptu Mundi* expression of the epilogue to the *Troilus* was religiously motivated, this motivation was not unrelated to Chaucer's gradual moving away from mediaeval literary conventions in general and toward the world of the *Canterbury Tales* in particular. It has been pointed out that the transitory theme is part of, if not intricately related to, the *De Contemptu Mundi* theme. The former is, however, compatible not only with courtly love poetry but with all subject matter of poetry; Shakespeare's wide use of the theme suggests this. The latter, however, is of course not compatible with love poetry and is in fact suitable only for religious poetry. This is seen in Chaucer's Retraction where he revokes his love poetry as "enditynges of worldly vanitees". The *Contemptus Mundi* of the Retraction, in fact, is the fullest expression and logical outcome of the mutability motifs in Chaucer's poetry. In the *Tales*, however, Chaucer's "compromise" was the acceptance of the world in all its transitoriness. From this acceptance stems much of the tension and universality of his poetry.

BIBLIOGRAPHY OF WORKS CITED

BOOKS

Aristotle, *Aristotle: On the Heavens*, trans. W. K. C. Guthrie (Cambridge, Mass., 1939).

——, *De Mundo*, ed. and trans. D. J. Furley, in *The Loeb Classical Library* (Cambridge, 1955).

Ayenbite of Inwyt, ed. Richard Morris, in EETS, Original Series, No. 23 (London, 1866).

Bede, *Bede: A History of the English Church and People*, trans. Leo Sherley-Price, in Penguin Books (Baltimore, 1955).

Bennett, J. A. W., *The Parlement of Foules: An Interpretation* (Oxford, 1957).

The Holy Bible, translated from the Vulgate (the Douay-Rheims version) (New York, 1938).

Boccaccio, *The Filostrato of Giovanni Boccaccio: A Translation with Parallel Text*, trans. N. E. Griffin and A. B. Myrick (Philadelphia, 1929).

Boethius, *Boethius' Consolation of Philosophy. Translated from the Latin by George Colvile*, 1556, ed. Ernest Belfort Bax, in *Tudor Library* (London, 1897).

Braddy, Haldeen, *Chaucer and the French Poet Graunson* (Baton Rouge, 1947).

Brandon, S. G. F., *Time and Mankind: An Historical and Philosophical Study of Mankind's Attitude to the Phenomena of Change* (New York, 1951).

Bronson, Bertrand H., *In Search of Chaucer* (Toronto, 1963).

Brooke, Stopford, *English Literature From the Beginning to the Norman Conquest* (London, 1930).

Brown, Carleton, *A Register of Middle English Religious and Didactic Verse*, 2 vols. (Oxford, 1916-20).

Brown, Carleton, and R. H. Robbins, *The Index of Middle English Verse* (New York, 1943).

Brusendorff, Aage, *The Chaucer Tradition* (London, 1925).

Bultot, Robert, *Christianisme et Valeurs humaines: La Doctrine du mépris du monde*, IV: *Le XIe siècle*, pt. 1: *Pierre Damien*; and pt. 2: *Jean de Fécamp, Hermann Contract, Roger de Caen, Anselme de Canterbury* (Louvain, Belgium, 1963, 1964).

Bury, J. B., *The Idea of Progress* (London, 1928).

Chambers, E. K., and F. Sidgwick (eds.), *Early English Lyrics* (London, 1911).

Charles, R. H., *Eschatology*, in Schocken Books (New York, 1963).

Chaucer, Geoffrey, *Canterbury Tales by Geoffrey Chaucer*, ed. J. M. Manly (New York, 1928).

——, *Chaucer's Translation of Boethius's "De Consolatione Philosophiae"*, ed. Richard Morris, in EETS, Extra Series, No. 5 (London, 1868).

Chaucer, Geoffrey, *The Complete Works of Geoffrey Chaucer*, ed. F. N. Robinson, 2nd ed. (Boston, 1957).

——, *The Complete Works of Geoffrey Chaucer*, ed. W. W. Skeat, 2nd ed., 7 vols. (Oxford, 1894-1900).

Cicero, *De Re Publica, De Legibus*, trans. C. W. Keyes, in *The Loeb Classical Library* (London, 1928).

——, *Macrobius: Commentary on the Dream of Scipio*, trans. William Harris Stahl (New York, 1952).

Clemen, Wolfgang, *Chaucer's Early Poetry*, trans. C. A. M. Sym (London, 1965).

——, *Der junge Chaucer: Grundlagen und Entwicklung Seiner Dichtung*, Kölner Anglistische Arbeiten (Bochum-Langendreer, 1938).

Coghill, Neville, *The Poet Chaucer* (Oxford, 1955).

Coulton, G. G., *Life in the Middle Ages*, 4 vols. in 1 (New York, 1933).

Curry, W. C., *Chaucer and the Mediaeval Sciences* (New York, 1960).

Dante, *The Divine Comedy*, trans. J. A. Carlyle, Thomas Okey, and P. H. Wicksteed, in The Modern Library (New York, 1950).

——, *Purgatory*, trans. Dorothy Sayers, in Penguin Classics (Edinburgh, 1955).

De Lorris, Guillaume, and Jean de Meun, *Le Roman de la Rose*, ed. Ernest Langlois, 5 vols. (Paris, 1914-1924).

——, *The Romance of the Rose*, trans. F. S. Ellis, 3 vols. (London, 1926-1940).

Dempster, Germaine, *Dramatic Irony in Chaucer* (New York, 1959).

Deschamps, Eustache, *Œuvres Complètes*, in SATF, 11 vols. (Paris, 1878-1903).

Empedocles, "On Purifications", in *The First Philosophers of Greece*, trans. Arthur Fairbanks (London, 1898).

Everett, Dorothy, *Essays on Middle English Literature*, ed. Patricia Kean (Oxford, 1959).

Fansler, D. S., *Chaucer and the Roman de la Rose* (New York, 1914).

Farnham, Willard, *The Medieval Heritage of Elizabethan Tragedy* (New York, 1936).

Fitts, Dudley, ed., *Greek Plays in Modern Translation* (New York, 1947).

Freeman, Kathleen, *Ancilla to the Pre-Socratic Philosophers* (Oxford, 1948).

Furnivall, Frederick J., *Trial-Forewords to My "Parallel-Text Edition of Chaucer's Minor Poems"*, Chaucer Society, Second Series, No. 6 (London, 1871).

Gill, Sister Anne Barbara, *Paradoxical Patterns in Chaucer's Troilus: An Explanation of the Palinode* (Washington, D. C., 1960).

Gilson, Étienne, *History of Christian Philosophy in the Middle Ages* (New York, 1955).

——, *Les Idées et les Lettres* (Paris, 1955).

Goldschmidt, Victor, *Le système stoïcien et l'idée de temps* (Paris, 1953).

The Greek Anthology, trans. W. R. Paton, in *The Loeb Classical Library*, 5 vols. (New York and London, 1916-1918).

Guitton, Jean, *Le Temps et l'éternité chez Plotin et Saint Augustin* (Paris, 1959).

Hesiod, *Hesiod: The Homeric Hymns and Homerica*, trans. Hugh G. Evelyn-White, in *The Loeb Classical Library* (New York, 1926).

Homer, *Homer: The Iliad*, trans. A. T. Murray, in *The Loeb Classical Library*. 2 vols. (New York, 1928).

Horace, *Horace: The Odes and Epodes*, trans. C. E. Bennett, in *The Loeb Classical Library* (New York, 1927).

Horstmann, C., ed., *Yorkshire Writers*. 2 vols. (London and New York, 1895-1896).

Huizinga, J., *The Waning of the Middle Ages*, in Anchor Books (New York, 1956).

Innocent III, *Lotharii Cardinalis De Miseria Humane Conditionis*, ed. Michele Maccarrone, *In aedibus Thesauri Mundi* (Lugano, Switzerland, 1955).

Jefferson, B. L., *Chaucer and the Consolation of Philosophy of Boethius* (Princeton, 1917).

Johnson, Aubrey R., *The Vitality of the Individual in the Thought of Ancient Israel* (Cardiff, U. of Wales Press, 1949).

Jones, Richard Foster, *Ancients and Moderns: A Study of the Background of the "Battle of the Books"*, in *Washington University Studies in Language and Literature* (St. Louis, 1936).

Kirby, T. A., *Chaucer's Troilus: A Study in Courtly Love* (Baton Rouge, 1940).

Kirk, G. S., *Heraclitus: The Cosmic Fragments* (Cambridge, 1954).

Kittredge, G. L., *Chaucer and His Poetry* (Cambridge, Mass., 1915).

Langlois, Ernest, *Origines et Sources du Roman de la Rose* (Paris, 1891).

Lewis, C. S., *The Allegory of Love*, in Galaxy Books (New York, 1958).

Lovejoy, Arthur O., *The Great Chain of Being*, in Harper Torchbooks (New York, 1960).

Lovejoy, Arthur O., Gilbert Chinard, George Boas, and Ronald S. Crane (eds.), *A Documentary History of Primitivism and Related Ideas* (Baltimore, 1935).

Lowes, John L., *Geoffrey Chaucer* (Oxford, 1934).

Lucretius, *De Rerum Natura*, trans. W. H. D. Rouse, in *The Loeb Classical Library* (New York, 1928).

Lumiansky, R. M., *Of Sondry Folk* (Austin, 1955).

Lydgate, John, *Lydgate's Troy Book*, ed. Henry Bergen, in EETS, Extra Series, Nos. 97, 103, 106, 126, 2 vols. (London, 1906-1935).

Machaut, Guillaume de, *Œuvres de Guillaume de Machaut*, in SATF, 3 vols. (vols. 102-104) (Paris, 1908, 1911, 1921).

Mâle, E., *L'Art religieux à la fin du moyen âge en France* (Paris, 1908).

Malone, Kemp, *Chapters on Chaucer* (Baltimore, 1951).

Marcus Aurelius, *The Meditations of Marcus Aurelius*, trans. George Long, in *Harvard Classics* (New York, 1909).

Marrou, H.-I., *L'ambivalence du temps de l'histoire chez saint Augustin* (Paris, 1950).

Mommsen, Theodor E., *Medieval and Renaissance Studies* (Ithaca, 1957).

Morris, Richard, *An Old English Miscellany*, in EETS, Original Series, No. 49 (London, 1872).

Muscatine, Charles, *Chaucer and the French Tradition* (Berkeley, 1957).

Ovid, *The Metamorphoses of Ovid*, trans. A. E. Watts (Berkeley, 1954).

——, *Ovid: The Art of Love, and Other Poems*, trans. J. H. Mozley, in *The Loeb Classical Library* (Cambridge, 1947).

——, *Ovid: Metamorphoses*, trans. Frank Justus Miller, in *The Loeb Classical Library*, 2 vols. (New York, 1926).

Patch, H. R., *The Goddess Fortuna in Mediaeval Literature* (Cambridge, Mass., 1927).

Patrologiae Cursus Completus, ed. J. P. Migne, Series Latina (Paris, 1879-87).

Plato, *The Collected Dialogues of Plato*, ed. Edith Hamilton and Huntington Cairns, *Bollingen Series*, LXXI (New York, 1961).

——, *Plato's Phaedo*, ed. and trans. R. S. Bluck (London, 1955).

——, *The Republic* and *Timaeus*, in *The Dialogues of Plato*, ed. and trans. B. Jowett, 4 vols. (New York, 1871).

——, *Symposium*, trans. W. R. M. Lamb, in *The Loeb Classical Library* (New York, 1925).

Poulet, Georges, *Studies in Human Time*, trans. Elliott Coleman, in Harper Torchbooks (New York, 1959).

Raby, J. F. E., *A History of Christian-Latin Poetry From the Beginnings to the Close of the Middle Ages* (Oxford, 1953).

Robertson, D. W., Jr., *A Preface to Chaucer* (Princeton, 1962).

Root, R. K., *The Poetry of Chaucer* (Gloucester, Mass., 1957).

——, ed., *The Book of Troilus and Criseyde by Geoffrey Chaucer* (Princeton, 1926).

Ruggiers, Paul G., *The Art of the Canterbury Tales* (Madison, Wisconsin, 1965).

St. Cyprian, "On the Mortality", in *The Ante-Nicene Fathers*, ed. A. Roberts and J. Donaldson, 10 vols. (Buffalo, 1885-1897), V, 469-75.

Salter, Elizabeth, *Chaucer: The Knight's Tale and The Clerk's Tale* (London, 1962).

Schaff, Philip, ed., *A Select Library of the Nicene and Post-Nicene Fathers*, 14 vols. (Buffalo, 1886-1889).

——, and Henry Wace, eds., *A Select Library of Nicene and Post-Nicene Fathers of the Christian Church*, Second Series, 14 vols. (Grand Rapids, 1952-1956).

Seneca, *Seneca: Moral Essays*, trans. John W. Basore, in *The Loeb Classical Library*, 3 vols. (London and New York, 1928-1932).

Sophocles, *Sophocles*, trans. Francis Storr, in *The Loeb Classical Library*, 2 vols. (New York, 1924).

Speirs, John, *Chaucer the Maker* (London, 1950).

Spencer, Theodore, *Death and Elizabethan Tragedy: A Study of Convention and Opinion in the Elizabethan Drama* (Cambridge, Mass., 1936).

Sypherd, W. O., *Studies in Chaucer's Hous of Fame*, Chaucer Society, Second Series. No. 39 (London, 1907).

Tatlock, J. S. P., *The Development and Chronology of Chaucer's Works*, Chaucer Society, Second Series, No. 37 (London, 1907).

Taylor, A. E., *A Commentary on Plato's Timaeus* (Oxford, 1928).

Thomas à Kempis, *The Imitation of Christ*, ed. Edward J. Klein, trans. Richard Whitford (New York, 1941).

Villon, François, *The Complete Works of François Villon*, trans. Anthony Bonner (New York, 1960).

Voegelin, Eric, *The World of the Polis*, Vol. II of *Order and History* (Baton Rouge, 1957).

Vossler, Karl, *Mediaeval Culture: An Introduction to Dante and His Times*, trans. William Cranston Lawton, 2 vols. (New York, 1929).

Wells, J. E., *A Manual of the Writings in Middle English, 1050-1400* (New Haven, 1916).

Whitehead, Alfred North, *Adventures of Ideas* (New York, 1935).

Willey, Basil, *The Seventeenth-Century Background*, in Anchor Books (New York, 1953).

Williams, Margaret, *Word-Hoard* (London, 1946).

ARTICLES

Battaglia, S., "Schemi lirici nell'arte del Boccaccio", *Archivum Romanicum*, XIX (1935), 61-78.

Baum, Paull F., "Chaucer's 'The House of Fame'", *ELH*, VIII (1941), 248-56.

Becker, C. H., "*Ubi Sunt* qui ante nos in mundo fuere", *Islamstudien*, I (1924), 501-508.

Bethurum, Dorothy, "The Center of the *Parlement of Foules*", *Essays in Honor of Walter Clyde Curry*, Nashville, 1954, 39-50.

——, "Chaucer's Point of View as Narrator in the Love Poems", *PMLA*, LXXIV (1959), 511-20.

Braddy, Haldeen, "The Date of Chaucer's *Lak of Steadfastnesse*", *JEGP*, XXXVI (1937), 481-90.

Bright, James W., "The *'ubi sunt'* Formula", *MLN*, VIII (1893), 187-88.

Bronson, Bertrand H., "Chaucer's *Hous of Fame*: Another Hypothesis", *University of California Publications in English*, III, No. 4 (1934), 171-92.

——, "In Appreciation of Chaucer's *Parlement of Foules*", *University of California Publications in English*, III, No. 5 (1935), 193-224.

——, "*The Book of the Duchess* Re-opened", *PMLA*, LXVII (1952), 863-81.

——, "*The Parlement of Foules* Revisited", *ELH*, XV (1948), 247-60.

Bultot, Robert, "Mépris du monde, misère et dignité de l'homme dans la pensée d'Innocent III", *Cahiers de civilisation médiévales (X-XII siècles)*, IV (1961), 441-56.

Cook, Albert S., "Chaucerian Papers I: Prologue 1-11", *Transactions of the Connecticut Academy of Arts and Sciences*, 23 (1919), 5-21.

Cross, J. E., " 'Ubi sunt' Passages in Old English – Sources and Relationships", *Vetenskaps-Societetens i Lund Arsbok* (1956), 25-41.

Cumming, William P., "The Influence of Ovid's *Metamorphoses* on Spenser's 'Mutabilitie' Cantos", *SP*, XXVIII (1931), 241-56.

Denomy, A. J., "The Two Mortalities of Chaucer's *Troilus and Criseyde*", *Transactions of the Royal Society of Canada*, Sec. 2, XLIV (1950), 35-46.

Fairchild, H. N., "Active Arcite, Contemplative Palamon", *JEGP*, XXVI (1927), 285-93.

Farnham, Willard, "The Lost Innocence of Poetry", in *Essays in Criticism by Members of the Department of English, University of California, University of California Publications in English*, I (1929), 25-47.

Frank, Robert Worth, Jr., "Structure and Meaning in the 'Parlement of Foules' ", *PMLA*, LXXI (1956), 530-39.

Frost, William, "An Interpretation of Chaucer's *Knight's Tale*", *RES*, XXV (1949), 289-304.

Garrett, A. C., "Studies on Chaucer's *Hous of Fame*", *Harvard Studies and Notes*, V (1897), 151-75.

Goffin, R. C., "Heaven and Earth in the 'Parlement of Foules' ", *MLR*, XXXI (1936), 493-99.

Greenlaw, Edwin, "Spenser and Lucretius", *SP*, XVII (1920), 439-64.

Ham, E. B., "*Knight's Tale*, 38", *ELH*, XVII (1950), 252-61.

Heninger, S. K., Jr., "The Concept of Order in Chaucer's *Clerk's Tale*", *JEGP*, LVI (1957), 382-95.

Hulbert, J. R., "What was Chaucer's Aim in the *Knight's Tale*?", *SP*, XXVI (1929), 375-85.

Huppé, Bernard F., "*The Wanderer*: Theme and Structure", *JEGP*, 42 (1943), 516-38.

Kellogg, Alfred L., "On the Tradition of Troilus's Vision of the Little Earth", *Mediaeval Studies*, XXII (1960), 204-13.

Kurtz, Benjamin, "Gifer the Worm: An Essay Toward the History of an Idea", *University of California Publications in English*, II, No. 2 (1929), 235-61.

Lowes, J. L., "Chaucer and Dante's 'Convivio' ", *MP*, XIII (1915), 19-33.

——, "Chaucer and the *Miroir De Mariage*", *MP*, VIII (1910-11), 165-86.

Lumiansky, R. M., "Chaucer's *Parlement of Foules*: A Philosophical Interpretation", *RES*, XXIV (1948), 81-89.

McDonald, Charles O., "An Interpretation of Chaucer's *Parlement of Foules*", *Speculum*, XXX (1955), 444-57.

Mogan, Joseph J., Jr., "Further Aspects of Mutability in Chaucer's *Troilus*", *Papers on English Language and Literature*, I (1965), 72-77.

Northup, Clark S., "*Ubi Sunt* Heroes?", *MLN*, XXVIII (1913), 106-107.
Nyrop, Kr., "Note sur une Ballade de Villon", *Bulletin de l'Académie royale des Sciences et des Lettres de Danemark*, II (1907), 78-82.
Owen, Charles A., Jr., "The Role of the Narrator in the 'Parlement of Foules' ", *College English*, XIV (1953), 264-69.
Patch, H. R., "Chaucer and Lady Fortune", *MLR*, XXII (1927), 377-88.
Patrick, G. T. W., "A Further Study of Heraclitus", *The American Journal of Psychology*, I (1888), 643-73.
Pratt, Robert A., "Chaucer's Use of the *Teseida*", *PMLA*, LXII (1947), 598-621.
——, " 'Joye After Wo' in the *Knight's Tale*", *JEGP*, LVII (1958), 416-23.
Rambeau, A., "Chaucer's 'House of Fame' in Seinem Verhältniss zu Dante's 'Divina Commedia' ", *Englische Studien*, III (1870), 209-68.
Rand, E. K., "Mediaeval Gloom and Mediaeval Uniformity", *Speculum*, I (1926), 253-68.
Robertson, D. W., Jr., "Chaucerian Tragedy", *ELH*, XIX (1952), 1-37.
Ruggiers, Paul G., "The Unity of Chaucer's *House of Fame*", *SP*, L (1953), 16-29.
Schlauch, Margaret, "Chaucer's 'Merchant's Tale' and Courtly Love", *ELH*, IV (1937), 201-12.
Silverstein, Theodore, "Chaucer's Modest and Homely Poem: The *Parlement*", *MP*, LVI (1959), 270-76.
Socola, E. M., "Chaucer's Development of Fortune in the 'Monk's Tale' ", *JEGP*, XLIX (1950), 159-71.
Stillwell, Gardiner, "Chaucer's 'O Sentence' in the *Hous of Fame*", *English Studies*, XXXVII (1956), 149-57.
——, "Convention and Individuality in Chaucer's *Complaint of Mars*", *PQ*, XXXV (1956), 69-89.
Tupper, Frederick, Jr., "The *ubi sunt* Formula", *MLN*, VIII (1893), 253-54.
Underwood, Dale, "The First of *The Canterbury Tales*", *ELH*, XXVI (1959), 455-69.
Varnhagen, Hermann, "Noch einmal zu den sprüchen des heiligen Bernhard", *Anglia*, III (1880), 285-92.
Vasiliev, A., "Medieval Ideas of the End of the World: West and East", *Byzantion*, 16 (1942-43), 462-502.
Wenzel, Siegfried, "Chaucer's Troilus of Book IV", *PMLA*, LXXXIX (1964), 542-47.
Williamson, George, "Mutability, Decay, and Seventeenth-Century Melancholy", *ELH*, II (1935), 121-50.
Wilson, H. S., "The *Knight's Tale* and the *Teseida* Again", *UTQ*, XVIII (1949), 131-46.
Wright, G. Ernest, "The Faith of Israel", *The Interpreter's Bible*, Nashville, 1952. I, 349-89.

UNPUBLISHED ITEMS

Gilbert, Jack G., "The 'Philosophy Group' in the *Canterbury Tales*: A Study of the *Knight's Tale*, the *Monk's Tale*, and the *Nun's Priest's Tale*", M.A. thesis, Louisiana State University, 1959.
Howard, Donald, "The Contempt of the World: A Study in the Ideology of Latin Christendom with Emphasis upon Fourteenth Century Literature", Ph.D. thesis, University of Florida, 1954.

Koonce, Benjamin, Jr., "Chaucer and the Tradition of Fame: A Study of the Symbolism in *The House of Fame*", Ph.D. thesis, Princeton University, 1959.

Litchfield, Florence, "The Treatment of the Theme of Mutability in the Literature of the English Renaissance: A Study of the Problem of Change Between 1558 and 1661", Ph.D. thesis, University of Minnesota, 1935.

Thackaberry, Robert E., "Chaucer's *The Parlement of Foules*: A Re-Interpretation", Ph.D. thesis, State University of Iowa, 1937.

INDEX OF NAMES